ROSE GUIDE TO
END-TIMES
PROPHECY

Timothy Paul Jones, PhD
David Gundersen, MDiv, ThM
Benjamin Galan, MTS, ThM

Rose Publishing, Inc.
Torrance, California

Managing editor: Lynnette Pennings

Design of cover and layout by Sergio Urquiza

Library of Congress Cataloging-in-Publication Data

Jones, Timothy P. (Timothy Paul)
  Rose guide to end-times prophecy / Timothy Paul Jones, David Gundersen, Benjamin Galan.
     p. cm.
  Summary: "Explains major Christian views on biblical prophecy regarding end times including the books of Revelation and Daniel, the tribulation, the millennium, and more. "--Provided by publisher.
  Includes index.
  ISBN 978-1-59636-419-6 (pbk.)
  1. End of the world. 2. Eschatology. 3. End of the world--Biblical teaching. 4. Eschatology--Biblical teaching.
I. Gundersen, David. II. Galan, Benjamin. III. Title. IV. Title: Guide to end-times prophecy.
  BT877.J66 2011
  236'.9--dc23
                        2011019504

Printed by Shenzhen Donnelley Printing Co., Ltd.
Shenzhen, China
April 2015, 5th printing

Contents

WHAT MATTERS MOST WHEN IT COMES TO THE END OF THE WORLD

Introduction

"Tell us," the disciples asked after their master predicted a future calamity in the city of Jerusalem, "when will this happen, and what will be the sign of your coming and of the end of the age?" (Matthew 24:3). Even after the death and resurrection of Jesus, his followers found themselves with at least a few unanswered queries about the end of the world as they knew it. Gathered on the Mount of Olives, the disciples questioned Jesus about how and when he would consummate his kingdom: "Lord," they wondered, "are you at this time going to restore the kingdom to Israel?" (Acts 1:6).

These disciples weren't the first or the last to ask such questions. In every generation since sin entered the cosmos, God's people seem to have wondered, "When and how will God make things right in the world?"

The Prophecy of the Destruction of the Temple in Jerusalem by James Tissot (1886–1894)

Two Common and Opposite Errors When Studying the End Times

Sometimes such wonderings degenerate into endless debates and unwarranted speculation about specific details. Other times, end times curiosity comes to a screeching halt as people throw up their hands at what they've begun to feel is an impossible and fruitless enquiry.

THE SLIP INTO UNWARRANTED SPECULATION	THE SLIP INTO SHOULDER-SHRUGGING CYNICISM
A slip into the rut of unwarranted speculation and guesswork results in a desire to wring more detailed data out of Scripture than Scripture clearly provides. The prophetic passages in Scripture are inflated until the rest of what Scripture has to say is marginalized, pushing Jesus and the gospel to the edges and corners of each page.	A slip into the rut of shoulder-shrugging cynicism about the end times results in down playing or ignoring end times texts. A balanced understanding seems unattainable, so Christians abandon careful study of the end times. Jesus is decentralized as readers fail to wait expectantly for their Savior as the consummation of God's plan for the ages.

These two possibilities represent two dangerous ditches in any study of the end times.

There's a saying that once crackled between truckers on their C.B. radios in the days before cellular telephones: "Keep your britches between the ditches." And, by God's grace, that's precisely what we plan to do in this book. Our aim is to steer carefully between the ditches of wild-eyed speculation and dreary-eyed disillusionment. As you peruse this text and the many charts and tables, you *will* gain much knowledge about the end of time. Yet the purpose of this book is not simply to raise your eschatological I.Q. This text focuses first and foremost on Jesus the crucified Messiah and risen King, the One in whom God the Father has made all things new and through whom God is setting the world right.

What the Bible Is Really All About

Why this single-minded focus on Jesus in a book about the end times?

Simply this: Our goal is to understand what the Scriptures have to say about the end times, and Jesus is the central focus of all Scripture—even of Scriptures that describe the end of time.

When some religious teachers questioned Jesus about his messianic credentials, Jesus retorted, "You study the Scriptures diligently because you think that in them you have eternal life. These are the very Scriptures that testify about me" (John 5:39).

Did you catch that?

"These are," Jesus said of the Scriptures, "the very Scriptures that testify about me."

The very Scriptures where the religious teachers looked for life by connecting themselves with particular patriarchs and laws were not primarily about those

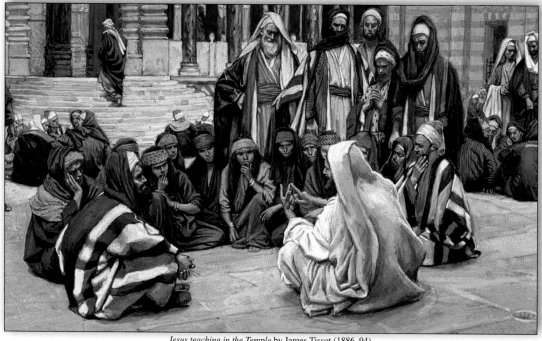

Jesus teaching in the Temple by James Tissot (1886–94)

rules or family identities at all! The Old and the New Testaments were—and are—about Jesus. That's why, when Jesus ran across a duo of downtrodden disciples on the road to Emmaus, he began "with Moses and all the Prophets" and showed them how he was the central subject of "all the Scriptures" (Luke 24:27). That's also why the apostle Paul pointed out to his pastoral protégé that the purpose of "the Holy Scriptures" was to make God's people "wise for salvation through faith in Christ Jesus" (2 Timothy 3:15).

Jesus with the disciples at Emmaus, by Abraham Blowmaert (1622)

What, then, will this book provide?

- Deeper understanding of Old Testament prophets and prophecies, especially the writings of Daniel.

- Insights into the New Testament prophecies, especially the apostle John's Book of Revelation, and what they meant to the people of that day.

- Different Christian interpretations of the Book of Revelation, and the biblical perspective for each.

- Various Christian understandings about key prophetic words and concepts: rapture, tribulation, seals, trumpets, Babylon, the Beast, Satan, 666, the millennium, and more.

- And what about a richer perspective on how Old Testament prophecies pointed both to Jesus and to the end of time?

- How about a clearer view of what the Jewish people expected the Messiah to be and why this matters for our understanding of the end times?

> What we are seeking is a deeper recognition of the majesty and sovereignty of Jesus in all of life—including the end of time.

- What about tools that will help you to develop your own biblically-based perspective on when and how time will end?

- Perhaps most important, how about a broader understanding of how Bible-believing Christians throughout church history have understood end-times prophecies in very different ways?

What this means for this book is that we are not searching for one more detailed road map to tell us the precise conditions of the Messiah's return. What we are seeking is a deeper recognition of the majesty and sovereignty of Jesus in all of life—including the end of time. God's promises and prophecies are not launching pads for our own speculations. They are a lens through which we can see clearly the supremacy of Jesus in the unfolding story of the cosmos. And so, if your deepest desire is to nail down the exact identity of the Antichrist or to calculate the precise date when time will end, you could be a bit disappointed as you read this book. If your desire is to understand how to view the end times in light of Jesus, read on. This book provides precisely what you've been looking for.

> **END TIMES**
>
> Events leading up to and including the physical return of Jesus to earth and the formation of new heavens and a new earth.

Keeping Your Eyes on the Right End

"It's a dangerous business, Frodo, going out of your door," Bilbo Baggins exhorted his nephew in J.R.R. Tolkien's *Lord of the Rings*. "You step into the Road, and if you don't keep your feet, there is no knowing where you might be swept off to."[1]

Much the same might be said about opening a book that focuses on the end of time. *Studying the end times is dangerous business.* Once you begin exploring this subject, there's no knowing where you might be swept off to.

© PHOTOCREO Michal Bednarek

A well-intended overemphasis on the end times has been known to drive people to sport prophetic placards on street corners, to stare at bar codes in search of that mysterious mark of the beast, to publish faulty predictions of the world's end, and to engage in a host of other behaviors that are likely to result in lots of blank spaces in social calendars. What's more, a quick glance at history shows that studying the end times has even had the capacity to bring out a bit of violence from time to time.

EXAMPLES OF END-TIMES PREDICTIONS GONE WRONG

1. Only a couple of decades after Jesus rose from the dead, false prophets in the city of Thessalonica proclaimed that Jesus had already returned (2 Thessalonians 2:2). This caused all sorts of worry when it occurred to the Thessalonian believers that, since they didn't recall seeing Jesus in the sky,

Eleventh-Century Illustration of the Beast in the Book of Revelation

they must have missed something significant. To this, Paul replied "that day will not come until ... the man of lawlessness is revealed" (2:3). This resulted in centuries of speculation about who "the man of lawlessness" might be, but it apparently made the Thessalonians feel better about their situation.

Bust of the Greek goddess Attis wearing a Phrygian cap. Marble, 2nd century AD.

2. A century later, in the mid-100s, a man named Montanus became a believer in Jesus and developed a strong interest in prophetic themes. Before long, Montanus had predicted that the New Jerusalem would soon show up in Pepuza, a backwoods parish in the province of Phrygia. Then, Montanus began to claim that he spoke as God, declaring, "I am Father, Word, and Comforter" and "I am the Lord God All-Powerful."[2] Churches typically frown on members who say things of this sort, and the congregation that Montanus attended was no exception. After his church disfellowshipped him, Montanus started his own religious community, but Pepuza never did play host to the New Jerusalem.

3. In the fourth century, a popular church leader named Martin of Tours declared that "the Antichrist has already been born" and that this ruler would rise to power in Martin's own lifetime.

4. A monk named Radulfus Glaber—translated, his name means "Ralph the Bald"—described a wave of apocalyptic worries in the decades around the year AD 1000. According to Bald Ralph the Burgundian monk, a blazing sign in the heavens had presaged a mysterious fire in a monastery. Fears of impending apocalypse and tribulation deepened when a famine struck on the thousandth anniversary of the death of Jesus.[3] Despite these many worries, the monastery was repaired, the famine passed, Ralph remained bald, and life went on.

Cages of the Muenster Rebellion at St. Lambert's Church

5. In 1534, a Dutch baker named Jan claimed that the New Jerusalem would soon appear in Muenster, Germany. After a supposed series of apocalyptic visions, Jan and his followers subjugated the city of Muenster. One of Jan's cohort declared himself the successor of the biblical King David and took sixteen wives for himself. In the end, the New Jerusalem did not arrive in Muenster, but a rival army did. The corpses of the apocalyptic revolutionaries were suspended above the city in iron cages. To this day, those cages still hang from the steeple of St. Lambert's Church, silent reminders of an apocalyptic expectation gone desperately wrong.[4]

6. Three hundred years later, Joseph Smith claimed that Jesus would establish the New Jerusalem in Jackson County, Missouri— and, in the process, launched a worldwide religious movement that denied essential biblical truths about Jesus. Still today, Mormons expect Jesus to return somewhere along the eastern outskirts of Kansas City.[5]

"Lieutenant" Joseph Smith, Jr. leading a militia in Illinois after he and his followers were expelled from Missouri.

7. Fast-forward to the twentieth century and we see the same patterns again: In 1987, a retired NASA engineer published a pamphlet entitled *88 Reasons Why the Rapture Will Be in 1988*. He targeted three days in September 1988 as the divinely-selected deadline for the return of Jesus. "Only if the Bible is in error am I wrong," he declared to the news media. A few months later, the NASA engineer published a subsequent set of pamphlets suggesting that he had made a mistake and that perhaps 1989 was the right date.[6] That date too appears to have been an error. The mathematical skills required to get a shuttle into orbit are apparently quite different from the ones needed to calculate the end of time.

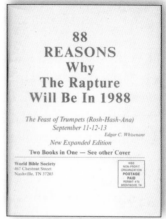

88 REASONS Why The Rapture Will Be In 1988

The Feast of Trumpets (Rosh-Hash-Ana)
September 11-12-13
Edgar C. Whisenant

New Expanded Edition
Two Books in One — See other Cover

World Bible Society
467 Chestnut Street
Nashville, TN 37203

This pamphlet from Edgar Whisenant caused one of the authors of this book several sleepless nights in October 1988.

8. About the time that the first copies of *88 Reasons* were rolling off the presses, a then-unknown leader of an obscure apocalyptic sect changed his name to David Koresh and urged his disciples to see themselves as "students of the

Seventy-five of David Koresh's "students of the Seven Seals" perished here after a 51-day siege in April 1995.

Seven Seals" in Revelation.[7] Koresh embraced polygamy and claimed that the end-times prophecies in Scripture would be fulfilled at his communal compound near Waco, Texas.[8] In 1993, David Koresh and seventy-five of his followers perished after a 51-day siege.

9. And still, in the opening decades of the twenty-first century, apocalyptic predictions and expectations show no signs of slowing down. There have been doomsday expectations surrounding the year 2000, one prediction that Jesus would return on May 21, 2011, and several claims that connected a convoluted Mayan prophecy about the end of time with the year 2012.[9] Thus far, these too have proven to be misguided predictions.

The Mayans calculated dates using a "long-count calendar." Dates were represented through glyphs, such as this small section of a stele. Some people have speculated that, because the Mayan calendar came to an end in December 21, 2012, the world would either come to an end or undergo a radical change on that date.

KEEPING OUR FEET—AND OUR HEADS—WHEN IT COMES TO THE END TIMES

After even the briefest survey of predictions that ended in disaster but not in the apocalypse, we might take a turn from Bilbo's exhortation to Frodo: "It's a dangerous business, studying the end of time. If you don't keep your feet, there is no knowing where you might be swept off to."

But don't take this book back to your local bookstore quite yet!

And, whatever you do, *don't* decide that a study of the end times isn't worth the risk.

REASONS TO STUDY THE END TIMES

The question is *not* whether we ought to study the end times. Christians should and must consider the end times! Here's why:

1. The apostles of Jesus commanded God's people to search the Scriptures (2 Timothy 3:14–17; 2 Peter 1:19–20), and Scripture testifies that God will bring the world as we know it to an end (Isaiah 65:17–25).

2. Jesus repeatedly reminded his disciples to watch for his future arrival (Matthew 24:42; see also Matthew 25:13; Mark 13:35–37; Luke 12:37).

3. Paul said to his hearers, "But you, brothers and sisters, are not in darkness so that this day should surprise you like a thief … let us be awake and sober" (1 Thessalonians 5:4, 6).

4. In Revelation, John recorded this blessing from the very lips of Jesus: "Look, I come like a thief! Blessed is the one who stays awake" (Revelation 16:15).

So our question shouldn't be whether to think about the end times; God clearly expects us to consider the end times. Instead, our question should be, "How can we 'keep our feet' in our study of the end of time? How do we study the second coming of Jesus without veering into dangerous doctrinal territory? How can we explore the end times in a way that focuses on Jesus?"

There's one simple fact that you need to know to keep yourself headed in the right direction when it comes to a study of the end times: *It's only dangerous when you focus on the wrong end.*

FOCUSING ON THE RIGHT END

According to Scripture, the endpoint and goal of God's work in human history is not a specific series of apocalyptic events or even a particular celestial place; it is, instead, a Person. The endpoint and goal of God's work in human history is Jesus.

Jesus himself declared, "I am the Alpha and Omega, the First and the Last, the Beginning and the End" (Revelation 22:13). Jesus is the source of the created order (John 1:3; Colossians 1:16), the one "for whom and through whom everything exists" (Hebrews 2:10). Jesus is the source of God's creation and God's story, and he is the goal of God's plan.

To be sure, God *will* end the world as we know it at some particular time and in a particular way—that's what we call the "end times"—but it isn't simply the termination of time for which the entire cosmos is groaning. What all creation expectantly awaits is the revealing of Jesus alongside a redeemed multitude of brothers and sisters (Romans 8:18–23).

"Alpha" and "omega" are the first and last letters of the Greek alphabet. © Zvonimir Atletic

ALPHA AND OMEGA

The first and the last letters of the Greek alphabet. The apostle John used these terms to describe Jesus as both the beginning and the goal of God's work in human history. John also used these terms to make it clear that Jesus is God in human flesh. In Revelation 1:8, the "Alpha and Omega" is "the Lord God"; then, in Revelation 22:13–16, the same words are applied to Jesus.

God's purpose is not simply to get people into heaven; God's plan has always been to display his glory throughout the cosmos in and through Jesus. According to the apostle Paul, God "set forth" his purpose "in Christ to be put into effect when the times reach their fulfillment—to bring unity to all things in heaven and on earth under Christ" (Ephesians 1:9–10). The present fellowship of Christians that will someday culminate in the communion of heaven is simply an outgrowth of God's plan to bring everything together in Jesus the Messiah. Jesus is the source of God's creation and the goal of God's plan. He is "the pioneer and perfecter of faith" (Hebrews 12:2).

But, before we wade any deeper into our study of the end times, there's one more issue involved in keeping our eyes on the right end: To keep our eyes on the right end is not only to recognize Jesus as the goal of God's creation. It's also to see that, through the work of Jesus on earth, the last days have already begun.

GREEK

Language in which the New Testament was written, in an ancient dialect known as *koine* or "common" Greek.

LOOKING FOR THE LAST DAYS

It's a question that someone eventually asks whenever I teach about the end times. The precise wording may differ, but the question always runs something like this: "So, do you think we're living in the last days right now?"

My answer is always an adamant, "Yes!" But what I say next is sometimes far from what the questioner expected: "And we have been in the last days ever since Jesus completed his Father's work on earth, almost two thousand years ago." What the individual asking the question typically wants is a list of specific signs of the times that somehow correlate to recent events in the news. What I provide is a reminder that the last days have already begun.

Why do I say that we have been in "the last days" ever since Jesus fulfilled his Father's will on the earth?

Because that is precisely what Scripture says.

When the Holy Spirit seized people's lives on the day of Pentecost, Peter proclaimed that this outpouring had been predicted "by the prophet Joel" and identified these events as part of "the last days" (Acts 2:16–17). Another New Testament text makes the point even clearer: "In these last days," the author of Hebrews wrote, "[God] has spoken to us by his Son" (Hebrews 1:2). The work of Jesus on earth was the ultimate sign of the times (Matthew 12:39–40) and, in him, "the last days" have already dawned.

Pentecost by Titian (1488–1576)

Because of the finished work of Jesus, Satan has been thrown down (John 12:31–33; Hebrews 2:14). Jesus has received the power over death, and he has demonstrated his triumph by means of his resurrection (Romans 1:4; 1 Corinthians 15:20–26; Revelation 1:18; 9:1; 20:1).

This work of Jesus on earth accomplished God's victory and inaugurated a kingdom that he will consummate at the end of time. And so, the biblical authors were able to describe the entire period between Jesus' victory over death and the end of time as "the last days" (Acts 2:17; Hebrews 1:2). In him, God's triumph has already been accomplished and guaranteed.

WHAT HAPPENS WHEN WE KEEP OUR EYES ON THE RIGHT END

Whenever a search for specific signs becomes the primary goal in our study of the end times, *we are focusing*

Three Marys at the Tomb by William Bouguereau (1825–1905)

on the wrong end. Such a misguided focus may drive some toward extremist cults. Others may become obsessed with increasingly specific schedules for the termination of time. But, even among the most stable persons, the results of fixing our eyes on the wrong end are far from the best. Such a focus tends to produce anxiety about the future and perhaps even a desire to stockpile more and more details about how time might end.

But how might our perspective change if we fix our eyes on the *right* end?

What would happen if we focused on the risen King Jesus himself as the goal of God's plan?

And how might this new focus reshape our perspective on the end times?

Thankfully, we aren't the first people to struggle with such issues. The first generations of Christians dealt with similar challenges—and what Jesus and Paul told these men and women is just as profitable for us as it was for them. Let's take a look at their words to discover what happens when we focus on the right end in our study of the end times.

READINESS, RESPONSIBILITY, AND REST: WHAT HAPPENS WHEN WE FOCUS ON THE RIGHT END

When we focus on the right end, we will be ready for Jesus to return at any time. When Jesus predicted the destruction of the Jewish temple, his first followers asked him, "Tell us, when will these things be, and what will be the sign of your coming and of the end of the age?" In response, Jesus *did* provide them with a few signposts that would precede the fall of the temple and the end of time. At the same time, the closing parable of his discourse makes it clear that his primary concern was not simply for them to have a detailed understanding of these signs. His desire was for them to be ready for his presence whenever and

Paul at His Writing Desk by Rembrandt (1629–30)

however these events might unfold (Matthew 24:3, 42–51). His purpose was not for his followers to become caught up in specifics of the end times; it was for them to be ready to welcome him at *any* time.

When we focus on the right end, we see our responsibility to proclaim the gospel all the time. After the resurrection, when the apostles demanded details about the end of time, Jesus replied quite curtly, "It is not for you to know times or seasons that the Father has set by his own authority"—then, he immediately reminded them of their responsibility to share with others what they had seen in him (Acts 1:7–8). Jesus turned their attention from "times or seasons" and focused them on his work and on their commission to proclaim the gospel. The words rendered "times or seasons" in English translations represent two different Greek words that describe time. "Times" translates a form of the word *chronos*, which points to chronological, linear time as measured by a calendar or a sundial or a clock; *chronos* includes years and months, days and hours. "Seasons" renders a form of the word *kairos*, a word that points to the quality or type of time; the focus of *kairos* is on the opportunity or significance of a particular time. By using both terms, Jesus made it clear not only that it wasn't his disciples' place to know *when* he might return but also that they wouldn't necessarily even know *what type of time* it would be when he returned.

When we focus on the right end, we rest in the certainty that God will make the world right again. Even after Jesus vanished into the eastern sky, his followers struggled with issues related to his return. Twenty years or so after the ascension, someone forged a letter in Paul's name and informed the Thessalonian church that Jesus had already returned (2 Thessalonians 2:2; 3:17). Not surprisingly, the thought that they might have missed their Savior's return caused quite a stir among the Christians in Thessalonica! Paul responded by making it clear that Jesus had not yet returned after all. Before the return of Jesus, there would be a rebellion of humanity against God and a revelation of a lawless man (2 Thessalonians 2:3). Yet Paul did not dwell long on these details! In fact, he spent fewer than a dozen verses on these issues. The outcome that Paul projected for these truths ("the teachings we passed on to you," 2:15) was not to drive the Thessalonians to speculate about who the lawless man might be or when the rebellion might come. It was, instead, that "our Lord Jesus Christ himself and God our Father" would "encourage [their] hearts and strengthen [them] in every good deed and word" (2 Thessalonians 2:16–17). Paul wasn't afraid to talk about the end times, but he knew that end times are not the endpoint of God's plan. And so, he called the Thessalonians to rest and to find comfort in God's promise that he will one day make all things new.

Notice the pattern in each of these New Testament discussions of the end times: The focus is not on the details of how time might end. Some future occurrences are certainly mentioned, but again and again, the emphasis is on the sufficiency of Jesus, the one through whom God will bring about the end in his own time. Jesus is the goal of God's plan and the ultimate sign of God's work in human history. Because Jesus perfectly fulfilled his Father's will, the last days are already underway and God's triumph is guaranteed. That emphasis is what it means to keep our eyes on the right end.

FINDING THE CORNER PIECES OF THE END-TIMES PUZZLE

From the words of the New Testament, it is clear that the result of considering the end times should not be smug satisfaction that comes from gaining more details about the future. Instead, where such study should drive us is toward a simultaneous sense of rest and responsibility that is found only in the gospel of Jesus. The result should not be increased speculation about the end of time but an increased capacity to work for the glory of Jesus the Messiah while watching and waiting patiently for his return.

That's why the primary goal of this book is not for you to learn intricate end times details but to learn more of the One whose arrival will fulfill a divine design that is more ancient than time. If the end of time is a puzzle, Jesus is the corner pieces; only when he stands in the most prominent place can the end-times puzzle begin to make sense.

It's a dangerous business, studying the end of time. If Jesus becomes the center point of your study, the danger won't completely go away—but the danger will take a quite different form. The danger won't be becoming caught up in all sorts of end-times kookiness. What will be endangered is our comfortable assumption that if only we can connect all the right charts with all the right verses, we can figure out exactly what God is doing when it comes to the end of time. During the days that he walked the dusty roads of Judea and Galilee, not even Jesus knew the precise details of the end of time (Mark 13:32). What Jesus did know was that his Father had a plan and that his Father's plan was glorious and good. And that's the truth about the end times that every follower of Jesus can rest in still today.

© Luminis

Apocalypse Now and Then

Imagine for a moment that several millennia pass before Jesus Christ returns to earth. Suppose that two thousand years from now, an intrepid forty-first century archaeologist unearths the opinion page from an early twenty-first century American newspaper.

Since our current form of English has faded from use, the archaeologist will have to wait many months while an expert on ancient texts decodes the faded words. Yet the archaeologist might still make a few preliminary observations based on an almost-wordless portion of the paper that's been preserved in pristine condition: the political cartoons.

Based on the political cartoons, what might this archaeologist conclude about the United States of America in the twenty-first century?

It's possible that the archaeologist would know a bit about traditional representations of American politics. If so, he might be able to see the meaning behind the donkeys and elephants, presidential caricatures, and sketches of national monuments. But what if he was not familiar with the style of communication that we know as the political cartoon? What if, for example, future generations had lost the knowledge that donkeys and elephants once symbolized the Democratic and Republican parties?

If the archaeologist read these political cartoons with wooden literalism, he might end up writing articles for popular magazines about how donkeys and elephants once ruled

© Madlen

the United States. He might even conclude that, every few years in the month of November, herds of pachyderms and burros went to war with one another to see who would rule America! Scientists could advance elaborate theories to explain how these creatures were once able to reason, debate, campaign, and rule a nation. Complex charts could even trace the devolution of donkeys and elephants from world rulers to dumb beasts.

But all of these theories would be utterly mistaken because these scientists and archaeologists were unaware of the signs, symbols, and styles that characterized American political cartoons in the twenty-first century. They would have completely misread these political opinions because they wouldn't know how these pages were read in the era when they were written.

Today, it's easy for Christians to make a similar mistake when reading biblical texts that tell about the end of time.

We are not suggesting, of course, that the prophecies in Ezekiel or Daniel or Revelation are nothing more than political caricatures! These are segments of God's own unerring Word. They were given by God's Spirit "for teaching, for reproof, for correction, and for training in righteousness," not only for ancient peoples but also for the church today and until the end of time (2 Timothy 3:16).

At the same time, God led the human authors of Scripture to write in particular styles and genres that were well-known to them and to their first readers. This is why careful study of the Scriptures means studying these texts according to their original historical and literary contexts.

Martin Luther (1483–1546).

How Christians Have Interpreted the Bible

Finding the original meaning of the text is what Christian teachers throughout church history have been getting at when they've urged students to search for the *sensus literalis*—the "literal sense" or "literary sense" of the biblical text.[10] When these Christians mentioned the "literal sense" they did *not* mean reading the text with rigid literalism, resorting to symbolic interpretation only when all other possibilities have been exhausted.[11] What they meant was to interpret the text within the literary style and historical context in which the text was originally written. In many cases, interpretation according to *sensus literalis* requires recognizing symbols and typologies in the biblical text.

Now, it's true that ancient and medieval scholars sometimes went overboard with symbols and typologies! For example, some ancient scholars around Alexandria, Egypt, claimed that biblical texts operated at three levels: literal meaning, moral meaning, and allegorical meaning.[12] By the fourth century, other interpreters were finding "tropological" and "heavenly" meanings in Scripture in addition to literal and moral meanings.

By the Middle Ages, many interpreters barely looked for the literal sense of the text at all.[13] Yet this wasn't always the case! One medieval theologian wisely pointed out, "Since the literal sense is what the author intends and since the author of Holy Scripture is God, who ... comprehends everything at once ... , it is not unfitting (as Augustine says) if many

Roman amphitheater in Alexandria, Egypt. Early influential Christians theologians like Origen, Clement, and Cyril came from this important coastal city in Egypt.

meanings are present even in the literal sense of a passage of Scripture." In other words, the literal or literary sense of a text doesn't rule out symbolic or typological interpretations. In fact, it's pretty clear that Peter, Paul, and the author of Hebrews saw certain parts of the Old Testament as typological symbols of New Testament realities (Romans 5:14; Colossians 2:17; 1 Peter 3:21; Hebrews 8:5; 9:9, 23–24; 10:1; 11:19).

Sensus literalis begins with historical-grammatical study of the text, but such study may reveal that the text was intended to be taken typologically or symbolically. In the sixteenth century, a pastor named Martin Luther called Christians to recover a focus on *sensus literalis* when reading the Scriptures.[14]

WAYS OF INTERPRETING THE BIBLE

Literal Interpretation	
Looks for: Historical-Grammatical-Literalistic Meaning	*Looks for:* Historical-Grammatical-Rhetorical Meaning
Method: Take every part of the text at its most literal meaning unless the immediate context makes this meaning impossible.	**Method**: Seek the meaning intended by the original human authors in their historical contexts as conveyed through their words and the literary genre, recognizing that the Holy Spirit superintended their words and their choice of genre. This does not exclude a later fulfillment of a text in a fuller and better way than what the original human author had in mind.
Challenge: Sometimes the larger context of the literary genre suggests a broader range of meanings for a word or idea. Not every literary genre was intended to be taken literalistically; may lead, for example, to reading certain texts like historical narratives even when those texts were not intended as historical accounts.	**Challenge**: In some cases, it can be difficult to identify the historical context correctly; in other instances, it can be a challenge to understand the nuances of a particular literary genre in its historical context, especially if a text combines different literary genres.
Example: "Temple" must be seen as a physical building.	**Example**: "Temple" is seen as the physical building in historical genres and contexts; but in other genres, "temple" might, for example, symbolize the people of God as God's dwelling place.

Moral Interpretation	Spiritual Interpretation	
Looks for: Ethical Meaning	*Looks for: Tropological (Spiritual) Meaning*	*Looks for: Anagogical (Heavenly) Meaning*
Method: Seek the underlying moral in each biblical story	**Method**: Look for ways in which parts of the story might prefigure or relate typologically to the life and ministry of Jesus	**Method**: Look for ways in which parts of the story might relate allegorically to the believer's union with God.
Challenge: If historical-grammatical-rhetorical interpretation does not remain primary, can lead to reading Scripture as a series of stories to improve our morals instead of seeing that all of Scripture testifies to Jesus Christ and that human morals can never measure up to God's perfect standard.	**Challenge**: If historical-grammatical-rhetorical interpretation does not remain primary, can allow the interpreter to read ideas into the text completely unrelated to the original author's intent, allowing the interpreter rather than the intent of the author to dictate the meaning of Scripture.	**Challenge**: If historical-grammatical-rhetorical interpretation does not remain primary, can allow the interpreter to read ideas into the text completely unrelated to the original author's intent, allowing the interpreter rather than the intent of the author to dictate the meaning of Scripture.
Example: "Temple" might symbolize the innermost part of the human soul.	**Example**: "Temple" might symbolize the people of God or the church, even in historical texts where this could not have fallen within the author's original range of intent.	**Example**: "Temple" might symbolize union with God in heaven.

WHY THE GENRE MATTERS

So what does all of this talk about literary styles and genres have to do with the end times?

Everything!

The biblical texts that tell us about the end of time were penned in particular historical contexts that deeply influenced how the authors recorded God's words. What's more, many of these end-times texts drew from literary backgrounds that had their own unique expectations for how readers would understand images and patterns in the book. Perhaps most important of all, if Scripture came about because people "spoke from God as they were carried along by the Holy Spirit" (2 Peter 1:21), the very Spirit of God was involved not only in the content of these texts but also in the styles and genres that were chosen.

> **GENRE**
>
> (from French *genre* [ZHAN-ruh] "kind, sort, style")
>
> A category of artistic or literary works that can be identified by shared elements in form or content (for example, prose, poetry, satire).

To interpret these texts without knowing their original contexts and literary styles is to risk missing the point completely—much like our imaginary future archaeologist who might misread a twenty-first century political cartoon and conclude that a fiercely-contested American election was actually a battle between two groups of mammals. Unless you keep in mind what genre of literature you are reading, it's easy to misinterpret and even to teach falsehoods about the Word of God.

WHAT MAKES APOCALYPTIC TEXTS DIFFERENT

Even if you don't know a lot about the Bible, one thing becomes quite clear as you read, for example, the book of Revelation and the latter chapters of Daniel: They are very different from other texts in the Bible.

Both Revelation and the last half of Daniel refer to historical characters and events—but not in the same way as purely historical texts like the Gospels or Acts or the opening books of the Old Testament.

The book of Revelation includes letters to seven churches in Asia Minor. Yet these letters from the hand of John aren't anything like the correspondence that Paul sent to churches throughout the Roman Empire; for that matter, they aren't even like John's other three letters in the New Testament.

APOCALYPTIC LITERATURE

(from Greek *apokalupsis*, "revelation" or "unhiding")

Genre of ancient Jewish literature presented in the form of visions that figuratively revealed hidden truths for the purpose of assuring God's people of the goodness of God's plans during periods of persecution.

The prophet Daniel and John the revelator both described dreams and visions. Yet, unlike the dreams of Joseph in the book of Genesis, the implications of these visions stretch far beyond one individual's personal destiny to include political events and even prophecies of the final resurrection. Much of the time, these texts can seem downright strange. John chews up a scroll and ends up with indigestion, and Daniel sees a flying leopard that leaps out of the sea and a one-horned goat that floats across the earth (Daniel 7:3–6; 8:5; Revelation 10:9–10). All of these experiences fall outside the usual boundaries of "normal," even by biblical standards.

So why are these books so different from other biblical texts?

It's partly because their authors drew from an ancient literary genre known as apocalyptic. The word "apocalyptic" comes from the Greek word *apokalupsis* ("revelation" or "unhiding"), a term that also happens to be the first word in the Greek text of Revelation. Ancient apocalyptic writings were filled with visions that revealed hidden truths in

John on Patmos by Alonso Cano (1646–50)

figurative language for the purpose of assuring persecuted people of the goodness of God's ways. Apocalyptic literature expressed both hope and lament during times of oppression—hope in God's sovereign rule over his world coupled with lamentation over the ways in which sin had distorted God's world.

Apocalyptic thinking began to blossom among the Jewish people in the aftermath of their defeat at the hands of the Babylonians, their deportation, and the destruction of their temple in the early sixth century BC. Ezekiel and Daniel were written during this time.[15] Ezekiel 37–39 and the last six chapters of Daniel represent "pre-apocalypses" or early expressions of apocalyptic thinking.

After the days of Daniel and Ezekiel, other Jewish writers penned more

Ottheinrich Bibel, The Woman in Revelation 12 by Matthias Gerung (1530–32)

elaborate apocalypses that don't appear in the Old or New Testaments: there are texts that falsely claim to come from Enoch, for example, and others that allege origins in the lifetimes of Abraham and Noah and Moses. Although the Jewish people never viewed these apocalyptic texts as part of their Scriptures, these documents probably did preserve a few truthful traditions, and the New Testament writers seem to have been familiar with them. Although the book of Revelation is not completely apocalyptic, John's imagery closely resembles the other apocalypses that were familiar to so many first-century Jews. The New

Testament book of Jude specifically references passages from two Jewish apocalypses: 1 Enoch (in Jude 14–15) and Assumption of Moses (in Jude 9).

So what are the primary patterns that Daniel and Revelation share with other ancient apocalyptic texts?

1. These texts reveal hidden truths through visions.

2. God's people are encouraged to remain faithful during a time of persecution.

3. God's people are assured that, despite the seeming hopelessness of their present circumstances, God will someday punish sin and make the world right.

CHARACTERISTICS OF JEWISH APOCALYPTIC LITERATURE[16]

1. *Assurance*: The author assures readers that God will break into the present age in a way that transforms the world and establishes a new and different existence for his people.

2. *Angels*: Angelic mediators convey God's message to a chosen recipient.

3. *Journey*: The human recipient journeys into a heavenly realm.

4. *Visions*: Highly symbolic and figurative visions describe present spiritual realities and future divine interventions.

5. *Warnings*: God's people are warned about coming distresses and trials.

6. *Encouragement*: The persecuted faithful are encouraged to persevere, knowing that God is working in present unseen realities and that God will intervene in the future.

7. *Final Judgment*: One or more portions of the text include a vision of final judgment.

ESCHATOLOGICAL

(From Greek *eschaton*, "final" or "last," and logos, "word" or "idea")

Pertaining to a study of the events leading up to the end of time.

THE DEVELOPMENT OF APOCALYPTIC LITERATURE

Writings	Dates
Pre-apocalyptic writings: Although not fully apocalyptic, certain texts written before and during the Babylonian exile set the stage for later apocalyptic writings. Daniel 7–14 represents the clearest expression of the apocalyptic thinking that would emerge later.	Seventh and sixth centuries BC
Early apocalyptic writings: Faced again with persecution at the hands of foreign nations, Jewish writers developed their own apocalypses.	Second and first century BC
	Early first century AD
Later apocalyptic writings: Christians and Jews were facing oppression at the hands of the Romans; some Jewish sects rebelled against Roman Empire in AD 66–73.	Late first century AD
Later Christian apocalypses: After the disastrous Jewish revolt against the Romans, Jewish apocalypticism faded; Christianity became increasingly Gentile and Christian apocalypticism took on different, less Jewish forms.	Second century AD

Biblical examples	Non-biblical examples
Isaiah 24–27 Ezekiel 37–39 Zechariah 12–14 Daniel 7–14	
	Book of Jubilees Psalms of Solomon Apocalypse of Moses 1 Enoch
	Testaments of Levi and Naphtali Assumption (Testament) of Moses
Mark 13 [Matthew 24; Luke 21] (not a full-fledged apocalypse but a discourse, delivered in the early first century, that draws from earlier apocalyptic themes) Revelation of Jesus Christ to John, AD 60's or 90's	4 Ezra (2 Esdras) Apocalypse of Abraham, around AD 80 Apocalypse of Baruch (2 Baruch), around AD 100 Martyrdom and Ascension of Isaiah
	Apocalypse of Peter Shepherd of Hermas

UNVEILING THROUGH VISIONS: THE CONTENT OF APOCALYPTIC LITERATURE

Ancient texts in the apocalyptic genre claimed to unveil divine truths that could not be discovered through human effort. This unveiling typically occurred through visions. In the Old and the New Testaments, these visions are divinely-inspired masterpieces that elaborately depict the workings of God in human history. Daniel's visionary descriptions ranged from a series of fantastic beasts with wings and horns to God himself on a fiery throne, from a ram and a goat and a manlike angel to people rising from the dead (Daniel 7, 8, 10, 12). Through these visions, God demonstrated to Daniel that God had not lost control of his

WHY AREN'T ALL THOSE OTHER APOCALYPSES IN THE BIBLE?

At least a dozen apocalypses circulated among ancient Jews and Christians—and two of these texts are quoted in the New Testament book of Jude! Why, then, aren't these apocalypses included in the Bible? Here's why:

- It was recognized even by the Jewish people living between the Old and New Testaments that the time of God-inspired prophets had ended until the Messiah arrived. This recognition is preserved in a Jewish historical text known as 1 Maccabees (9:27; 14:41). So the apocalyptic texts written after the Old Testament but before the coming of Jesus should not be considered part of Holy Scripture.

- The primary standard for whether texts written after the time of Jesus were authoritative for Christians was, "Can this text be clearly connected with an apostolic eyewitness of the risen Lord Jesus or a close associate of an eyewitness?" With the exception of the Revelation of Jesus Christ to John, none of the apocalypses of the Christian era could be clearly traced back to an apostle. Apocalypse of Peter did not come from Peter, and the Shepherd of Hermas was written after the apostolic era had ended. Around AD 160, some Christians in Rome wanted to include Shepherd of Hermas in their lists of authoritative books. A leader in the Roman church responded with these words: "Hermas composed 'the Shepherd' quite recently—in our own times, in the city of Rome.... While it should indeed be read, it cannot be publicly read for the people of the church. It is counted neither among the Prophets (for their number has been completed) nor among the Apostles (for it is after their time)."[17]

world; God had a plan to bring new life to his people and to destroy their oppressors. The book of Revelation presents similar visions that use extravagant language and cryptic numbers to point to transcendent realities. Like Daniel, John used these visions to assure his readers that God had not lost control of his world.

In one sense, the visions of Revelation are, however, quite different from other apocalyptic writings: What is revealed in Revelation is not merely a plan but a plan centered in one particular person, Jesus Christ. Over and over in Revelation, Jesus stands at the center of John's

The Adoration of the Lamb by Beringarius (c. 870)

visions. Jesus is the Lion and Lamb who breaks the Seven Seals (Revelation 5–8). It is he who takes his stand on Mount Zion (14:1) and he who embraces his people as his beloved bride (19:7). In the end, Jesus is the conquering King of kings, the Lord of lords, and the light who illumines his people's lives forevermore (17:14; 21:23; 22:3). From the very first sentence, the book of Revelation is a revelation "of Jesus Christ" (Revelation 1:1).[18]

ENCOURAGEMENT DURING PERSECUTION: THE CONTEXT OF APOCALYPTIC LITERATURE

Apocalyptic writings developed during times of exile and persecution. In some cases, the apocalyptic literary style concealed elements of the author's message that the dominant political powers might have perceived as subversive. During the decades that Daniel preserved his visions for his people, King Nebuchadnezzar of Babylon besieged Jerusalem and hauled away captives four times—first in 605, then again in 597 and in 586 when he destroyed the Jewish temple, and one last time in 581 or 580 BC. Another prophet graphically described the oppression in Daniel's hometown during these years: "Our inheritance has been turned over to strangers, our homes to foreigners.... Our skin is hot as an oven, feverish from hunger. Women have been violated in Zion, and virgins in the towns of Judah. Princes are hung up by their hands; elders are shown no respect.... Mount Zion ... lies desolate, with jackals prowling over it" (Lamentations 5:2–18). Daniel seems to have been taken captive in 605, after Nebuchadnezzar defeated the Egyptians at the Battle of Carchemish. He and his fellow Israelites were marched nearly 500 miles to Babylon under heavy guard.[19]

Building inscription of King Nebuchadnezzar II (604–562 BC)

And what about the New Testament apocalypse known as Revelation? It's uncertain whether John wrote Revelation during Emperor Nero's reign in the AD 60s or in the AD 90s when Emperor Domitian ruled the Roman Empire. Either way, persecution and exile were definite threats for Christians in Asia Minor and Rome. That's clear even in the first verses of Revelation. There, John described himself as "your brother and companion in the suffering and the kingdom and patient endurance that are ours in Jesus ... on the island of Patmos

© Vladislav Gajic

because of the word of God and the testimony of Jesus" (1:9). John's statement regarding exile on Patmos is historically credible: The Roman historian Tacitus repeatedly reported how persons suspected of being potential political threats to the peace of Rome were exiled to islands in the Aegean Sea.[20]

ASSURANCE OF GOD'S GOODNESS: THE PURPOSE OF APOCALYPTIC LITERATURE

When people today read apocalyptic literature, the first question they often ask is, "What will be the precise order and timing of events between now and the end of time?" When apocalyptic writings first circulated, however, that probably wasn't the primary question that the saints were asking. What readers then were likely asking was not what or how but who: "Who's really in charge of history?"

When Daniel proclaimed his prophecies, for example, it seemed like the Babylonians, Medes, and Persians controlled the world. To many Israelites, it looked as if God was no longer working for the good of his people. Through divinely disclosed visions, Daniel made it clear that God's kingdom was "an everlasting kingdom" and that Israel's oppressors would one day be condemned to "everlasting contempt" (Daniel 2:44; 4:3, 34; 12:2). What God provided through Daniel's prophecies was an eschatological hope—an assurance that God was working in a definite direction and, in the end, God would make all things good, right, and new.

When John wrote Revelation, the Roman Empire ruled the known world. Christians seem to have been losing their positions, their property, and even their lives because they refused to offer sacrifices on the emperor's behalf. The Jewish faith remained legal—albeit unpopular—in the Roman Empire. As a result, some Christians may have downplayed their trust in Jesus and tried to blend in at local synagogues (see Revelation 2:9; 3:9).

In this context, John proclaimed that the rightful king of the world was not the emperor in Rome; Jesus was the "King of kings," and his power extended far beyond the heavens to encompass every kingdom on earth (11:15; 21:23). Like Daniel, John offered his readers eschatological assurance and hope: Not only was God working even in times of persecution; someday, God would consign his foes to eternal punishment, recreate the fallen cosmos, and cleanse every tear from his people's eyes (20:12–21:8). Through visions of spiritual realities that transcended present circumstances, apocalyptic writings pointed persecuted people toward hope that is greater than any human eye can see.

© mountainpix

What Christians Agree About When It Comes to the End of the World

THREE ESSENTIAL TRUTHS THAT CHRISTIANS HAVE ALWAYS BELIEVED, AND THREE KEY THEMES THAT BRING BELIEVERS TOGETHER

A Christian philosopher was debating a Jewish rabbi who wasn't convinced that Jesus was the Messiah. The philosopher and the rabbi wrangled over whether the ancient prophets had really predicted the coming of Jesus, whether the Old Testament manuscripts were reliable, and precisely how the angels revolted against God. Then, their discussion turned to Jerusalem and the end of time.

"Do you really think that Jerusalem is going to be rebuilt?" the rabbi asked. "And do you really expect your people to be gathered with the Messiah and the patriarchs?"

"I and others that are right-minded Christians do indeed expect that there will be a thousand years in Jerusalem," the philosopher responded, then he added: "But many who belong to the pure and pious faith and who are truly Christians think otherwise.'[21]

> **MESSIAH**
>
> (from Hebrew *Mashiakh*, "Anointed One")
>
> Savior-king anticipated throughout the Hebrew Scriptures (Genesis 3:15; Deuteronomy 18:15; Isaiah 53; 61). Also known as "Christ" (from Greek *Christos*, "Anointed One").

The Christian philosopher's beliefs about the end times were clear—but he knew that many faithful Christians disagreed with him about the specifics.

Now, when do you suppose this dialogue took place?

Maybe in the latter decades of the twentieth century, sometime between *The Late*

Great Planet Earth and *Left Behind*? Or maybe a little earlier, in 1948, around the founding of the modern nation of Israel?

Perhaps in the nineteenth century, when politicians began to discuss the possibility of establishing a Jewish homeland?[22]

Or what about the years approaching 1666, when a rabbi known as Menasseh Ben Israel told the British Parliament that the Jews would soon be returning to their native land?[23]

Not even close.

This dialogue took place in the middle of the second century, only a generation or two after John wrote the book of Revelation. The philosopher was Justin, one of the most famous Christian thinkers of his day. The rabbi was Tarphon, a prominent interpreter of Jewish law and tradition.

So what do we learn from this dialogue between Justin and Tarphon?

Justin Martyr, AD 103–165

As early as the mid-second century AD, faithful Christians already disagreed about the details of how time would end.

In some ways, this is encouraging. It means that you aren't the first person to struggle with these issues! At the same time, it can also be discouraging. After all, if Christians in the second century couldn't agree on what would happen before the end of time, how can twenty-first-century Christians possibly reach consensus on these issues?

If all of this does seem a bit discouraging to you, stop for a few moments before slumping into the slough of eschatological despondency! There are two important truths that you could be missing:

1. Complete consensus among all Christians is not the most important goal when exploring the end times! The goal of God's work and the church's fellowship is to glorify Jesus, the "beginning and the end" of God's plan (Revelation 22:13).

2. And so, the question shouldn't be, "What needs to happen for all Christians to agree?" Instead, what we should be asking is, "How can our knowledge of the end times reveal more of the splendor of Jesus and the wonder of his gospel?"

Believers today can still practice a pattern that Christians followed even in the first generations of Christian faith: *Learn to distinguish between essential and nonessential beliefs.* Whenever a biblical truth is clear and held dear by Christians throughout the ages, the church must lovingly discipline anyone who denies or dilutes this truth. But what about the times when Scripture is not explicit on a particular detail? Christians should be able to disagree agreeably. A century

DISTINGUISHING THE ESSENTIAL FROM THE NON-ESSENTIAL

To help Christians to distinguish between essential and nonessential beliefs, theologian Albert Mohler has suggested a "theological triage" with three orders of theological issues:[24]

First-order issues: Doctrines that are essential to the Christian faith, such as the Trinity, the full deity and humanity of Jesus Christ, justification by faith, the authority of Scripture, and the bodily return of Jesus. "First-order doctrines represent the most fundamental truths of the Christian faith, and a denial of these doctrines represents nothing less than an eventual denial of Christianity itself."

Second-order issues: Doctrines on which believing Christians may disagree but which will result in significant boundaries between congregations. Whether to baptize infants or believers is a second-order issue. The question of whether women should be ordained as church leaders also belongs to the second order.

Third-order issues: Nonessential issues over which Christians should learn to disagree agreeably. "Christians who affirm the bodily, historical, and victorious return of the Lord Jesus Christ may differ over timetable and sequence without rupturing the fellowship of the church. Christians may find themselves in disagreement over any number of issues related to the interpretation of difficult texts or the understanding of matters of common disagreement. Nevertheless, standing together on issues of more urgent importance, believers are able to accept one another without compromise when third-order issues are in question."

before Justin's debate with the rabbi, the apostle Paul pointed out the importance of this principle to the church in Rome. Paul's specific prescription for dealing with these points of disagreement was "without quarreling over disputable matters" and that people "should be fully convinced in their own mind" (Romans 14:1, 5). Notice that Paul did not forbid the formation of biblically based beliefs about nonessential issues—otherwise, the Roman Christians couldn't have been "fully convinced" in their own minds! Yet Paul reminded them to hold these beliefs with humility and gentleness, because "we will all stand before God's judgment seat" (Romans 14:10).

THREE ESSENTIAL TRUTHS ABOUT THE END TIMES THAT CHRISTIANS HAVE ALWAYS BELIEVED

© Janaka Dharmasena

This pattern of learning to distinguish between essential and nonessential beliefs persisted far past the pages of the New Testament. As Christianity spread throughout the Roman Empire in the first and second centuries AD, deviant forms of faith developed in some areas. People who held these deviant beliefs claimed to be Christians. Yet these same persons denied essential truths that the apostles had taught in the churches.

Some false teachers, for example, claimed that the physical world was completely evil; thus, they rejected the physical resurrection and return of Jesus. Others of these false teachers claimed that the God who created the world and the God revealed in Jesus were two different deities. A few even butchered their Bibles to match their false beliefs, cutting out the entire Old Testament and much of New Testament until only Paul's epistles and Luke's Gospel remained. Then, they doctored Luke's Gospel to remove references to the physical birth and resurrection of Jesus!

To protect congregations from these false teachings, a summary of essential beliefs that could be traced back to the apostles emerged very early in the church's history. This summary became known as the "Rule of Faith."

Beginning in the second century AD, new believers memorized the truths found in the Rule before they were baptized. Although the precise wording of the Rule of Faith varied slightly from church to church, the same essential truths could be found in each variation.

So what did the Rule of Faith have to say about eschatology, the study of the end times? When it comes to the end times, Rule of Faith clearly affirmed three essential truths:

1. Against those who claimed that Jesus would not return to earth in bodily form, the Rule of Faith declared that Jesus "sat at the Father's right hand and will come again."

2. Against those who claimed that Christians would not be resurrected physically, the Rule of Faith confessed a belief in "the resurrection of the flesh."

3. Against those who denied a future judgment, the Rule of Faith affirmed that Jesus would "judge the living and the dead."[25]

In the early centuries of Christian faith, many churches required new converts to affirm the Rule of Faith before being baptized. "Wade in the Water." Postcard of a river baptism in New Bern, North Carolina, around 1900.

THREE ESSENTIAL TRUTHS

Essential truth about the end of time	What Scripture says
Jesus will return to earth in bodily form at some point in the future	"The Son of Man will come at an hour when you do not expect him" (Matthew 24:36–44; Mark 13:32–37). "Jesus, who has been taken from you into heaven, will come back in the same way you have seen him go into heaven" (Acts 1:11). "We wait for the blessed hope—the appearing of the glory of our great God and Savior, Jesus Christ" (Titus 2:13). "Christ was sacrificed once to take away the sins of many; and he will appear a second time, not to bear sin, but to bring salvation to those who are waiting for him" (Hebrews 9:28). " ... continue in him, so that when he appears we may be confident and unashamed before him at his coming" (1 John 2:28).
Jesus will judge all humanity	"He has fixed a day on which he will judge the world in righteousness by a man whom he has appointed; and of this he has given assurance to all by raising him from the dead." (Acts 17:31; see also 10:42). "We must all appear before the judgment seat of Christ" (2 Corinthians 5:10). "Christ Jesus ... is to judge the living and the dead" (2 Timothy 4:1).
God will physically resurrect all humanity at some point in the future	"The rest of the dead did not come to life until the thousand years were ended.... And I saw the dead, great and small, standing before the throne.... The sea gave up the dead who were in it, and death and Hades gave up the dead who were in them, and each person was judged according to what they had done" (Revelation 20:5, 12–13).

What early Christians said	Nonessential details about this essential truth
"This prophecy [Isaiah 33:13–19] is about the bread that the Messiah gave us to eat ... and the cup that he gave us to drink; ... this prophecy proves that we shall behold this very same King in glory."[26] "The church believes in ... the ascension into heaven in the flesh of the beloved Messiah Jesus our Lord, and in his revelation from heaven in the Father's glory to gather all things into one."[27] "He sat at the Father's right hand ... and will return in splendor."[28]	Whether the return of Jesus will be one single event after a time of tribulation, or if Jesus will return to remove his church before the great tribulation and then return to reign after the time of tribulation.
"John prophesied ... the eternal resurrection and judgment of all."[29] "He shall execute righteous judgment toward all, so that he may send spiritual wickednesses and the angels who transgressed and became apostates together with the ungodly, unrighteous, wicked, and profane into eternal fire. He will by his grace confer immortality on the righteous, holy, and those who have kept his commands and persevered in his love-—some from the beginning and others from their repentance-—and will surround them with eternal glory" (Irenaeus). Jesus will "take the holy ones to the enjoyment of eternal life and of the heavenly promises, and he will condemn the wicked to eternal fire" (Tertullian).	Whether Jesus will judge all humanity at the same time or if he will judge Christians at the judgment seat of Christ (2 Corinthians 5:10) and non-believers at the great white throne (Revelation 20:11–15).
"If you have fallen in with some so-called Christians but ... who say there is no resurrection of the dead, ... do not imagine that they are Christians."[30] Jesus will "raise up anew all flesh of the whole human race" (Irenaeus). Judgment will occur "after the resurrection of both these groups, ... with the restoration of their flesh" (Tertullian).	Whether the resurrection will occur all at once at the end of time, or if some will be resurrected before the great tribulation, some after the great tribulation, and the remainder after a thousand-year reign of Jesus on earth.

THREE ESSENTIAL TRUTHS IN THE APOSTLES' CREED

Over time, the Rule of Faith became standardized in a statement that we know today as the "Apostles' Creed." Even with a few slight shifts in wording across the centuries, the essential components of the original Rule of Faith remain unaltered. Consider this amazing truth: Less than a century after Jesus walked the dusty roads of Judea and Galilee, churches throughout the world were confessing the same essential truths about the end times that Christians still confess today when they recite the Apostles' Creed. Like the Rule of Faith, the Apostles' Creed affirmed that:

- Jesus will return physically to earth.

- God will physically resurrect all humanity.

- Jesus will judge all humanity.

APOSTLE

(from Greek *apostolos*, "commissioned one").

An eyewitness of the risen Lord Jesus (Acts 1:2, 21–22), commissioned by Jesus to testify authoritatively to the meaning of Jesus' identity and ministry (Luke 10:16).

Apostles' Creed	Summary of Meaning
I believe in... (Isaiah 44:6)	The basic meaning of *creed*. *Credo* means "I believe." It expresses the beliefs that unite all Christians. The words that follow preserve the teaching of the Apostles.
God, the Father Almighty (Isaiah 44:6)	Not just belief in an impersonal force or in many gods, but rather, a deep trust in a personal, caring, loving God.
Maker of heaven and earth. (Gen. 1:1; John 1:1)	God is powerful. Just as God created the universe, God can heal, save, guard, comfort, and guide us. The whole universe is his.
And in Jesus Christ, his only Son, (John 9:38; 20:28)	We believe Jesus is the promised Messiah. Believing in God is also believing in Jesus.
Our Lord; (Phil. 2:9–11)	No nation, no king, no Caesar comes first: only Jesus is Lord. He has all authority and power; only he deserves praise and worship.
Who was conceived by the Holy Spirit, and born of the Virgin Mary; (Luke 1:35)	Jesus' birth and life were a miracle: he was both fully divine and fully human. By being fully human, Jesus has shown us how to live, taken upon himself the penalty of sin, and given us a new life and a new future.
Suffered under Pontius Pilate, (Luke 23:23–25)	Many have blamed Jews for Jesus' death. The Creed makes it clear that Pilate decided Jesus' death. Jesus died an innocent man. Pilate's injustice contrasts with God's justice; Pilate's arrogance contrasts with Jesus' humility.
Was crucified, died, and buried (1 Cor. 15:3–4)	These events really happened. Jesus' crucifixion and death were not staged; Jesus' death was real and a sad necessity for our sake.

Apostles' Creed	Summary of Meaning
He descended into hell; (1 Peter 3:18–19)	The meaning of this line is not clear; some think it refers to 1 Peter 3:19: "He went and preached to the spirits in prison." It is also possible to translate this line as "he descended to the dead," emphasizing the reality of Jesus' death. The phrase was not in the oldest available copy of the creed.
On the third day he rose from the dead; (1 Cor. 15:4)	Jesus' resurrection is fundamental. His resurrection points to the fulfillment of all justice and the hope for all believers. Jesus is the "firstborn from among the dead" (Col. 1:18).
He ascended into heaven and is seated at the right hand of the Father; (Luke 24:51)	Ascending to heaven and sitting at the right hand of the Father demonstrate Jesus' authority over the whole creation.
From thence he will come to judge the living and the dead. (2 Tim. 4:1; John 5:22)	Jesus' second coming will not be like a humble lamb. He will return like a triumphant king and judge. With his authority, he will judge all of creation. Christians rest assured that there is "no condemnation for those who are in Christ Jesus" (Rom. 8:1).
I believe in the Holy Spirit, (John 15:26; 16:7–14)	Jesus promised to send us a Comforter, Guide, Equipper, and Advocate. The Holy Spirit is God's presence in our midst.
The holy catholic church, (Gal. 3:26–29)	God has called his people out of sin and death; it is a group separated (holy) and from the whole world and throughout all time and space (the word catholic with small "c" means "universal"). The church is a people bought with the precious blood of Jesus on the cross.
The communion of saints, (Heb. 10:25)	In Jesus, all believers from all places and all times are brothers and sisters; we all share the same fellowship, the same Spirit, and the same Lord. We, who were many, are now one people in Jesus. In Jesus, all believers are saints (Acts 9:13, 32; 26:10; Phil. 4:21).
The forgiveness of sins, (Heb. 8:12; Luke 7:48)	Sin had broken our relationship with God, with creation, and with one another. Jesus has reconciled us with God, freeing us from our sin and death.
The resurrection of the body, and the life everlasting. (1 Thess. 4:16; John 10:28)	Unlike the Gnostics who viewed every physical reality as evil, Christians believe that they will receive new bodies and a new creation. Jesus' resurrected body was real (he could eat and could be touched); our resurrection bodies will also have a physical nature. And we will live with Jesus forever in a new creation.

THE PROBLEM WITH MARCION (AD 140)

- One prominent heresy began with a preacher's kid. His name? Marcion. His father was an overseer or elder in a city on the southern coast of the Black Sea. At first Marcion followed a different path from his father. He became a ship-owner, sailing passengers and cargo throughout the Roman Empire. During his travels, Marcion developed a distaste for the physical world and a theology that mingled this distaste with a heretical form of Christian faith.

- While a member of the church in Rome, Marcion developed his heretical ideas into a full-fledged system. According to Marcion, the wrathful God of the Jewish Scriptures was not the same deity as the Father of Jesus. The God of the Jewish people was, Marcion claimed, a lower deity, the Creator of the physical world. The supreme God of the universe was the all-loving Father of Christ—a deity who would never punish anyone or resurrect anyone's physical body. Marcion even reduced the Savior to a spirit; according to Marcion, Christ only seemed human. This belief later became known as Docetism.

- Because they believed the earth was evil, Marcion's followers denied every earthly desire. When they celebrated the Lord's Supper, Marcion's followers drank only water. Why? Drinking the fruit of the vine might incite physical pleasure. They banned all sexual relations—even between spouses.

- As he proclaimed this perspective on life, Marcion perceived a problem: Some portions of the apostles' writings challenged his teachings. And what was his solution? Marcion created the earliest known list of authoritative writings for Christians. Only eleven books made Marcion's list—an edited version of Luke's Gospel and ten of Paul's letters. The good news was that, in Marcion's Sunday school, learning the books of the Bible was easy. The bad news was that Marcion had rejected the God of Israel—the very God that, according to the earliest eyewitnesses of Jesus, had been revealed in Jesus Christ. This placed Marcion's beliefs far beyond the boundaries of faith that had been passed down through the apostles.

- In 144 the Roman church returned the money Marcion had donated. Several Christians, including Polycarp of Smyrna, tried to turn Marcion away from his wayward teachings. In the end, Marcion refused, and he was removed from the church's fellowship. He responded by forming his own congregations in Italy and Asia Minor.

Three Essential Truths at the Council of Nicaea

A couple of centuries after the Rule of Faith and Apostles' Creed circulated throughout the Roman Empire, another controversy arose to threaten the truths that had been "once for all entrusted to God's holy people" (Jude 3). The followers of an Alexandrian elder named Arius were singing in the streets, "There was a time when the Son did not exist!"—denying not only the Trinity but also the unique deity of Jesus. To counter these false claims, more than three hundred church leaders gathered in a village known as Nicaea (modern Iznik, Turkey) to reaffirm what the churches had long believed about Jesus. From this council in Nicaea, another statement of faith emerged. Once again, even in this expanded creed, the same three essential truths about the end times remained intact. According to the creed that developed from Nicaea:

- Jesus "ascended into heaven, ... [from] thence he shall come again."
- "We look for the resurrection of the dead."
- "He shall come again, with glory, to judge the living and the dead."

NOTE: The words in italics in the following chart are additions made after the First Council of Nicaea in AD 325. The Council of Constantinople made these additions in AD 381.

Nicene Creed	Meaning	Comments
We believe in one God, the Father Almighty, Maker *of heaven and earth, and* **of all things visible and invisible.**	As in the Apostles' Creed, the foundation of the Christian faith is the uniqueness of God. He alone is God. The Father is a distinct person, or individual reality, within the Godhead. In addition, God created all things. He is not created, but the Creator.	In Gnosticism, the God of the Bible is just the *demiurge*, an evil god who brought about the material world. This god is himself a created being.
And in one Lord Jesus Christ, *the only-begotten* **Son of God, begotten of the Father** *before all worlds,* **Light of Light, very God of very God, begotten, not made, being of one substance with the Father; by whom all things were made;**	The creed affirms Jesus' • Lordship: The creed gives him the same title applied to God the Father in the Old Testament. • Equality: Jesus is as much God as the Father. They share the same divine *essence*. Thus, Jesus is eternal. • Distinctness: Although they share the same essence, Jesus is a *person* distinct from the Father.	In the New Testament, Jesus' Lordship is directly connected to his divinity. He is not Lord simply because he earned it; rather, he is Lord because he is God. Arius tried to understand the Incarnation, but his approach ignores the broad context of the Scriptures.

Nicene Creed	Meaning	Comments
Who for us, and for our salvation, came down *from heaven,* **and was incarnate** *by the Holy Ghost of the Virgin Mary,* **and was made man;** *he was crucified for us under Pontius Pilate,* **and suffered,** *and was buried,* **and the third day he rose again,** *according to the Scriptures,* **and ascended into heaven,** *and sits on the right hand of the Father;* **from thence he shall come** *again, with glory,* **to judge the living and the dead;** *whose kingdom shall have no end.*	The creed emphasizes both Jesus' divinity and humanity. • The image of coming down from heaven shows his divinity. • His miraculous virgin birth shows his humanity. • His suffering and death on the cross, again, show his full humanity. • His resurrection and ascension show his perfect work of salvation on behalf of humanity. • His final judgment shows his authority over the whole creation.	Heresies about Jesus denied either his full divinity or his full humanity. • Denying Jesus' divinity removes his ability to save humanity from sin and death. Jesus is reduced to being a *model* of perfection. • Denying Jesus' humanity removes his ability to intercede and represent humanity in his death.
And in the Holy Spirit, *the Lord and Giver of life, who proceeds from the Father [and the Son], who with the Father and the Son together is worshiped and glorified, who spoke by the prophets.*	The creed confirms the Bible's doctrine of the Trinity: The Holy Spirit is fully divine, of the same *essence* as the Father and the Son, and is a distinct person within the Godhead. In the sixth century, Western churches added "who proceeds from the Father *and the Son.*" It is this last addition, known as the *filioque* (Latin for "and the Son") that has caused division and conflict between the Eastern Orthodox and Western churches.	The natural consequence of denying Jesus' divinity is that the Holy Spirit is not divine either. After the creed of AD 325, the heresy about the Holy Spirit arose as a follow-up to Arianism.
In one holy catholic and apostolic church; we acknowledge one baptism for the remission of sins; we look for the resurrection of the dead, and the life of the world to come. Amen.	One of the main purposes of the creed was to promote the unity of all believers in one universal church within the Apostolic tradition. Baptism represents this unity, as does the forgiveness of sins, the resurrection, and the world to come. These are all promises and hopes that link all Christians everywhere and at every time.	The Arian controversy threatened to split the young and growing church. The creed allows the possibility of unity of belief and practice. The word *catholic* means "universal," in the sense of the whole world. It refers, then, to the worldwide fellowship of all believers.

What do we learn from looking at these early creeds and confessions of faith?

When studying the differences between end times views, it's easy to feel like no one really agrees about *anything* when it comes to the end of time. That's when it seems appealing to declare oneself a "*pan*-millennialist" and say "I don't know what will happen, but it will all *pan* out in the end!" Or how about a "*pro*-millennialist" who declares, "Whenever God does it, I'm *for* it"? But such flippant responses overlook a beautiful truth that is crystal-clear in these ancient creeds and confessions of faith: Regardless of the particulars of their perspective, Christians throughout the world and throughout time have shared a common confession when it comes to the end of time. *The same Savior who was crucified also conquered death, and he will return to earth in bodily form; the dead will be raised, and the judge of the living and the dead will be Jesus himself.*

THREE KEY THEMES THAT BRING BELIEVERS TOGETHER: KINGDOM, TRIBULATION, AND PATIENT ENDURANCE

Throughout time and throughout the world, Christians have agreed on three essential truths about the end of time—but the agreement doesn't stop there! In the opening verses of Revelation, John listed three eschatological themes that he and his readers shared in the experiences of their daily lives: "the suffering [or tribulation] and kingdom and patient endurance that are ours in Jesus" (1:9). Despite the differences and the distance that separated John from the seven churches in Asia Minor, he was a "brother and companion" with these believers when it came to tribulation, kingdom, and patient endurance (1:9).

Two thousand years later, when looking at the end times, these same three themes provide a worthwhile spot to conclude our consideration of where Christians agree on the end times. You may take a different view on the Antichrist or the thousand-year reign of Christ than other persons in your church—but when it comes to kingdom, tribulation, and patient endurance, there is far more that draws you together than pulls you apart. Regardless of your differences, you and every other believer in Jesus have experienced God's kingdom, you live through times of tribulation, and you wait with patient endurance.

© Mr. Arakelian

First Theme: The Glory of the Kingdom

The kingdom of God is God's people living in God's domain under God's rule.[31] Christians in a multitude of times and places have agreed that God inaugurated a kingdom through the life, death, and resurrection of Jesus. From the very beginning of his earthly ministry, the gospel of Jesus was, after all, the good news of the kingdom of God (Matthew 3:2; 4:17, 23; 24:14). This kingdom will not be consummated or fully realized until King Jesus returns to earth—but that doesn't make the kingdom of God any less true or real here and now! Another term for the kingdom of God is "the kingdom of heaven." The ancient Hebrews occasionally used "heaven" or "the heavens" as a respectful way of referring to God. In keeping with this custom, the Gospel According to Matthew employed "kingdom of heaven" as a synonym for "kingdom of God"—but not because the kingdom of heaven is somehow different from the kingdom of God! When we compare parallel passages in the Gospels, it is very clear that the kingdom of God and the kingdom of heaven are two different phrases that describe one identical reality (compare Matthew 8:11 with Luke 13:29, for example, or Matthew 11:11 with Luke 7:28).

THE KINGDOM OF HEAVEN = THE KINGDOM OF GOD	
"I tell you, many will come from east and west and recline at table with Abraham, Isaac, and Jacob in **the kingdom of heaven**" (Matthew 8:11)	"And people will come from east and west, and from north and south, and recline at table in **the kingdom of God**" (Luke 13:29)
"This is he of whom it is written, 'Behold, I send my messenger before your face, who will prepare your way before you.' Truly, I say to you, among those born of women there has arisen no one greater than John the Baptist. Yet the one who is least in **the kingdom of heaven** is greater than he" (Matthew 11:10–11).	"This is he of whom it is written, 'Behold, I send my messenger before your face, who will prepare your way before you.' I tell you, among those born of women none is greater than John. Yet the one who is least in **the kingdom of God** is greater than he" (Luke 7:27–28).

Second Theme: The Reality of Tribulation

Christians throughout the ages have also recognized that this Christ-inaugurated kingdom is not yet fully realized on earth. Because the full realization of God's kingdom is yet to come, God's people endure times of tribulation even as they rejoice in the truth of God's eternal kingdom—and this should not surprise us. Jesus clearly predicted tribulation for his followers: "In the world you will have trouble," Jesus said, "but take heart! I have overcome the world" (John 16:33; see also Matthew 24:9; Acts 14:22; Romans 8:35; 12:12; Revelation 1:9).

© Jaco van Rensburg

Christians differ on the particulars of the period described in Scripture as "the great tribulation" ("great distress" in the NIV) (Matthew 24:21; Revelation 7:14). Also, there's disagreement on whether Christians will endure this time of terror. However, on one point all believers agree: ***Until the return of Jesus Christ, God's people will experience persecution, tribulation, and distress***. Although many of us haven't experienced persecution firsthand, Christians around the world suffer terrible persecution and martyrdom for the sake of Christ.

And it isn't only human beings that share in the pain of a sin-shattered world: Throughout this time of waiting for kingdom come, all creation "groans together" with God's children in expectation of a revelation that will mark the end of all tribulation. The center-point of this revelation will be the unveiling of the Son of God alongside a multitude of blood-redeemed brothers and sisters, the adopted sons and daughters of Almighty God (Romans 8:22–23).

© Evgeni Gitlits

WHERE ARE THE MOST DANGEROUS PLACES FOR CHRISTIANS TO LIVE?

The World Watch List (at www.OpenDoorsUSA.org) ranks the countries where persecution of Christians is most severe. For the past two decades, North Korea, Saudi Arabia, and Iran have topped the list.

- North Korea allows only the worship of "the beloved leader" Kim Jong Il and his father Kim Il Sung. Christians are seen as a threat, so increasing numbers of Christians have been sentenced to torture and starvation in labor camps or secretly executed. North Korea's border with China is virtually closed. Chinese authorities vigilantly pursue North Korean defectors and return them to North Korea to face a painful, prolonged death in labor camps.

- In Saudi Arabia, public non-Muslim worship is forbidden. Although Christians are generally allowed to worship in private, some have been arrested, issued with death threats, and forced into hiding. Most Saudi believers must keep their faith secret or else risk being killed by family members in honor killings.

- In Iran, the police closely watch and crack down on house churches. Muslims found guilty of converting to Christianity could face a death sentence. Church services may be monitored by the secret police. Believers are often discriminated against, making it difficult to find and keep jobs.

100 million: The number of Christians living in areas where they face persecution

400 million: The number of Christians living under the threat of persecution

Third Theme: The Responsibility to Endure Patiently

So what are Christians called to do while they await this revelation? Every believer in Jesus Christ is a partner with other believers not only in kingdom and tribulation but also in "patient endurance" (Revelation 1:9). Until the consummation of God's kingdom, Christians wait and work together "patiently" (Romans 8:25). Patient endurance is very different from laziness or passive waiting. Patient endurance means working together to expand the kingdom of Christ into the lives of people around us while finding contentment in the goodness of God's providential care in each present moment.

IT'S NOT JUST ABOUT THE FUTURE

Kingdom. Tribulation. Patient endurance.

If you are a believer in the Lord Jesus, these three themes are not simply theoretical aspects of your future life. They are woven into every moment of your life here and now. The themes of kingdom, tribulation, and patient endurance are as near to you as the events of this very day.

You have confessed Jesus as the king of all kings. Yet your gas tank still gets empty, your baby's diaper still gets full, and some months still outlast the balance in your checking account. What's more, sometimes you still struggle to submit yourself to the Messiah's reign in your life. Other times, you may be treated unjustly because of your faith in Jesus.

And so, what do you do?

You patiently endure tribulation; you rejoice in God's ever-present presence while never ceasing to pray, "Your kingdom come, your will be done, on earth as it is in the heavens." And you wait—you wait and work toward the glorious future that Christians have anticipated in every time and every place, a future in which Jesus will return to earth, God will raise the dead to life, and the Jesus himself will judge all humanity.

© *Galyna Andrushko*

CHAPTER 4
Words You Need to Know When It Comes to the End of the World

TWELVE KEY TERMS TO HELP YOU UNDERSTAND THE END TIMES

By this point, perhaps you have asked yourself, "If there's so much common ground among Christians, why are there different views of the end time? What causes people to read the same texts so differently? Why can't everyone agree on one view?"

These are good questions, but they aren't easily answered.

The entire issue would be far simpler if every Bible-believing Christian held one particular view of the end times while all slanderers of Scripture pursued other perspectives. Yet that's simply not the case. In the study of eschatology, Christians who sincerely trust the truth of Scripture have arrived at very different perspectives. That's been the case at least since the second century AD and will probably continue until the end of time—at which time God could prove us all wrong about the specifics of Christ's second coming!

© Vitaly M

So why *doesn't* everyone agree on one view of the end times?

Here's a primary reason why: At different times in the history of Christianity, Bible-believing followers of Jesus have taken:

> **APOCALYPSE**
>
> From the Greek words *apo*, "away from" and *kalupsis* "cover." It is the unveiling (revelation) of God's plan concerning the end times.

- Three different perspectives on how God will fulfill his promises to Abraham and Israel.
- Four different approaches to interpreting biblical apocalypses.
- These differences have resulted in four distinct views of the end times.

Let's take a closer look at each of these views, approaches, and perspectives to gain a better understanding of how Jesus will be glorified through God's work at the end of time!

TWELVE KEY TERMS TO HELP YOU UNDERSTAND THE END TIMES

One word to describe the reign of Jesus

Millennium (from Latin *mille* [thousand] and *annum* [year]) The reign of Jesus that John described in Revelation 20:1–6.

Three perspectives on how God will fulfill his promises to Abraham and Israel

Dispensational God has two plans with two people, the church and Israel. God will fulfill his promises to Abraham and Israel by giving to ethnic Jews the land that he promised to Abraham.

Covenantal God has one plan with one people, with one covenant of grace that extends from the fall of humanity to the end of time. God's work with Israel was preparatory for his work with the church.

New Covenantal God has one purpose that he has worked out through multiple covenants. God's work with Abraham and Israel was a temporary picture of what God had already purposed to do in Jesus. God's promises to Abraham find their fulfillment in Jesus.

Four approaches to interpreting apocalyptic literature

Futurist Apocalyptic texts in the Bible are predictive prophecy about events that, even now, have not yet occurred.

Historicist Apocalyptic texts in the Bible are symbolic retellings of certain epochs of history.

Idealist Apocalyptic texts in the Bible are idealized expressions of struggles between good and evil that occur in every age.

Preterist (from Latin *praeteritus*, "past" or "bygone") Apocalyptic texts in the Bible are symbolic descriptions of events that happened near or soon after the time when the text was written. In other words, they happened soon after Jesus' death and resurrection.

Four views of the end times

Amillennial—There will be no future, earthly millennium. The millennium is the present spiritual reign of Jesus with his people. Jesus will return physically to earth at the end of the millennium. (*See Chapter 16.*)

Postmillennial—The millennium is a spiritual reign of Jesus on earth through the widespread proclamation and acceptance of the gospel. Jesus will return physically to earth at the end of the millennium. (*See Chapter 17.*)

Dispensational Premillennial—The millennium will be a future, physical one-thousand year reign of Jesus on the earth, following a time known as "the great tribulation." Jesus will return to rapture Christians from the earth before God pours out his wrath on the earth. (*See Chapter 18.*)

Historical Premillennial—The millennium will be a future, physical one-thousand reign of Jesus on the earth after all times of tribulation have ended. Christians endure the great tribulation. (*See Chapter 19.*)

THREE PERSPECTIVES ON HOW GOD FULFILLS HIS COVENANT WITH ABRAHAM[32]

If you spent any time in children's church in your childhood years, you may have heard a song that ran something like this: "Father Abraham had many sons, and many sons had father Abraham"—go ahead and start humming the tune if you know it—"I am one of them and so are you, so let's just praise the Lord." What typically followed this line was a hodgepodge of physical movements that had nothing to do with father Abraham and everything to do with expending the children's excess energy. It's sort of like a church version of "The Hokey-Pokey," but without the whole "shake it all about" bit.

Abraham's Departure by Jozsef Molnar (1850)

Despite the lighthearted lilt of this tune, the lyrics lead to a serious theological dilemma: If I am a son of Abraham "and so are you" because of our faith in Jesus, what about the physical progeny of Abraham? How will God fulfill his promises to Abraham, Isaac, Jacob, and their descendants? What about the Jewish people?

The dilemma is as ancient as the first generation of Christians. "Know then," Paul admonished a congregation in Asia Minor, "that those who have faith are children of Abraham" (Galatians 3:7), clearly identifying believers in Jesus as Abraham's children.

In other places, Paul made it clear that God has not given up on his work with the physical descendants of Abraham. "Did God reject his people?" Paul asked the Christians at Rome. "By no means! I am an Israelite myself, a descendant of Abraham, from the tribe of Benjamin. God did not reject his people, whom he foreknew" (Romans 11:1–2).

And so, according to Paul, anyone who trusts in Jesus becomes a son of Abraham; yet, at the same time, God has not given up on persons who have physically descended from Abraham.

> ## GOD'S PROMISE TO ABRAHAM
>
> God made an agreement with Abraham. In this agreement, God makes the following promises:
>
> 1. To make a great nation from Abraham's descendants (Genesis 12:1–3)
>
> 2. To give to Abraham's descendants all the land of Canaan (Genesis 15:18–21)
>
> 3. To make Abraham a father of many nations (Genesis 17:2–9)

Up to this point, nearly every person who professes faith in Jesus would agree. But here is also where questions emerge that reveal significant disagreements among sincere believers: For example, does God have distinct and separate purposes for Israel and the church? Or were God's dealings with Israel primarily a preparation for what he has accomplished in Jesus Christ? How will God fulfill the covenant of land and blessing that he made to Abraham? What role does the modern nation of Israel play in the fulfillment of these promises?

There are three primary perspectives when it comes to how God will fulfill his covenant:

Dispensationalism: Two purposes, two people

Dispensationalists believe that "throughout the ages God is pursuing two distinct purposes: one related to the earth with earthly people and earthly

> ## DISPENSATION
>
> The unique pattern of expectations and purposes that God has for particular group of people during a divinely-designated period of time. See chart on pages 312–313.

objectives involved, which is Judaism; while the other is related to heaven with heavenly people and heavenly objectives involved, which is Christianity."[33] God's distinct purposes with different peoples are organized into "dispensations." Within each dispensation, there are different ways that someone can be a child of Abraham:[34]

1. ***Children of Abraham through physical descent***: The Jewish people are children of Abraham through natural lineage from Abraham, Isaac, and Jacob; some of these persons simultaneously share in a spiritual lineage because they have faithfully kept God's law. Dispensationalists contend that faithful Jews with a natural lineage that stretches back to Abraham must someday rule the land "from the Wadi of Egypt to the great river, the Euphrates" (Genesis 15:18). At some point in the future, near the end of a terrible time-period known as "the great tribulation," the physical descendants of Abraham will repent of their rejection of Jesus Christ and return to their rightful God.

> **GENTILE**
>
> (from Latin *gentilis*, "tribe")
> Anyone who is not Jewish.
> Also *goyim* (Hebrew,
> "nations") or *ethne*
> (Greek, "nations").

2. ***Children of Abraham through spiritual adoption***: Believers in Jesus Christ are children of Abraham through a spiritual lineage. God's purpose in this spiritual lineage is separate from his purpose and work with the nation of Israel. God offered the kingdom to the Israelites through Jesus Christ, but the leaders of Israel rejected this offer. As a result, God offered Gentiles the possibility of becoming spiritual children of Abraham. This offer of grace to the Gentiles was "an unexpected and unpredicted" spiritual parenthesis within God's work with the physical descendants of Abraham.[35]

Covenantalism: One plan, one people

The **covenantal** perspective takes a quite different view of God's plan.[36]

- According to covenantalists, *God has always had one plan and one people*.
- God's people in every age have been those who live by faith in Jesus as the divine Messiah and King.

- In the New Testament and in the Old, it was only through faith in the Messiah that anyone could become a true child of Abraham and enter into right relationship with God (Galatians 3:7–9).

- Before Jesus arrived on earth, faithful Israelites—as well as some who weren't Israelites at all—trusted in Jesus by looking expectantly for the Messiah who was yet to come (Hebrews 11:13, 39–40).

> **HEBREWS 11:39–40**
>
> "These were all commended for their faith, yet none of them received what had been promised, since God had planned something better for us so that only together with us would they be made perfect."

- Because persons in every age have been saved only through faith in Jesus as their Lord and Messiah, one single covenant of divine grace stretches from the promise of the Messiah in Eden (Genesis 3:15) to the triumph of the Messiah at the end of time (Revelation 20:6–10).

- The purpose of Israel was to prepare the way for the Messiah's coming and to provide a people through whom God could display his glory.

- From a covenantal perspective, God's purpose when he chose Abraham was for the descendants of Abraham to be the people through whom Jesus came into the world.

- Even then, God intended his promises to Abraham and to the Israelites to find their fulfillment in Jesus. The Old Testament tells the story of how God preserved the descendants of Abraham so that he could reveal himself to the world through Jesus.

© Natalia Rex

When it comes to how God fulfills his promises of land and blessings, covenantal theologians take a variety of viewpoints—and none of these viewpoints excludes the others. Here are three common covenantal views on how God keeps his promises to Abraham and Israel:

1. ***"Don't you remember? I already gave you the land!"—Fulfillment during King Solomon's reign.*** According to some covenantal theologians, God fulfilled his promise to Abraham during the reign of King Solomon. According to 1 Kings 4:21, Solomon ruled all the kingdoms from the Euphrates River to the border of Egypt. This fulfilled God's promise to Abraham (Genesis 15:18).

2. ***"I warned you that this would happen if you worshiped those other gods!"—A promise with a condition.*** Some see God's covenant as a promise with a condition. God promised that the descendants of Abraham would receive land regardless of their deeds (Deuteronomy 9:5), but they would retain the land only if they remained faithful to their God (Joshua 23:15–16). When the Israelites turned to other gods, they lost this aspect of God's blessing (Deuteronomy 4:26).

3. ***"There are some new kids in town, and they've taken your place"—Fulfillment through the church.*** From the perspective of some covenantalists, *the church has superseded Israel as God's people.* According to this view—known as "supersessionism," because theologians like making up words that are bigger than necessary—God is fulfilling his promises to the Jewish people through the church.[37]

   - Paul referred to followers of Jesus Christ as "the Israel of God," and James used "the twelve tribes" as a description for Christians (Galatians 6:16; James 1:1). This suggests to supersessionists that the church fulfills God's plans for Israel.

   - A supersessionist might also point to these words that Jesus himself spoke to the Jewish leaders of his day: "The kingdom of God will be taken away from you and given to a people who will produce its fruits" (Matthew 21:43).

   - Some supersessionists suggest that God's promise of the land to Abraham is being fulfilled as believers in Jesus Christ reign alongside their Savior and King (Revelation 20:6).

   - The supersessionist view was widespread in the early church. Lactantius (c. 240–320) declared that, because the Jewish people had not turned to Jesus, "God changed his covenant—that is, he bestowed the inheritance of eternal life on foreign nations—and collected to himself a more faithful people."[38]

- Sadly, in several instances throughout church history, persons who claimed to be Christians have misconstrued such thinking to excuse violence toward Jews. This is not the fault of supersessionism, however; it's the result of a sinful human choice to distort God's Word and to pin blame on a particular ethnic group. Regardless of one's view of the end times, persecution of Abraham's descendants represents an inexcusable repudiation of the passionate love for the Jewish people that pervades the New Testament (see, for example, Romans 1:16; 9:1–5).

> **ROMANS 9:1-4**
>
> "I speak the truth in Christ—I am not lying, my conscience confirms it through the Holy Spirit—I have great sorrow and unceasing anguish in my heart. For I could wish that I myself were cursed and cut off from Christ for the sake of my people, those of my own race, the people of Israel."

New Covenant Theology: One plan, more than one covenant

New covenantalists see God's workings in the Old Testament as a separate covenant with a preparatory purpose that pointed people toward the new covenant that God made through Jesus (Jeremiah 31:31–34; Hebrews 8:7–13). Paul did, after all, refer to God's work with Israel and his work in Jesus as covenants, in the plural (Galatians 4:24).[39]

In this distinction between Israel and the church, there are similarities between new covenantalism and dispensationalism. But there are also distinct differences:

- According to new covenantalists, God's work with Abraham and Israel was always intended to be a temporary picture of a more permanent reality (Hebrews 3:5; 8:5–13; 9:8–10; 10:9). And what was the permanent reality that God had planned before time began? *To redeem sinners for his glory through Jesus Christ and to provide those people with a place of contentment and peace.*

- New covenantalists—as well as many covenantalists—take God's promises to Abraham and Israel as promises that find their fulfillment in Jesus.

- As proof of this pattern, new covenantalists might point out how Paul explained a singular noun in God's promises to Abraham: "The promises were spoken to Abraham and to his seed. Scripture does not say, 'and to seeds,' meaning many people," Paul emphasized, "but, 'and to your seed,' meaning one person, who is Christ" (Galatians 3:16; see Genesis 12:7). In other words, God's promises to Abraham find their fulfillment in Christ.

- And so, God's promise to give Abraham all the land from the Nile River to the Euphrates River (Genesis 15:18) *will* be fulfilled—but *not* because the modern nation of Israel will somehow gain this land! The promises were made to one particular descendant of Abraham, Jesus Christ ("to one," Galatians 3:16).

- Old Covenant Israel was a type or temporary picture that anticipated the coming of Jesus—the true Israelite, the true servant, and the true vine (compare Isaiah 5; Hosea 11:1; Matthew 2:15; John 15). The church is "the Israel of God" only because the church is united with Jesus, the true Israelite (Galatians 6:16).

> **GALATIANS 3:7–9**
>
> "Understand, then, that those who have faith are children of Abraham. Scripture foresaw that God would justify the Gentiles by faith, and announced the gospel in advance to Abraham: 'All nations will be blessed through you.' So those who rely on faith are blessed along with Abraham, the man of faith."

- It is through the kingdom reign of Jesus over all the earth that God's covenant with Abraham will be fulfilled. The gospel includes the claim that God's reign has been inaugurated in Jesus (Mark 1:14-15). And so, every time we proclaim the gospel, we are also proclaiming God's fulfillment of his promises to Abraham and Israel through Jesus.

- The commands of Jesus and his apostles provide a law ("the law of Christ," Galatians 6:2) for New Testament believers. However, neither this law nor the Old Testament law was ever intended to save anyone.

- The purpose of these laws was to reveal the holiness of God, the depth of humanity's sin, and the patterns of a God-centered life. In Old and New Testament alike, salvation came through personal faith in the promised Messiah (Galatians 3:7–9; Hebrews 11:13, 39–40).

Hints of this Jesus-centered perspective were common among the earliest generations of Christians. Less than a century after the New Testament writings were completed, Justin Martyr seems to have taken a similar position to new covenantalism.[40] Melito of Sardis put it this way in the late second century: "The [Old Testament] law was a parable, a sketch. The gospel became the explanation of the law and its fulfillment."[41]

THREE VIEWS ON FULFILLMENT

PERSPECTIVE ON FULFILLMENT	PRECISE FORM OF FULFILLMENT
Dispensationalism	
Fulfillment in the future through the nation of Israel	At some point in the future, physical descendants of the ancient Israelite people will possess the land promised to Abraham (Genesis 15:18; 17:8).
Covenantalism	
Fulfillment during Solomon's reign	When Solomon ruled the region from the Euphrates River to Egypt, God fulfilled his promise to Abraham (1 Kings 4:21).
Conditional promise	When the Israelites turned to other gods, they forfeited the land that God had promised (Joshua 23:15-16).
Fulfillment through the church	Because Israel rejected the Messiah, the church has superseded Israel in God's plan (Matthew 21:43). Also known as "replacement theology" or "supersessionism."
New covenantalism	
Old covenant as temporary picture of new covenant	As a temporary picture, the covenant with Abraham and Israel was intended to be fulfilled in Jesus and then to pass away (Hebrews 3:5; 8:5-13; 9:8-10; 10:9). The present and future reign of Jesus over all the earth fulfills God's promise to Abraham.
Fulfillment in Jesus Christ (also affirmed by many covenantalists)	God's promise was made primarily to one offspring of Abraham, Jesus the Messiah (Genesis 12:7; Galatians 3:16). Through the present and future reign of Jesus over all the earth, including the promised land, God fulfills his promise to Abraham.

FOUR APPROACHES TO APOCALYPTIC TEXTS: FUTURIST, HISTORICIST, IDEALIST, PRETERIST

How you read depends on *what* you're reading.

Suppose you're reading a comic book. Even if you pore carefully over every "ungh!" and "whump" in the white balloons, you're likely to make it through a page of superhero duels far quicker than you'd finish a page from Leo Tolstoy's *War and Peace*. That's because these are two very different forms of literature (and perhaps also because, when reading a comic book, you are more likely to remain awake).

Did you read the newspaper this morning? Even though you might take both a newspaper and a thought-provoking novel seriously, you approach these texts with two different sorts of seriousness. The newspaper quickly informs you about current events and weather patterns while the novel provokes questions deep in your soul. Once again, *what* you're reading influences *how* you read.

It's that way when it comes to biblical apocalypses too (see definition on page 54). How you read these writings depends on what you think you are reading. If you take these texts primarily as predictions of events yet to come, you will scour them for clues about what could happen in the future. But if you see Daniel and Revelation mostly as elaborate illustrations of temptations that Christians face in every age, you'll probably look for connections between your present struggles and the temptations of past believers. If you read them as writings that provide a God-centered perspective on what was happening in the times when the texts were written, you will spend your time seeking hints of first-century events.

When it comes to biblical apocalypses, all of this becomes a bit more complex because the authors wove together different styles in the same text. For example, Daniel's prophecies include apocalyptic elements—but the book of Daniel is also full of historical vignettes from life in Babylon.

© Elnur

Since Revelation is primarily an apocalyptic text, how are we to understand the letters to real-life local churches at the beginning of the book of Revelation?

- Are these epistles to be read simply as introductory letters for the seven original recipients of this apocalypse?
- Or do they represent examples of churches that exist in every age?
- How do the letters connect to the visions in the rest of the book? Might they even be historical retellings of the entire story of Christianity, encoded in the form of letters?

Here's one way to think about the apocalyptic texts that are found between the bonded-leather bindings of your Bible:

- *Road maps for the future?* If you see Daniel, Revelation, and other apocalyptic texts mostly as road maps for the future, you are probably taking what's known as a *futurist* view.
- *History textbooks about the past, present, and future?* If you think apocalyptic texts prophetically provide information about a long period of history— perhaps the history of Christianity or some other significant epoch—that's a *historicist* approach.
- *Allegories for all times and places?* If all the visions seem to you to be allegories of struggles that God's people in every age, that's closer to an *idealist* view.
- *Long-lost newspapers from the past?* If you see the biblical apocalypses as books that mostly tell about current events from the times when the texts were written—something like a lavishly-written newspaper report—that's a *preterist* perspective.

It's important to notice that none of these four approaches completely excludes the others. Partly because the biblical writers mixed literary genres, nearly every interpreter of the end times draws from more than one of these approaches when reading biblical apocalypses and end-times prophecies.

FOUR APPROACHES TO APOCALYPTIC TEXTS

Approach	Analogy	Assumption about Biblical Apocalypses	Analysis of Approach	Aim of Studying Biblical Apocalypses
Futurist	A road map for the future	Apocalyptic texts tell what will happen in the future, before and during the end times.	Futurism treats the text as a predictive prophecy about events that, even now, have not yet occurred. The emphasis in futurism is on events that will happen near the end of time.	To understand the events that will occur before and during the end times.
Historicist	A history textbook for the past, present, and future	Apocalyptic texts tell what is happening from God's perspective throughout a particular period of history.	Historicism treats apocalyptic writings as symbolic retellings of certain epochs of history; if someone reads Revelation in this way, that person might expect, for example, that John is using lavish language to retell the history of early Christianity, the rise and fall of the Roman Empire, or some other series of events.	To understand God's perspective on the events of human history.
Idealist	An allegory for all times and places	Apocalyptic texts tell in picturesque language the conflict that is always happening between good and evil.	Idealism treats apocalypses as symbolic expressions of struggles between good and evil that occur in every age. Idealism sees the scenes and symbols in biblical apocalypses as picturesque expressions of the conflict between the reign of God and the powers of evil.	To understand God's perspective on the conflict between the reign of God and the powers of evil.
Preterist	An ancient newspaper	Apocalyptic texts tell about events that happened around the time that the texts were written or soon afterward.	The word "*preterist*" comes from the Latin *praeteritus* ("past" or "bygone") and suggests that most or all the events described in apocalyptic text have already passed. A *preterist* treats apocalyptic texts as descriptions of events that happened near or soon after the time when the text was written. Typically, preterists understand the fall of Jerusalem and destruction of the temple in AD 70 as the time when many apocalyptic prophecies were fulfilled.	To understand God's perspective on the events that happened around the time in which the text was written.

WHEN AND HOW THE KINGDOM COMES

How long is a thousand years?

When it comes to the end times, it all depends on who you ask.

Near the end of his visions on the island of Patmos, John glimpses a glorious angelic being. The angel bursts forth from the heavens with a chain and a key in hand. Suddenly, a dragon appears as well—the same dragon who had slithered into Eden as a serpent and who whispered temptations in the Messiah's ear in the deserts of Judea. The divinely-empowered angel seizes the dragon, chains him, and hurls him into a bottomless pit where he will remain for "a thousand years" (Revelation 20:1-3). Throughout this span of a thousand years, the souls of martyrs and faithful witnesses live and reign with Christ (Revelation 20:4–5). In Christian theology, this thousand-year reign has become known as the "millennium," from the Latin terms for "thousand" (*mille*) and "year" (*annum*).

But this notion of a millennium leads to a long litany of difficult questions: Are these ten centuries intended to be taken as a precise time-period or as a symbol of something greater? And when in human history does the chaining of the dragon take place? Has it already happened? Or is this event yet to come? Will Jesus physically return to earth before the millennium or afterward?

How you reply to these questions depends on the perspective that you took on some of the earlier questions in this chapter. Are you reading the biblical apocalypses from a futurist perspective or more idealistically? More as a historicist or as a preterist? Do you see covenantal continuity or dispensational discontinuity between the Old and New Testaments?

© Linda Armstrong

Over the past two thousand years, these differences in interpretation have resulted in four primary perspectives on how time will end. All four views agree when it comes to every essential truth about the end times: Someday, Jesus will return to set the world right; God will resurrect all humanity, and Jesus will be their judge. Yet each view takes a very different perspective on how the return of Jesus relates to the millennial kingdom.

Kingdom Came and Is Still Coming: Amillennialism: (A-Millennial: "No millennium") The "thousand years" is *not* ("a-") a future, earthly reign. But the millennium is no less real simply because it does not include an earthly kingdom! For the amillennialist, the millennium symbolizes the present and ongoing reign of Jesus with his people. It is a spiritual reign that extends from the ascension of Jesus to his glorious return. Amillennialists tend to see the relationship between Israel and the church from a covenantal or new covenantal perspective.

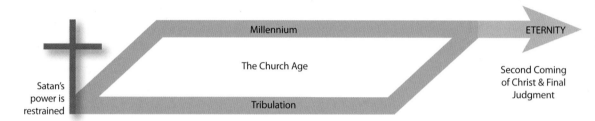

Kingdom Came and is Yet to Come—but Jesus Won't Return Until the Millennial Kingdom Is Complete: Postmillennialism: (Post-Millennial: "After the millennium") Jesus will return to earth *after* ("post-") a millennium when the overwhelming majority of persons throughout the world embrace the gospel. This millennium may last exactly one thousand years, or "thousand years" may symbolize an extended era of gospel peace. In either case, Jesus will not be physically present on the earth during the millennium; he reigns spiritually through the spread of his gospel around the globe. Postmillennialists see covenantal continuity between Israel and the church.

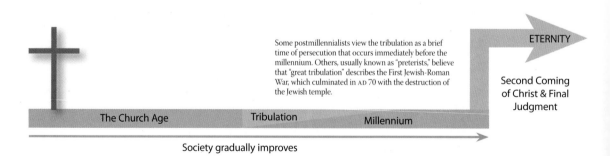

Kingdom Is Yet to Come—But, Before the Kingdom Comes, Christians Will Leave the World Behind: Dispensational Premillennialism: (Pre-Millennial: "Before the millennium") Jesus will return to earth *before* ("pre-") the millennium. Before Jesus returns to establish his millennial kingdom, seven years of "tribulation" will afflict the earth. Most dispensational premillennialists expect Christians to be "raptured" from the world before the tribulation. A few dispensationalists do, however, expect God to remove Christians from earth partway through the tribulation. Dispensationalists see Israel and the church as two separate groups for whom God has two separate plans. During the great tribulation, God will renew his work with the earthly nation of Israel.

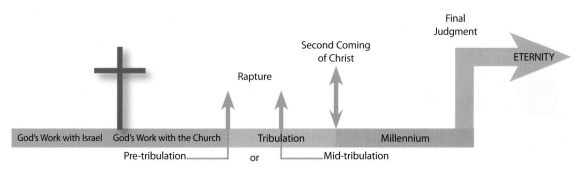

Kingdom Came and is Yet to Come—and Christians Will Still Be on Earth When the Kingdom Is Consummated: Historical Premillennialism: Jesus will return to earth *before* ("pre-") the millennium described in Revelation 20, after a time of tribulation. Christians endure the time of tribulation. Historical premillennialists tend to take a covenantal or new covenantal perspective on the relationship between Israel and the church.

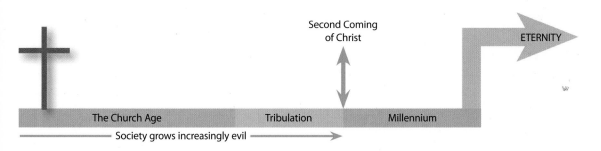

69

FOUR APPROACHES TO THE BOOK OF REVELATION

Approaches to Revelation	Amillennialism	Postmillennialism
The seven churches (Rev. 1–3)	**Preterist**—John was addressing seven local churches in the first century **Idealist**—Each church symbolized a type of church that can be found in every age	**Preterist**—John was addressing seven local churches in the first century **Idealist**—Each church symbolized a type of church that may be found in every age
The time of tribulation (Rev. 4–19)	**Historicist**—Tribulation describes distresses that God's people endure throughout history **Preterist**—Tribulation describes first-century persecutions and conflicts **Idealist**—Tribulation symbolizes distresses that God's people endure in every age	**Historicist**—Tribulation describes distresses that God's people have endured throughout history **Preterist**—Tribulation described first-century persecutions and conflicts **Idealist**—Tribulation symbolizes distresses that God's people endure in every age **Futurist**—Tribulation describes a time of distress immediately before the millennium begins
The millennial kingdom (Rev. 20)	**Idealist**—Millennial kingdom symbolizes the reign of Jesus in the lives of his people or with the glorified people of God in heaven **Historicist**—Millennial kingdom is the reign of Jesus through his people from the establishment of the Church to the end of time	**Historicist**—Millennial kingdom is the reign of Jesus through his people **Futurist**—Millennial kingdom describes a future time when Jesus begins to reign through his gospel
The New Creation (Revelation 21—22)	**Futurist**—God will glorify all who trusted Jesus and condemn all who rejected him	**Futurist**—God will glorify all who trusted Jesus and condemn all who rejected him

Dispensational Premillennialism	Historical Premillennialism
Preterist—John was addressing seven local churches in the first century **Historicist**—Each church represents an era of church history **Idealist**—Each church represented a type of church that may be found in every age	**Preterist**—John was addressing seven local churches in the first century **Idealist**—Each church represented a type of church that may be found in every age
Futurist—Tribulation describes a seven-year time of distress between the rapture and Jesus' return to establish his millennial kingdom	**Historicist**—Tribulation describes distresses that God's people have endured throughout history **Preterist**—Tribulation described first-century persecutions and conflicts **Idealist**—Tribulation symbolizes distresses that God's people endure in every age **Futurist**—Tribulation describes a time of distress immediately before the millennium begins
Futurist—Millennial kingdom describes a future time when Jesus will physically reign on earth	**Futurist**—Millennial kingdom describes a future time when Jesus will physically reign on earth
Futurist—God will glorify all who trusted Jesus and condemn all who rejected him	**Futurist**—God will glorify all who trusted Jesus and condemn all who rejected him

WHY DOES IT MATTER?

After hearing so many different perspectives on eschatology, some Christians find themselves wondering, "Why do different views of the end times even matter? What's the point of knowing what Christians throughout the ages have believed about the end of time? There are so many disagreements!"

If your sole goal is simply to increase your knowledge about the end times, you're right: there is no point in such study. It is a trivial pursuit of knowledge, and knowledge without love leads only to arrogance (1 Corinthians 8:1).

It doesn't have to be that way, though. With love for God and for fellow believers firmly in place, increased knowledge of God's workings and God's Word can help to grow your soul.

So what can happen when knowledge of the end times mingles with love divine? As you hear the voices of past Christians, you learn to appreciate believers who have different understandings of nonessential beliefs. As you recognize the essential truths that have been cherished throughout the church's history, you become more able to identify false teachings here and now. Perhaps most important of all, as you develop clear expectations for the end of time, you are likely to look for the coming of Jesus with a deeper and more urgent sense of anticipation. That's when you find yourself speaking in joyous unison with Christians throughout the ages, saying, "Come, Lord Jesus!" (Revelation 22:20)

CHAPTER 5 What Happens After the End

LOOKING PAST THE END

As early as the second century AD, Christians have differed when it comes to *how* God will bring the world to an end. Yet there has been widespread agreement about *what happens after* God's final triumph over evil (Revelation 20:7-9).[42] *There will be a final judgment of all humanity.*

The consensus among early Christians about the outcome of this judgment was consistent and clear:[43] Faithful followers of Jesus would be welcomed into a new heaven and a new earth while all who failed to submit to the Son of God would experience unending torment. According to Irenaeus, God will "send spiritual wickednesses and the angels who transgressed and became apostates together with the ungodly, unrighteous, wicked, and profane into eternal fire. He will by his grace confer immortality on the righteous, holy, and those who have kept his commands and persevered in his love ... and will surround them with eternal glory."[44] These teachings from the early church are rooted deeply in the words of Jesus and his apostles (Revelation 20:10–21:8).

But what will this "eternal glory" be like? Will it be an unearthly existence without physical bodies? And what does it mean to be cast "into eternal fire"? What is the biblical perspective on heaven and hell?

© PHOTOCREO Michal Bednarek

WHAT DO WE MEAN BY *HEAVEN*?

In popular culture, and for many believers, heaven evokes images of cloudy, ghost-like existence, or angelic beings floating about among the clouds. This image comes radically and wrongly separates the physical and spiritual worlds. Some of the resulting misconceptions in popular culture are:

POPULAR VIEW OF HEAVEN

- A place for disembodied, ghost-like beings
- A place where people sing all the time
- A place up among the clouds
- A place everyone goes after death
- A place where all beings live as angels

BIBLICAL VIEW OF HEAVEN

However, the final destination of believers is not an ethereal place like that. The final destination of all believers is *the renewed heavens and earth* anticipated in Revelation 21. A very physical future awaits us when Christ comes back.

WHAT CAN WE KNOW ABOUT HEAVEN?

Perhaps not as much as we would like! Still, we can be confident of these truths:

- God's promises are trustworthy, including his promises about heaven.
- We will be with God and with our fellow believers in heaven.
- God's plan for his people is far greater than anything we can ask or imagine.

A non-biblical understanding of the universe

Behind the cloudy, ethereal idea of heaven lies the old Greek belief that the physical world is evil and the spiritual is good. Thus, one must focus on the spiritual to escape this evil world. This is not a biblical idea. It ignores some basic biblical facts:

A biblical understanding of the universe

1. God made the whole universe and called it *very good* (Genesis 1:31).

2. Satan is a spiritual being and is evil—thus, not all *spiritual* is good and not all *physical* is evil.

3. God promises a renewed heavens and earth at the end of time (Revelation 21).

WHAT IS HEAVEN?

- In Scripture, the word "heaven" can refer both to the physical reality beyond the earth (see, for example, 1 Kings 21:24; Psalm 19:1; Acts 1:11) and to the spiritual dimension wherein God dwells in glory (see 1 Kings 8:27; Amos 9:6; Acts 7:55).

- Heaven is where the final judgment will occur (Revelation 20:7–15).

- After the final judgment, the distinction between heaven and earth will pass away. The "New Jerusalem" will descend from heaven to earth (Revelation 21:2–10).

Unfortunately, many people gain their ideas of heaven from popular literature, movies, and television instead of Scripture. Popular media often portray heaven as boring, ethereal, and unearthly—but this is not the perspective of Scripture.

Although sin has profoundly affected creation, God never called creation evil. It is under a curse. However, Jesus came to lift that curse and turn it into blessing. God is redeeming all of creation. At the end of time, God will renew all things to their original intention.

WHAT WAS GOD'S ORIGINAL INTENT FOR CREATION?

God created the whole universe for his own glory and relationships. He intended all his creatures to relate to each other, to nature, and to himself in harmony. Humanity's main and great goal in life is to glorify God (Isaiah 60:21; 1 Corinthians 6:20; 10:31) and enjoy him forever (Philippians 4:4; Revelation 21:3–4).

Human sin twisted God's original intentions. However, because of God's grace and faithfulness, his plans would not be frustrated. He planned to rescue his creation from the effects of sin (Romans 8:18–27). Through the saving work of Jesus on the cross, people can find peace with God and each other. Through the same process, believers can begin the reconciliation with one another and God's world.

WHAT IS THE RENEWED HEAVEN AND EARTH?

This process will have a glorious ending when Christ returns. He will renew all things (Revelation 21:1). It will not be a different creation or a non-creation. It will be *this* creation renewed; God will restore his creation to its original glory and purpose. As if to close the circle, what God began at Eden he will fulfill in Revelation. Not everything will be the same. Some things from the biblical idea of Eden will continue in the renewed creation; others will end (see page 92).

From the beginning, God's intent was for his glory to cover the earth as water fills the seas (Numbers 14:21; Isaiah 11:9; Habakkuk 2:14). Adam and Eve were commanded to expand the family of humanity beyond Eden until the image of God encompassed the earth (Genesis 1:26–28), but they chose sin

instead. Israel was called to extend God's glory throughout all creation (Psalm 2:8; 72:8–19), but they chased after other gods. Jesus alone perfectly exemplified the glory of God. Through the new heaven and new earth where Jesus will reign over all creation, God's original intent will be fulfilled; his glory will fill the entire cosmos like water that fills the seas.

NEOS AND KAINOS

Greek has two different words for the idea of *new*. *Neos* is a newness of time; *kainos* is a newness of quality. A *neos* object would mean that the object did not exist and now is there. A *kainos* object means that the object was there but its quality has changed: it is better, it is made different. In this sense, the *new heavens and earth* in Revelation 21:1 are not *neos* but *kainos*. That is, God will renew, transform, improve, and refresh his creation. It will be a *kainos* heaven and earth.

© Andrejs Pidjass

WHAT IS OUR HOPE FOR THE FUTURE?

Our hope for the future is firmly rooted in God's faithfulness. We can trust that God will do what he has promised us because he has been faithful in the past. We can safely conclude that many features and characteristics of this world will continue in the renewed creation. Of course, there will be things that will end as well. Based on biblical testimony, we can identify many things that will continue and some that will not.

> *This is the will of Him who sent Me, that of all that He has given Me I lose nothing, but raise it up on the last day*—John 6:39 (*NASB*).
>
> Besides referring to people, this text could also refer to God's creation. The neuter pronoun *it* (Greek *auto*) would seem to extend Jesus' mission from people to all of creation (see Romans 8:19–22 and Colossians 1:20). Jesus' words in John 6:39 are a guarantee that no good thing shall be lost, but rather shall have some new and fulfilled form in the renewed creation. Everything good belongs to Christ, who is the life of the whole world as well as the life of every believer (John 6:33, 40). All things good in this world will continue to exist in the next, but they will be transformed in the renewed creation.

What Will Continue in our Glorified Bodies	What Will End in Our Glorified Bodies
• Relationship with God (Revelation 21:3) • Relationships with fellow human beings (Luke 24:39; John 20:27) • Physical bodies (1 Corinthians 15:42–44) • Ethnic backgrounds (Revelation 21:24) • Eating and drinking (Revelation 22:2; see also Luke 24:36–42; Acts 10:41) • The natural world (Revelation 22:2) • Learning (1 Corinthians 13:12)	• Sin (Revelation 21:8, 27) • Death (Revelation 20:14; 21:4) • Curse (Revelation 22:3) • Hunger and thirst (Revelation 22:1–2) • Weeping (Revelation 21:4) • Sadness (Revelation 21:4) • Sickness and pain (Revelation 21:4) • The need for marriage and childbearing (Matthew 22:30; Mark 12:25)

WHY DOES JESUS' RESURRECTION MATTER?

Jesus' resurrection gives us a good idea of what heaven may look like. The Apostle Paul makes it clear that our future is tied to Jesus' own resurrection (1 Corinthians 15:12–34). He concludes, "And if Christ has not been raised, your faith is futile" (15:17).

- Because Christ has been raised from the dead, our hope is true and secured.
- Christ is the firstfruits or first example of all who will be raised into new life (1 Corinthians 15:20).
- Our future includes a resurrected body; that is, it will be a physical reality. Our future resurrected bodies will be like Jesus' own resurrected body (1 Corinthians 15:42–49).
- The women and the disciples recognized Jesus after his resurrection (Matthew 28:9, 17).
- Jesus' body was physical (Luke 24:39). Jesus ate with his disciples (Luke 24:41–43). Yet, it was not a body like ours. The Apostle Paul uses two ways to explain this difference:

© R. Gino Santa Maria

  1. Just as different animals have bodies suited for their environment (for the sea, the air, and the ground), so our resurrected bodies will be suited for the renewed creation (1 Corinthians 15:39).

  2. There are also "natural bodies" and "spiritual bodies." Both Jesus' pre- and post-Resurrection bodies were physical; the difference has to do with whether this body will perish. Natural bodies die; spiritual bodies do not. Sin has polluted and damaged our natural bodies; our bodies die, decay, and are unfit for a future in God's presence. Just as God will renew this creation, also marred by sin, God will give us renewed bodies that will not be polluted by sin, will not decay, and will be fit to continue forever in the presence of God.

Natural Bodies	Spiritual Bodies
Psychikos	*Pneumatikos*
Derived from *psyche*, meaning "soul"	Derived from *pneuma*, meaning "spirit"

The ending *-ikos* is used in Greek to make an adjective, and it means "in reference to." It does not describe the material out of which something is made. Rather, it refers to the force that animates an object. In this case, *psychikos* refers to the human soul that animates our bodies. In the case of *pneumatikos*, it refers to the Spirit, God's Spirit, as the source of existence (see, for example, Romans 1:11 and Galatians 6:1). Thus, both kinds of bodies are physical. The difference is that a "natural body" dies and a "spiritual body" does not die.

WILL WE BE ABLE TO RECOGNIZE OUR LOVED ONES IN HEAVEN?

Yes! When Jesus rose from the dead and appeared to his friends and disciples, they recognized him (Luke 24:39; John 20:27). There will be continuity between our bodies today and our resurrected bodies in the renewed creation.

© Tiffany Chan

JOB 19:25–27

"I know that my Redeemer lives, and that in the end he will stand upon the earth. And after my skin has been destroyed, yet in my flesh I will see God; I myself will see him with my own eyes—I, and not another. How my heart yearns within me!"

WHAT KINDS OF RELATIONSHIPS WILL EXIST IN HEAVEN?

Emotions and relationships are a very important part of what it means to be human. There will be emotions and relationships in heaven, though they may not be exactly the same. They will be renewed emotions, emotions as they were meant to be from the beginning: joyful, satisfying, enriching, intimate, and refreshing.

The most important relationship in heaven will be our fellowship with God the Father, Son, and Holy Spirit. We will be his people and he will be our God in an intimate and perfect relationship that lasts forever (Revelation 21:3). God himself will provide everything that we need (Revelation 21:6), and we will worship him face-to-face (Revelation 22:3–5).

© Monkey Business Images

WILL THERE BE DISABILITIES, INJURIES OR DEFORMITIES IN HEAVEN?

No. There will be no brokenness at all, either emotional or physical. God will renew our bodies; they will be beautiful and work as God intended them to. Because Jesus' scars were visible after his resurrection (Luke 24:39; John 20:27), some think that martyrs, those who died for the name of Jesus, will wear their healed scars as badges of honor. Although it is possible, it remains, like so many other things about heaven, just speculation.

© Florin C

Will our bodies need food, clothing, and language in heaven?

Because we do not understand the nature of the future bodies, it is difficult to know whether they will need food, clothing, and languages. However, since our bodies will preserve much of their characteristics, we could imagine that language, food, and clothing will have very similar functions. Jesus drank and consumed food in his glorified body (Luke 24:36–42; Acts 10:41). John's descriptions of the new heaven and new earth include fruit trees and a river, so it certainly seems possible that glorified believers will eat and drink in heaven (Revelation 21:6; 22:1–2).

© Monkey Business Images

Jesus, in his glorified body, was seen wearing "a long robe, with a golden sash around his chest" (Revelation 1:13). Jesus promised his faithful followers that they would receive "white garments" (Revelation 3:5). Throughout Revelation, John mentioned robes and clothing in connection to the glorified people of God (Revelation 4:4; 6:11; 22:14). Much of this language may be symbolic, but it certainly suggests that Christians could wear some form of clothing in eternity.

In this fallen world, clothing can be a status symbol to serve our pride or a covering to prevent shame. Whatever clothing may exist in heaven, its purpose will not be to serve pride or to prevent shame. Its purpose will be somehow to point to the glory and purity of Jesus, the sacrificed and risen King.

Will heaven be boring?

Definitely not! People may get the idea that heaven will be boring because we will worship God all day long in heaven. It is true—we will worship God non-stop! But let's revisit what we mean by *worship*.

Worship is not just the singing and praying part of Christian church services. Everything we do can be worship: from the moment we wake up, take our meals, relate to others, do our work, play games, and live life. Worship is not just an activity; it is primarily an attitude. Worship is the attitude that arises when we recognize who God is and who we are:

God	Human
He is the creator	We are the creatures
He is in control of our lives	We depend completely on God's grace and mercy
He is all powerful	We are limited and weak
He knows all things	We know imperfectly
He loves us unconditionally	We are just learning to love in the same way

Worship is the attitude that acknowledges God's presence at every moment in our daily lives, sometimes moving us to tears, sometimes to great joy, to repentance, to humility, to gratitude, to hard work, to commitment, to compassion, to love.

In the busyness of our lives, we often miss this reality: God is interested and active in our lives! We may go days or weeks without realizing that our words, actions, and thoughts have brought glory or sadness to God. This forgetfulness will find no place in the renewed creation; we will not miss God in our lives because he will dwell in our midst.

WORSHIP

An attitude of awe and gratitude, of humble submission to God's greatness and grace, of obedience and love.

WHAT WILL WE DO IN HEAVEN?

The Bible does not give many details about activities in heaven. But we can be sure that:

- God loves his creation. He proclaimed it good (Genesis 1:31).
- Nature itself reflects God's greatness and glory (Psalm 19).
- Nature will be renewed so it may fulfill God's purposes.

So it is at least possible that much of the new creation will be similar to what we experience now. The best things about this world will become better in the renewed creation.

WHAT WILL WE SEE IN HEAVEN?

John described heaven as a place that has:

- A city that looks like a rare jewel, with a high wall, golden streets, twelve gates, and twelve foundations (Revelation 21:11–21).
- No need for sun or moon because of the splendor of the Lord God Almighty and the Lamb (Revelation 21:23).
- A river surrounded by fruit trees (Revelation 22:1–3).

Some of these descriptions may be metaphors. For example, the streets of gold could symbolize the fact that the wealth of the old earth has no value in the new earth. Regardless of whether these descriptions are metaphors or physical realities, one thing is certain: "No eye has seen, nor ear heard, nor the heart of man imagined, what God has prepared for those who love him" (1 Corinthians 2:9).

The New Jerusalem, Kimon Berlin

WILL THERE BE WORK?

In the aftermath of humanity's fall, work often feels like painful toil (Genesis 3:17–19). As a result, we may wonder if heaven means that we will never need to work again. But don't forget that:

- Work preceded humanity's fall into sin (Genesis 1:28; 2:15).
- Work was part of what God declared to be "very good" in his original creation (Genesis 1:31).
- Work was one of the means by which Adam would have expanded Eden to fill the earth with God's glory.

As such, it seems quite possible that glorified believers will enjoy some form of work in heaven—but none of this work will be to impress others or to earn favor. Whatever work we do will be a free and joyous response to all that Jesus has already accomplished. Jesus has completed every work that is needed to provide "eternal salvation" that will satisfy our souls forever (Hebrews 5:8–9; 10:12–22). Every crown and honor in heaven is placed at his feet, for he alone is worthy of such glory and praise (Revelation 4:10–11; 21:24).

© Lilun

WILL THERE BE LEARNING OR ARTS IN HEAVEN?

Worship seems to be a central activity of the heavenly realm (Revelation 4:10; 5:14; 7:11; 11:16; 22:3). In Scripture, worship often includes singing and playing music (2 Chronicles 29:28–30; Psalm 66:4), so music will likely be part of the experience of heaven. Dedication of physical structures provided opportunities for worship in Scripture (Ezra 3:10–13); perhaps art and architecture could provide opportunities for praise in heaven as well. Certainly, there may be learning in heaven; believers could grow for all eternity in their knowledge of the infinite perfections of Jesus (see 1 Corinthians 13:12).

> **COLOSSIANS 3:23-24**
>
> "Whatever you do, work at it with all your heart, as working for the Lord, not for men, since you know that you will receive an inheritance from the Lord as a reward. It is the Lord Christ you are serving."

WHAT WILL HAPPEN TO ME BETWEEN DEATH AND THE FINAL JUDGMENT?

Most Christian theologians throughout church history have affirmed an "intermediate state"—a spiritual existence that lasts from an individual's death until the final judgment. Jesus taught that, even though the fathers of the Israelite nation were physically dead, they were still alive (Matthew 22:31–32). Jesus also promised the dying thief that they would be together in Paradise "today" (Luke 23:43). Paul expected to be with Jesus immediately when he died (Philippians 1:20–24). Scripture does not provide details about this intermediate state, but it is clear that human beings continue to exist even after death.[45]

THE LONGING FOR A LASTING CITY

- Heaven is not an escapist idea; our longing for heaven provides an orientation and a goal to guide our lives here and now. G.K. Chesterton once wrote, "We must be fond of this world ... in order to change it. ... We must be fond of another world ... in order to have something to change it to."[46]

- In the Old Testament exodus, Moses led the Israelites to the Promised Land; this exodus provided a picture of what Jesus would do in

Heavenly Jerusalem, Mattias Gerung, 1530–32

the New Testament. Jesus inaugurated a new exodus that will lead his people to a "lasting city" in a glorious new heaven and earth (Hebrews 13:14).

WHO WILL BE IN HEAVEN AND HOW DO WE GET THERE?

© David Huntley

- Jesus is the only source of lasting life (John 11:25; 14:6; Colossians 3:4), and heaven is only for those whose names have been inscribed in "the book of life" (Revelation 20:15). Apart from explicit faith in Jesus, no human being will enjoy God's glorious presence in heaven. "There is salvation in no one else, for there is no other name under heaven given among men by which we must be saved" (Acts 4:12).

- There is nothing that we can do to get to heaven. We can only respond to what God has already done by trusting in Jesus and surrendering our lives to him.

- Sin is rebellion against the infinite holiness of God; even sins that seems slight to us deserve eternal judgment. Jesus took this eternal judgment on himself in place of everyone who would trust in him. Anyone who does not trust in Jesus will endure eternal torment in a "lake of fire" (Revelation 20:11–15).

- Scripture does not provide specific details about this eternal torment in the lake of fire, and much of the language about hell seems to be metaphorical. This much is certain, though: If the language about hell is metaphorical, the reality will be worse than the metaphors.

- According to Scripture, hell is a place of "fire" (Revelation 20:15); "weeping and grinding of teeth" (Matthew 13:50; 24:51; 25:30); "darkness" (Matthew 22:13; 25:30); and never-ending agony (Mark 9:48). In hell, those who have never trusted Jesus will receive their due for "things done while in the body" (2 Corinthians 5:10; 2 Peter 2:13; Jude 1:15).

WHAT IS THE NEW JERUSALEM?

The book of Revelation provides another image of the renewed creation: the city of Jerusalem (Rev. 21:2). The city is described as a bride and its dimensions are detailed. Believers understand this text in different ways. Some understand the city to be a literal city, and the dimension an accurate representation of what the city will be like. The resulting picture is an enormous cube of about 1,400 miles per side.

Others take this image as a symbolic representation of God's people. Since the image of the bride ready to marry the Lamb occurs before, and it seems applied to God's people (Rev. 19:7), it is possible that the Holy City stands for God's holy people. It is perfectly possible that there will be no seas (21:1), or sun and moon (21:23). It is also possible that the language is symbolic—the text in Revelation says the "city does not need the sun or the moon" not that they will not exist. If there is continuity between this creation and the renewed creation, as we have suggested, then the beauty of the sun and the moon will be present, even if not needed.

> There is much about heaven and hell that God does not tell us. But we can rest in this certain truth: God has revealed to us all that we need to know for us to be fully faithful to Jesus. Even though Scripture may not give us every detail, Scripture provides a "more sure" word than human experience or speculation (2 Peter 1:19).
>
> And so, as we consider what will happen after the end of time, it is to these written words that we "do well to pay attention as to a lamp shining in a dark place, until the day dawns and the morning star rises in [our] hearts" —(2 Peter 1:19).

In any case, it is clear that:

- The renewed creation is God's work, since it comes from above.
- It is large enough to fit all of God's people.
- It points at the beauty and splendor of the renewed creation.
- God dwells in its midst.
- It closes the circle from Paradise in the Garden of Eden to the Holy City in the new heavens and new earth.

Original Creation (Genesis)	Renewed Creation (Revelation)
Heaven and earth created (1:1)	Heavens and earth renewed (21:1)
Sun created (1:16)	No need of sun (21:23)
The night established (1:5)	No night there (22:5)
The seas created (1:10)	No more seas (21:1)
The curse enters the world (3:14–17)	No more curse (22:3)
Death enters the world (2:19)	Death is no more (21:4)
Humanity is cast out of paradise (3:24)	Humanity is restored to paradise (22:14)
Sorrow and pain begin (3:17)	Sorrow, tears, and pain end (21:4)

THE END OF THE WORLD IN THE OLD TESTAMENT

Introduction

- ***In the beginning***, God created the heavens and the earth (Genesis 1:1).
- ***In the middle***, God promised to create new heavens and a new earth (Isaiah 65:17).
- ***And in the end***, John glimpsed the long-promised new heavens and new earth (Revelation 21:1).

The story of the Bible runs from creation to new creation, from the cradle of civilization to the consummation of all things, from Eden's garden to the New Jerusalem.

© Mario Tarello

There is so much complexity and conjecture about the end times that it's tempting to skip ahead to the juicy parts—to debates about the rapture and Armageddon, winged beasts and darksome dragons, coded numbers and the end of all things.

But the end times don't start at the end.

They start in the beginning.

And, no matter how great the ending of a story may be, you don't begin at the ending; you begin at the beginning.

The end times don't start at the end.

They start in the beginning.

When the apostle Peter wrote about the end of time, he urged his first-century readers to look back at the Old Testament (2 Peter 3:2–7). There, he knew that they would see the many threads that cross over, split off, then come together again to form the stunning tapestry that God will reveal at the end of time.

How the Beginning Points to the End

CHAPTER 6

IT ALL BEGINS IN AN ORCHARD CALLED EDEN

The story of humanity begins simply and elegantly. Out of nowhere and from nothing, God created the cosmos beautiful and good. Day and night, sun and moon, dawn and dusk flashed into existence with a divine word. Then land and sea, flora and fauna, plant and animal, bird and beast, fish and fowl—all obeyed God's mere command to exist.

Then, near the end of this creative process, God chiseled out the crown jewel of the cosmos: humanity. He crafted Adam from Eden's soil and sculpted Eve from Adam's side. He made them as his mirrors, bearing his own likeness. "And God blessed them. And God said to them, 'Be fruitful and increase in number; fill the earth and subdue it'" (Genesis 1:28). Adam and Eve were placed in a luscious garden at the convergence of four life-giving rivers. Adam was commissioned to

Garden of Eden, Thomas Cole, 1825

"work" and "take care of" the garden (Genesis 2:15).

But Adam's job description ran far deeper than tilling the soil in an ancient

paradise. ***Eden was the special place of God's presence***. God "walked" in the garden—the same word used later for his presence in Israel's tabernacle (Leviticus 26:12; Deuteronomy 23:14; 2 Samuel 7:6–7). When the two verbs "work" and "take care of" occur together elsewhere in the Old Testament, they imply keeping God's word and serving as God's priest.[47]

The Creation of Adam. Jan Breughel, 1601–78.

So what does all this mean, and why does it matter for the end times?

Eden was a botanical temple where Adam had a priestly and kingly role.[48] The divine plan was for Adam to enjoy fellowship with God, to expand the garden, and to "be fruitful and multiply." Over time, this garden paradise would spread around the face of the globe and fill the earth with a holy humanity living in harmony with one another and reflecting God's own image. Then the cosmos itself would be God's temple, and his glory would emanate throughout the entire planet (Numbers 14:21; Psalm 72:19; Isaiah 6:3; Habakkuk 2:14).

The divine plan was for Adam to enjoy fellowship with God, to expand the garden, and to "be fruitful and multiply."

All of which sounds a lot like heaven, doesn't it?

You see, Eden was not just for the beginning. Eden points toward the end. Throughout the biblical story, we see God continuing to set apart people and places where his glory can dwell. Then at the end of time, in the book of Revelation, we see Eden restored, renewed, and revamped.

The last two chapters of the Bible (Revelation 21–22) are an amplified echo of the first two chapters (Genesis 1–2). In the final paragraphs of Revelation, the elder John sees a new heaven and a new earth, a holy city where God himself dwells with humanity, a place where tears have evaporated and mourning is muted and pain has passed and death has died. A sparkling river flows from the throne room of God and fruit hangs ripe from trees of life on either side of the river.

So what are we really awaiting and anticipating when we talk about the end of time? The return of Eden.

Eden and the End	Gen. 1–2	Rev. 21–22
God dwelling with humanity	3:8	21:3, 22–23; 22:3–5
No sin, mourning, pain, death	1:31	21:4, 8; 22:3
River flowing from God's presence	2:10	22:1–2
Tree of life bearing fruit	2:9; 3:22	22:2

FROM FIRST ADAM TO LAST ADAM

Adam and Eve failed in their charge. They succumbed to the serpent's cunning deception and threw the cosmos into disarray. Toil, pain, death, and broken relationships began to set the rhythms of the created order. And still, only a few pages into the Bible's story, God makes his first eschatological promise.

"I will put enmity between you and the woman," God said to the satanic serpent, "and between your offspring and hers; he will crush your head, and you will strike his heel" (Genesis 3:15). This statement has been called the *protoevangelium*, which means "first gospel," because this is the first hint of God's good news. One of Eve's descendants would be wounded by Satan ("you will strike his heel") but this same descendant would ultimately defeat Satan ("he will crush your head").

PROTOEVANGELIUM

(from Greek *protos* ["first"] + *eu* ["good" or "fortuitous"] + *angelion* ["message" or "news"])

The first prediction in Scripture of the coming of Jesus the Messiah to shatter the power of Satan. "The LORD God said to the serpent, ... 'And I will put enmity between you and the woman, and between your offspring and hers; he will crush your head, and you will strike his heel'" (Genesis 3:15).

© Sergei Chumakov

A continuation of this cosmic conflict stands at the center of the book of Revelation. A great dragon—the same serpent that slithered into Eden so long ago—makes war with a woman, her Son, and her offspring. Yet the dragon is ultimately defeated (Revelation 12:1–17). Jesus of Nazareth, the seed of Eve and the Messiah of Israel, was bruised by the serpent on Golgotha's cross (Isaiah 53:5, 10). Yet he also sealed the serpent's defeat when he rose from the dead. Through his defeat of the dragon, Jesus opened the way to a new Eden; in Jesus, a new exodus began that will lead God's people to a new heaven and a new earth.

Temptation of Christ, by Ary Sheffer (1854).

Adam Failed	Jesus Conquered
Adam was tempted in fantasy-like surroundings and failed.	Jesus was tested on the verge of starvation in the wilderness and triumphed (Matthew 4:1–11).
Adam's sin plunged the human race into wickedness, ruin, and death.	The obedient sacrifice of Jesus brought righteousness and life (Romans 5:12–21; 1 Corinthians 15:21–22).
The first Adam's actions brought about a curse.	Jesus broke the curse of the first Adam and became the "last Adam" (1 Corinthians 15:45; see also Romans 5:14).
Adam brought about death and despair to humanity.	As the last Adam, Jesus brought a new beginning for humanity and new hope for the human race.

Eden and Adam stand at the beginning of God's story line, but they are prototypes for the end. The second Adam has come, and a second Eden is assured. So as you read the rest of this book—whenever, in fact, you consider the end of time at all—remember the beginning of the story. ***Remember Eden, because Eden is coming back.***

As the last Adam, Jesus brought a new beginning for humanity and new hope for the human race.

Blessing the World: God's Covenant with Abraham

Studying the end times without considering Abraham is like researching the American Civil War without making any reference to Abraham Lincoln. You cannot understand the Civil War without some knowledge of Lincoln, and you cannot understand the end times without taking a look at God's promises to Abraham. On this, premillennialists, postmillennialists, and amillennialists can all agree: God's promises to Abraham play a central role in God's plan not only in the Old Testament but also all the way to the end of time.

- One day some four thousand years ago, God called an idol-worshiper named Abram out of the clear blue Mesopotamian sky and told him to pack up, leave his homeland, and head to a land that God would reveal (Genesis 12:1).

- The blessings that awaited him were incredible:
  » His offspring would multiply into a great nation;
  » These descendants would inherit a special land;
  » And one particular offspring would be the means by which God would bless the whole world (Genesis 12:1–3; 13:14–17; 15:1–20; 17:1–8).

- God even gave him a new name with such a great meaning that Abram probably didn't even mind switching his signature: Once he had been Abram, "the father is exalted" (which really wasn't such a bad name to begin with), but God expanded his name to Abraham, a name that identified him as "father of a multitude."[49]

God gave Abraham three primary promises that pulse like a wave throughout the rest of the biblical story and wash up on the shores of the new creation:

1. Innumerable descendants,
2. exclusive land,
3. and worldwide blessing.

> You cannot understand the end times without taking a look at God's promises to Abraham.

This ripple begins in Genesis and runs through the rest of Scripture. From Genesis 12 onward, the saving mission of God traces a path directly down Abraham's family line.

So what does all of this have to do with eschatology and the end of time?

Everything!

The nation of Israel arises from the seedbed of God's promises to Abraham, and Israel is central to biblical prophecy—on this point, nearly every Christian interpreter of prophecy agrees.

Past that point, differences begin to emerge. These differences hinge on precisely *how* Israel is central to God's plans for the end of time. Will God's promises to Israel be fulfilled through the ethnic descendants of Abraham? Or do these promises find their primary fulfillment through one particular Israelite, a descendant of Abraham known as Jesus of Nazareth?

TRACING GOD'S COVENANT WITH ABRAHAM THROUGH THE BIBLE

- **Patriarchs**: The promise to Abraham is repeated to Isaac, Jacob, and their descendants throughout Genesis (Isaac—26:3–5, 24; Jacob—28:3–4, 13–15; 35:9–12; 48:3–4; descendants—50:24).

- **Descendants**: Abraham's descendants multiply in Egypt (Exodus 1:7), escape through the exodus (Exodus 12:40–41), and enter the promised land of Canaan (Joshua 21:43–45).

- **Land**: The guarantee of land saturates the Old Testament story (Exodus 6:8; Leviticus 26:42; Numbers 32:11; Deuteronomy 6:3; Joshua 21:43–45; Judges 2:1; 1 Kings 8:34; Nehemiah 9:23–25; Psalm 105:8–11).

- **Prophets**: The prophets' hopes that God will fulfill his promises spring from God's covenant with Abraham (Isaiah 41:8; 51:1–3; Jeremiah 33:25–26; Micah 7:20).

- **The Messiah**: The royal genealogy of Jesus begins with Abraham (Matthew 1:1).

- **Church**: Paul announces that those who trust Jesus are Abraham's descendants and heirs (Galatians 3:7–9, 29).

- **Blessing**: God blesses the nations through Jesus the Messiah, the offspring of Abraham (Galatians 3:7–9).

God's Promises to Abraham

Offspring	"I will make you into a great nation" (Genesis 12:2). "To your offspring I will give this land" (Genesis 12:7). "I will make your offspring like the dust of the earth, so that if anyone could count the dust, then your offspring could be counted" (Genesis 13:15–16). "Look up at the sky and count the stars—if indeed you can count them.... So shall your offspring be" (Genesis 15:5). "Walk before me faithfully and be blameless. Then I will make my covenant between me and you and will greatly increase your numbers. ... You will be the father of many nations. ... I have made you a father of many nations. I will make you very fruitful; I will make nations of you, and kings will come from you.... The whole land of Canaan, where you now reside as a foreigner, I will give as an everlasting possession to you and your descendants after you; and I will be their God" (Genesis 17:1–8). "I will surely bless you and make your descendants as numerous as the stars in the sky and as the sand on the seashore. Your descendants will take possession of the cities of their enemies, and through your offspring all nations on earth will be blessed, because you have obeyed me" (Genesis 22:17–18).
Land	"At that time the Canaanites were in the land. The LORD appeared to Abram and said, 'To your offspring I will give this land'" (Genesis 12:6–7). "All the land that you see I will give to you and to your offspring forever.... Go, walk through the length and the breadth of the land, for I will give it to you" (Genesis 13:15–17). "I am the LORD who brought you out of Ur of the Chaldeans to give you this land to take possession of it" (Genesis 15:7). "To your descendants I give this land, from the Wadi of Egypt to the great river, the Euphrates" (Genesis 15:18). "The whole land of Canaan, where you now reside as a foreigner, I will give as an everlasting possession to you and your descendants after you; and I will be their God" (Genesis 17:8).
Blessing	"I will bless you; and I will make your name great, and you will be a blessing" (Gen. 12:2). "I will establish my covenant as an everlasting covenant between me and you and your descendants after you for the generations to come, to be your God and the God of your descendants after you" (Genesis 17:7). "Abraham will surely become a great and powerful nation, and all nations on earth will be blessed through him" (Genesis 18:18). "I will surely bless you ... and through your offspring all nations on earth will be blessed, because you have obeyed me" (Genesis 22:17–18).

HOW IS GOD'S COVENANT WITH ABRAHAM CENTRAL TO GOD'S PLAN FOR THE END OF TIME?

Dispensationalism

God will still give the land to Abraham's physical descendants

Some Christians see the centrality of Israel from a *dispensationalist* perspective. **Dispensationalism emphasizes the differences and discontinuity between the physical descendants of Abraham and followers of Jesus.**

> **DISPENSATIONALISM**
>
> God is pursuing two distinct purposes with two distinct peoples: one purpose has earthly objectives and involves the ethnic descendants of Abraham; the other purpose has heavenly objectives and involves believers in Jesus.[50] Each distinguishable outworking of God's plan in human history is known as a "dispensation."

Here's how dispensationalists see the covenant with Abraham in relation to the end times: God's promises to Abraham included unconditional guarantees of land and blessings for Abraham's physical descendants. When God made his covenant with Abraham, the presence of God passed between animal pieces that had been cut in two. Through this ritual, God declared a curse on himself if he failed to keep his promises to Abraham (Genesis 15:7–21; see Jeremiah 34:18–19). God called this covenant an "everlasting covenant" (Genesis 17:7, 13, 19).

Because this covenant was unconditional and everlasting, God must still fulfill his promises to Israel's first father—and this fulfillment must meet the expectations of the first hearers of this promise. Despite Israel's constant disobedience, "it is not as though the word of God had failed" (Romans 9:6). And so, at some point before the end of time, ethnic Israel must thrive in the land that stretches from the Euphrates River to the Nile and thereby bless the world (Genesis 12:2–3; 15:18).

Covenantalism

The promised land wasn't the point of God's promise to Abraham

On the opposite side of the eschatological aisle from the dispensationalists are **those who believe that the church replaces Israel as God's people**. Here's what a covenantalist might point out: Didn't Paul himself emphasize that Jesus Christ is Abraham's one offspring, the perfect covenant-keeping Israelite? And isn't it faith in Jesus that brings together Jews and Gentiles to inherit the promises given to Abraham? (Galatians 3:7–9, 13–14, 16).

And what about the land that was promised to Abraham? Some say God fulfilled his land promise to Abraham's offspring by establishing Israel in the land through Joshua's conquest (Joshua 11:23; 21:43–45; Nehemiah 9:22–25) or later during Solomon's reign (1 Kings 4:21; 5:4).[53] If so, no literal earthly millennium is needed for God to keep his word to Israel. Others claim that Abraham's physical descendants forfeited these promises by rebelling against God and rejecting his Messiah.

> **COVENANTALISM**
>
> In the Old and New Testaments alike, salvation came through faith in Jesus as Lord and Messiah; therefore, God has always had one plan with one people. Old Testament believers looked forward to the Messiah with expectant faith; New Testament believers look back to Jesus. After Adam and Eve sinned, "the Lord was pleased to make ... the covenant of grace; wherein he freely offers unto sinners life and salvation by Jesus Christ; requiring of them faith in him, that they may be saved."[51] All other covenants in Scripture were simply renewed expressions of this one covenant of grace;[52] the "new covenant" is the fulfillment of the covenant of grace (Jeremiah 31:31; Luke 22:20).

Right now, Jesus reigns as king over all the earth. In the consummation, the saints—including ethnic descendants of Abraham who have trusted Jesus—will reign over the new creation. This geographical inheritance includes and yet far exceeds the land promised to Abraham. This could fit with Paul's perspective that God's promise to Abraham was ultimately "that he would be heir of the world" (Romans 4:13).

New Covenantalism

The promised land was a temporary picture of what God would provide in Jesus

According to new covenantalists, God's promises of land were a temporary picture of what he was preparing to do through Jesus. The new covenant is not simply a fuller expression of a covenant of grace that began in the Garden of Eden. The covenant that Jeremiah predicted and Jesus fulfilled is truly a *new covenant* (Jeremiah 31:31; Luke 22:20). The old covenant was a temporary type and a picture that was intended to last only until the new covenant came along (Galatians 3:25; Hebrews 3:5; 8:5–13; 9:8–10; 10:9). Everything in the Old Testament

> ### NEW COVENANTALISM
>
> God's work with Israel in the Old Testament was a temporary picture of what God had already purposed to accomplish through Jesus. The promises of land and blessings pointed forward to Jesus; these promises are fulfilled through the reign of Jesus over all the earth.

must be interpreted in light of what God accomplished through Jesus.[54]

So what about the "everlasting covenant" with Abraham that included promises of land? (Genesis 17:7, 13, 19). These promises were made to the offspring of Abraham—not to many "offsprings," the apostle Paul pointed out, but to one single "offspring" (Galatians 3:16). Jesus, this one offspring of Abraham, will one day rule far more than the land promised to Abraham. Through Jesus, the divine promises to Abraham will be fulfilled in a way that is truly everlasting. The people that Jesus will rule—in full fulfillment of God's promise to Abraham—will be believers from many nations (Genesis 17:1–8; Revelation 7:9).

According to Exodus 23:31, God promised Israel to extend the borders "from the Red Sea to the Mediterranean Sea, and from the desert to the Euphrates River." See also Numbers 34:1–15 and Ezekiel 47:13–20. © AridOcean

Of course, Abraham wasn't completely aware of all this when he received God's promise. He was simply walking by faith. In the midst of this walk of faith, Abraham and his descendants faced unbelievable challenges. The elderly Abraham found his wife infertile, the promise-child Isaac found himself tied to an altar, the cunning Jacob found himself fleeing his own family, and dreaming Joseph found himself bullied, betrayed, and imprisoned in a nation far from the land of promise. And still, in all of this, God was at work, building a kingdom for his glory from this fragile family line.

THE FOREVER KING: GOD'S COVENANT WITH DAVID

At the foot of Mount Sinai, God called Israel to be a "kingdom of priests" (Exodus 19:6). God intended Israel to become a lighthouse nation that would settle into a culture of comprehensive righteousness and establish an Eden-like kingdom to broadcast God's glory to the nations. A priest stood between God and the people. Israel the priestly kingdom was to stand between God and the nations.

Israel Around Mt. Sinai by Stan Stein.

But Israel failed in this calling. Israel turned from God while still camped in the shadow of Sinai, stiffened at the border of Canaan, compromised during the conquest, then ran wild during the days of the judges. Yet God had a plan to rescue Israel and to establish a kingdom for his glory. This time, the plan would require turning a shepherd-boy from Bethlehem into a mighty king.

At the pinnacle of his power, King David was rolling out blueprints for what he thought would be God's house—a grand temple. But God turned the tables and declared that God himself would be the one doing the building, but not of a temple for himself. God pledged to construct a "house" for David, a dynasty with an heir from David who would reign forever from a royal throne (2 Samuel 7:1–16).

The Promised Reign of David's Heir		
	Timing	**Throne**
Dispensational	Future physical reign of the one heir of David, Jesus the Messiah, during the millennium, with ethnic Israelites occupying the land promised to Abraham	Earthly throne in restored Israel during the millennium
Covenantal and New Covenantal	Present spiritual reign from heaven (amillennial) Present or future spiritual reign through gospel (postmillennial) Future physical reign of the one heir of David, Jesus the Messiah, during the millennium (historical premillennial)	Heavenly throne at the right hand of the Father (amillennial and postmillennial) Earthly throne ruling the earth from Jerusalem during the millennium (historical premillennial)

Although the word "covenant" is not found in God's promise to David, one of the psalmists made it clear that this promise was a covenant: "You have said, 'I have made a covenant with my chosen one; I have sworn to David my servant: 'I will establish your offspring forever, and build your throne for all generations''" (Psalm 89:3–4). But neither David's son Solomon nor any of the long line of dreadful kings who followed him were the ultimate Davidic king. Jesus was.

The New Testament is not shy about promoting this lineage. The genealogies document it (Matthew 1:1, 6; Luke 3:31), the angel announced it (Luke 1:32–33), the outcasts hoped for it (Matthew 15:22; Luke 18:35–39), the gospel requires it (Romans 1:1–2), the apostles proclaimed it (Acts 13:22–23, 34), and Jesus himself declared it (Revelation 22:16). This means that, if he is indeed the Messiah, Jesus of Nazareth must rule from David's throne, and this kingdom must have no end. The only questions are *how* and *when.*

NEW COVENANT BLESSINGS

- Everlasting covenant (Ezekiel 16:59–63)
- Full forgiveness (Jeremiah 31:34)
- Law in hearts (Jeremiah 31:33)
- Pure community (Jeremiah 31:34)
- Renewed land (Jeremiah 32:36–37)
- Physical security (Jeremiah 32:37b)

Stained glass window at the Melkite Catholic Annunciation Cathedral depicting Christ the King.

Dispensational Premillennialism and the Davidic Kingdom

When Jesus was born in Bethlehem, Herod the Great was king by might, but Jesus was king by right (Matthew 2:1–18). Yet Jesus was rejected by his own people, and so—according to dispensationalists—the kingdom failed to come in its fullness. That's why dispensationalists anticipate a future earthly kingdom in which Jesus, an ethnic Jew from the line of David, will return to earth after a seven-year tribulation. Jesus will rightfully inherit David's throne (Isaiah 9:6–7), govern the nations from Jerusalem (Psalm 2:6–9), and usher in an unparalleled age of abundant peace (Micah 5:2–9). But these blessings will not flow from the simple spring of health, wealth, and prosperity. The nation of Israel will repent of their rejection of Jesus as Messiah. Jesus himself will clear away the blockage of sin and provide national forgiveness and spiritual cleansing for the repentant nation (Zechariah 12:10–13:2).[55] Their hearts will be changed (Jeremiah 31:31–34) and their nation will be restored (Jeremiah 32:37–40).

> According to dispensationalists, the kingdom failed to come in its fullness. That's why dispensationalists anticipate a future earthly kingdom in which Jesus, an ethnic Jew from the line of David, will return to earth after a seven-year tribulation.

Amillenialism, Postmillennialism, and the Davidic Kingdom

> Amillennialists think that Jesus inherited David's throne when he ascended into heaven and sat down at the right hand of the Father. Postmillennialists take a similar perspective.

Amillennialists think that Jesus inherited David's throne when he ascended into heaven and sat down at the right hand of the Father. The everlasting nature of the covenant with David was fulfilled when Jesus rose from the dead, never to die again and always to reign as king (Acts 2:31). Now, he is reigning spiritually over his people; when he returns, he will consummate the kingdom that he has already inaugurated.

Postmillennialists take a similar perspective but place the beginning of this reign at the beginning of the millennium, when the gospel begins to transform the world.

Historical Premillennialism and the Davidic Kingdom

Historical premillennialists understand that Jesus inaugurated an eternal reign when he ascended to his Father (Acts 2:29–36)—but they see far more in the covenant with David than a spiritual reign from heaven. God's covenant with David does not require a restoration of the modern nation of Israel to the land because this covenant was made with Jesus in mind. The temple that David's son would construct (2 Samuel 7:13) was a temporary picture of the house that Jesus would build—a house that he is constructing through the spirit and flesh of his new covenant people (Hebrews 3:6; 1 Peter 2:5). During the future millennium, Jesus will fulfill God's covenant with David by reigning over David's domain and more, alongside followers from every nation.

> Historical premillennialists understand that Jesus inaugurated an eternal reign... God's covenant with David does not require a restoration of the nation of Israel because this covenant was made with Jesus in mind.

THE CONSUMMATION OF THE COVENANTS

Regardless of our view of the end times, every Christian can agree on this truth: Jesus is the key to the fulfillment of God's covenants (see Isaiah 22:22; Revelation 3:7). He is the last Adam. He is the offspring of Abraham. He is the Davidic king. And he is the final sacrifice, sealing the new covenant with his very own blood (Luke 22:20). That's why Paul proclaimed to the Corinthian believers that "all the promises of God find their 'Yes' in him" (2 Corinthians 1:20). These promises form the backbone of the Old Testament story, and the Old Testament is the springboard for end times prophecy.

Now, are you beginning to see how much the beginning matters whenever we look at the end?

© José Luis Gutiérrez

QUICK GUIDE TO GOD'S COVENANTS

Royal grant covenants were unconditional grants of property or position, given by a king as a free gift to a loyal servant. **Vassal-treaty covenants** were conditional diplomatic treaties and depended on whether the servant remained loyal to the king.

From the perspective of *covenantalists*, all the covenants from Noah through the New Covenant are simply reiterations of one covenant of grace.

Although *dispensationalists* and *new covenantalists* may differ on the precise nature of each covenant, they agree that the New Covenant was more than merely a renewal and fulfillment of the Old Covenant.

Covenant participants	Type of covenant	Meaning of covenant
God and Creation	May include elements of both types of covenants	God will preserve his creation and bless faithfulness; Adam and Eve must obey or die (Genesis 1–3)
God and Noah	Renewal of covenant with creation	God will never again destroy all life in a flood (Genesis 9:8–17)
God and Abraham	Unconditional royal grant given to Abram as believer in God's promise	God will give the Promised Land to Abram's seed (Genesis 15:9–21) Abraham expresses his continued faithfulness to this covenant by circumcising his son (Genesis 17); some see this as a conditional vassal-treaty
God and Israel	Conditional vassal-treaty	If Israel is faithful, God will remain their God (Exodus 19–24)
God and Israel's Priesthood	Unconditional royal grant, perhaps not a separate covenant but an upholding of God's previous covenant	God will provide his people with a perpetual faithful priesthood (Numbers 25:10–31)
God and David	Unconditional royal grant	God will establish a perpetual king in the line of David (2 Samuel 7:5–16; Psalm 89)
God in Jesus with all who believe	Unconditional royal grant	God will forgive the sins of his unfaithful people and of all who believe (Jeremiah 31:31–34; Luke 22:20; 2 Corinthians 3:6; Hebrews 8:8; 9:15; 12:24)

The Kingdom That Was, Kingdom That's Yet to Be

What goes up must come down.

Unsupported by a firm foundation of some sort, most things will tumble downward. It's that way with kingdoms too.

At their peak, kingdoms appear eternal and invincible. Yet, they inevitably falter and fall. Consider how the mighty kingdoms of the past have fallen: Egypt, Babylon, Greece, Rome. Kingdoms are contexts for conflict, and every kingdom except one is ultimately destined to fall.

It's been that way ever since the beginning—ever since before the beginning, in fact.

Thus, the inevitable story of every human kingdom became the story of Israel as well: things fall apart.

© Subbotina Anna

A Time Line of Kingship: Rebellion, Failure and Hope

Heavenly Kingdom
Before time began, God reigned over a heavenly kingdom, and one of God's own angels, Satan, tried to usurp his throne (Jude 1:6; Revelation 12:4).

Rebellion Against the King
Then God formed a kingdom on the earth only to see it too invaded by this fallen angel.[56] The satanic serpent entered the garden and enticed God's image-bearers to join his rebellion (Genesis 3:1–8).[57]

A Kingdom in Chaos
Humanity's rebellion plunged the planet in a flood of sickness and sorrow, darkness and death. And yet, the hope and promise of a righteous king persisted.

A Promised King
Even as Adam and Eve watched Eden fade in the rearview mirror, God's last words to them had included the promise of a king so powerful that he would shatter the serpent's power (Genesis 3:15).

A Kingdom of Priests Failed
God commissioned Abraham's descendants to be a "kingdom of priests and a holy nation" (Exodus 19:6). They received land, laws, and leadership, but the leaders continually broke the laws and eventually lost the land.

A King Like the Nations
God yielded to the Israelites' copycat demand for a king "like all the nations" (1 Samuel 8:5, 20) and Saul got the popular vote because he was tall, dark, and handsome, but God's forewarnings about the resulting misery came true time and again (1 Samuel 8:10–17).

King David
What about David, the pure-hearted, psalm-singing, giant-slaying shepherd boy? Even with his sincere love for God, he committed adultery, failed at fatherhood, and joined his ancestors in the grave.

King Solomon
Then Solomon, David's son bowed at the feet of his thousand-plus women and their thousands of idols (1 Kings 11:1–8).

A Kingdom Divided
Rehoboam listened to his frat-boy peers instead of his grey-haired counselors (1 Kings 12:1–20), and Jeroboam set the bar so low that he became the default standard of wickedness to which later kings were compared (1 Kings 15:25–26, 30, 34; 16:2, 7, 19, 26, 31; 22:52).

Failed Kingdoms
This dismal trajectory would only continue; the remainder of Israel's kings proved to be a parade of disappointments with only a few shining lights scattered among them.

God's Promise: A New King that Will Last Forever

But this constant crumbling of kingdoms is not the final word! Throughout history, God made the same promise over and over: a new kingdom is coming, and this perfect kingdom will last forever. It is a kingdom that has risen never to come down. That's why the final book of the New Testament is filled with references to a King whose kingdom will never end:

- "The kingdom of the world has become the kingdom of our Lord and of his Messiah, and he shall reign forever" (Revelation 12:10).

- "Your works are great and amazing, Lord God Almighty! Your ways are righteous and true, King of the nations!" (Revelation 15:3).

- "He is Lord of lords and King of kings" (Revelation 17:14; 19:16).

The Tree of Jesse, detail. Stained glass from the 13th century, restored in the 19th century, in the cathedral of Saint-Pierre-et-Saint-Paul de Troyes

A Long Line of Broken Kings[58]

United Kingdom under Saul	
Saul	1051–1011
United Kingdom under David and Solomon	
David	Reigns in southern kingdom from 1011 Reigns over both kingdoms 1003–971
Solomon	971–931

Chronology in the Divided Kingdom

After King Solomon died, his son, Rehoboam, refused to make changes to forced labor laws. Led by Jeroboam, the northern tribes rebelled against Rehoboam. Ten northern tribes formed the Kingdom of Israel, with Jeroboam as their king. Two southern tribes formed the Kingdom of Judah, with Rehoboam as their king.

The Kings of the Divided Kingdom

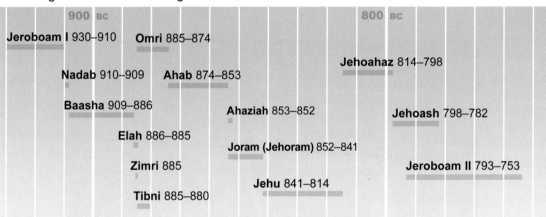

900 BC 800 BC

Jeroboam I 930–910 Omri 885–874

Jehoahaz 814–798

Nadab 910–909 Ahab 874–853

Baasha 909–886 Ahaziah 853–852 Jehoash 798–782

Elah 886–885 Joram (Jehoram) 852–841

Zimri 885 Jeroboam II 793–753

Jehu 841–814

Tibni 885–880

Divided Kingdom of Israel (Northern Kings)

Divided Kingdom of Judah (Southern Kings)

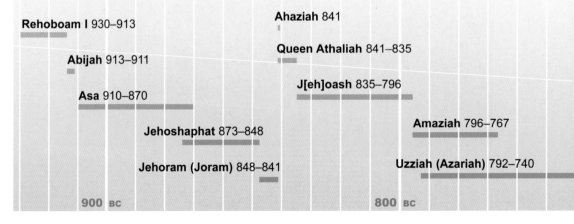

Ahaziah 841

Rehoboam I 930–913 Queen Athaliah 841–835

Abijah 913–911 J[eh]oash 835–796

Asa 910–870

Jehoshaphat 873–848 Amaziah 796–767

Jehoram (Joram) 848–841 Uzziah (Azariah) 792–740

900 BC 800 BC

The time line of the kings in the divided kingdom era is difficult to establish with great accuracy because:

- Co-regencies existed. Two kings could rule at the same time.
- Sometimes the counting of a king's reign began at his coronation during his father's lifetime. At other times, they started counting when he began his reign as an independent king.
- They had two different new years. In the Northern Kingdom, the new year began on 1 Nisan (around April), while in the Southern Kingdom it began on 1 Tishri (around September).

The system of counting changed during this period. The North switched from antedating (counting the year of coronation as a full year) to postdating (counting begins during the first full calendar year after the king's coronation). *All dates are approximate.*

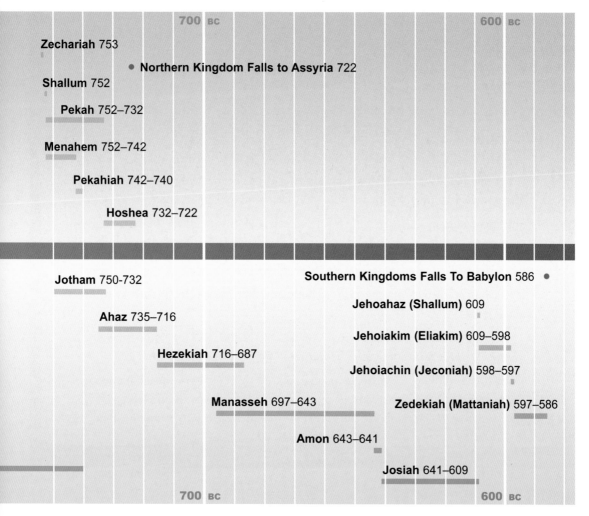

700 BC   600 BC

Zechariah 753

● **Northern Kingdom Falls to Assyria** 722

Shallum 752

Pekah 752–732

Menahem 752–742

Pekahiah 742–740

Hoshea 732–722

Jotham 750-732

Southern Kingdoms Falls To Babylon 586 ●

Jehoahaz (Shallum) 609

Ahaz 735–716

Jehoiakim (Eliakim) 609–598

Hezekiah 716–687

Jehoiachin (Jeconiah) 598–597

Manasseh 697–643

Zedekiah (Mattaniah) 597–586

Amon 643–641

Josiah 641–609

700 BC   600 BC

FOUR VIEWS OF THE KINGDOM

Dispensational premillennialism:

- The promised kingdom will be established when Jesus returns to earth after the rapture of the church and the seven-year tribulation.

- Jesus will reign from David's throne in Jerusalem, restore the Jewish nation, and rule over Israel and the nations for 1,000 years.

- Jesus offered this millennial kingdom to Israel during his earthly ministry with the apostles, but the religious leaders of his day rejected this offer.

- So God postponed the millennial kingdom and established a new form of the kingdom, never predicted in the Old Testament. This kingdom includes anyone who trusts in Jesus.[59]

Historical premillennialism:

- The promised kingdom was inaugurated in the first coming of Christ and will be fulfilled when he returns and reigns on the earth for 1,000 years.

- This millennial reign will fulfill God's kingdom promises to the Israelites.

Amillennialism:

- The promised kingdom began with the first coming of Christ.

- Ever since his resurrection and ascension, Jesus has been sitting at the right hand of God's throne, ruling over the world in a heavenly reign.

- His final triumphant return will reveal and establish this reign on the earth.

Postmillennialism:

- The promised kingdom will grow and spread through the proclamation of the gospel.

- It will expand throughout the earth as more and more people believe the good news about Jesus.

- The nations will become increasingly open to the gospel, and the kingdom will eventually cover the entire planet, ushering in God's eternal kingdom.

Although Christians differ on the exact nature and timing of God's promised kingdom, there is one point on which nearly all believers agree: ***Jesus himself inaugurated a kingdom, and he will consummate the kingdom when he returns to reign on earth.***

A NEW KINGDOM DAWNS

> "Although the burden of Jesus' message was the kingdom of God, he nowhere defined it. It is not recorded that anyone asked him what 'the kingdom of God' meant. He assumed that this was a concept so familiar that it did not require definition."[60]

When Jesus arrived on the scene, he immediately began proclaiming the message of a new kingdom: "The time has come. ... The kingdom of God has come near. Repent and believe the good news!" (Mark 1:15). If you didn't know the rest of the story already, you might have said, "A kingdom is arriving? Just give it time. What goes up must come down." And in fact, that is precisely what some religious leaders seem to have thought. They feared that, if Jesus continued to proclaim this royal domain, the Romans would destroy their temple and any hope for a kingdom (John 11:47–48).

But this kingdom was different. He never provided a detailed verbal definition of his kingdom. Instead, he told stories—and his parables rarely included the typical trappings of kingship. There were no horses or chariots or battles in these stories. Instead, Jesus told about a woman who was kneading some dough, a farmer whose neighbor mixed weeds with his wheat, and a man who planted some mustard seeds (Matthew 24:24–33).

Why would Jesus make such a monumental assumption? How could he assume that a word so freighted with past failures could stand without definition? The answer is simple: the Old Testament! You see, even though the history of the kingdom of Israel may have looked like one massive train wreck, it was not because

The Sermon of the Beatitudes, by James Tissot, 1886–1894

113

there were no tracks for people to follow. Even though many of Jesus' first hearers did not catch the message, the blueprints for his future kingdom were all laid out in the Old Testament.

What does this mean for our study of the end times?

- It shows that we can't neglect the first two-thirds of our Bibles when we study the end times.
- It reminds us that the words of Jesus in the New Testament draw deeply from Old Testament expectations and images.
- It reveals that sometimes the New Testament authors do not explain what we want to know because they assume that we already know our Old Testament.

WHAT IS A KINGDOM?

Sometimes the most basic questions are the most easily neglected. So before leaping into the deep end of the pool, let's wade in with a simple question: "What is a kingdom?"

A kingdom requires three elements: a ruler, a realm, and a reign:[61]

- The ruler is the person whose position puts him above all others, the one who has the authority and the power to reign.
- But a ruler must also have a realm over which to rule, a defined area or people over whom his authority is legitimate.
- Finally, the ruler and the realm are merely dead facts without an active reign. The reign of a ruler is active exercise of authority that results in decisions and decrees, legal treaties and heroic triumphs.

SO . . . WHAT KIND OF KINGDOM?

With these elements in mind, what kind of kingdom did the Old Testament writers proclaim? What did God reveal to his people in the Old Testament to shape their kingdom hope? And what do these hopes mean for our hope today? Let's take a look at the Old Testament expectation from the perspective of a **ruler**, a **realm**, and a **reign**.

THE RULER OF THE KINGDOM

The Once, Future, and Always King

WHAT KIND OF KINGDOM DID THE OLD TESTAMENT PROPHETS PREDICT?

Six Spirit-Inspired Expectations:

Aspects of the Kingdom	Expectations for the Kingdom
The Ruler	The king would be God himself (Zechariah 14:9).
	The king would also be a human representative of God (Is. 9:6–7).
The Realm	The kingdom would fill the earth (Isaiah 11:9).
	The kingdom would include non-Jews (Isaiah 19:23–25).
The Reign	The kingdom would last forever (Daniel 7:14, 18, 27).
	The kingdom would be righteous (Isaiah 9:7)

God is already king of the entire cosmos (Psalm 29:10), including planet earth (2 Kings 19:15; Psalm 47:2). Yet, Scripture also suggests that the king is coming. If God already reigns as king, how can the king and his kingdom possibly be coming in the future?

Once again, to understand the end of time, it's necessary to look back to the ancient Hebrew Scriptures. The Old Testament expectation was not simply that God would continue to reign but that God would come to reign (Isaiah 24:23; 33:22; 52:7; Zephaniah 3:15; Obadiah 21; Zechariah 14:9).[62] **What this meant was that God would someday be revealed to all people as the rightful king.** At this time, he would exercise his reign in an immediate and direct way. That's why the eyes of faithful Israelites were turned toward the future, watching and waiting for the Lord himself to inaugurate an unhindered and uninterrupted rule.

Statue of King David by Nicolas Cordier

The Royal Representative

Although God is the king, he chose human representatives to rule, even in the beginning. The first of these representatives was Adam. He bore God's image and functioned as his appointed earthly ruler. The divine commission for Adam was simple yet royal: "subdue" and "have dominion" (Genesis 1:26, 28).[63]

Despite the royal disaster that ensued, God never gave up on his plan to send an ultimate representative—someone who would institute the perfect government that every faithful Israelite longed to experience. This ruler would be a

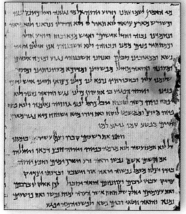

descendant of Adam, Abraham, and David, making him fully human, ethnically Jewish, and rightfully king.

This final representative is identified as "the servant of the LORD" throughout the second half of Isaiah (Isaiah 42:1–9; 49:1–13; 50:4–9; 52:13–53:12). This servant would be obedient to God but rejected by men (50:4–9), he would suffer and die for the sins of others (52:13–53:12), he would restore Israel and reach the nations (49:1–13), and he would establish mercy and justice throughout the earth (42:4).

Portion of the Great Isaiah Scroll from the Dead Sea Scroll manuscripts found in 1929 in the southern desert of Israel. Photo by Ardon Bar Hama.

Dispensationalists and amillennialists, historical premillennialists and postmillennial preterists—all of them agree that Jesus fulfilled Isaiah's prophecy of the servant who would be king.[64]

But there is also some disagreement when it comes to the precise nature of his restoration of Israel and his outreach to the nations:

- The dispensational conviction is that Jesus will establish Israel and bless the nations by descending to earth after the great tribulation and reigning for a thousand years.

- Historical premillennialists agree that Jesus will reign on earth for a thousand years—but the fulfillment of promises to ethnic Israel will not be the primary point of this reign. God's kingdom promises are fulfilled because Jesus, the true and perfect Israelite, reigns over all the earth.

- Amillennialists and many postmillennialists envision Jesus already reigning in the heavens while reaching the nations through the ongoing spread of the gospel.

© paul prescott

THE REALM OF THE KINGDOM

On Earth as It Is in Heaven

Surrounded by twelve disciples and untold multitudes of hearers on a rise of land overlooking the Sea of Galilee, Jesus provided his audience with a model prayer. In this prayer, he prayed, "Your kingdom come, your will be done, on earth as it is in heaven" (Matthew 6:10).

In heaven, God's will is done perfectly. On earth, the opposite seems to be true. This stark contrast leads many Christians to believe that they are headed for the skies while the earth is destined for the rubbish heap.

But does such a sharp distinction between earth and heaven reflect the Old Testament's portrayal of God's promised future kingdom? Did the patriarchs, prophets, priests, and kings anticipate an ethereal, spiritual kingdom existing somewhere beyond the skies?

Jesus proclaiming the Kingdom of God in the Sermon on the Mount. Carl Bloch.

The Hebrew prophets answer that question with a resounding "No!" The Old Testament hope was an earthly hope.[65] **The Israelites expected a comprehensive renewal that would touch all aspects of human existence.** They looked forward to a time when the earth would be "full of the knowledge of the Lord as the waters cover the sea" (Isaiah 11:9).

That's why Isaiah envisioned not a mass evacuation from the earth but a full transformation of the earth. He portrayed a time when life on earth buds, blossoms, and flourishes (35:1–2, 6–7). The carnivorous food chain that previously dominated animal life will become a calm fellowship (Isaiah 11:6–7). Patterns of mutual harm and hurt will fade away (Isaiah 11:9). And all of these effects will be rooted in the work of Jesus (Isaiah 11:1–9); they will be "the result of righteousness" (Isaiah 32:17).

A Kingdom for Everyone

Even in the opening book of the Bible, the realm of the kingdom was intended to extend beyond the Jewish people. After all, God had guaranteed Abraham that "in you all the families of the earth shall be blessed" (Genesis 12:3).

At times, Israel struggled to embrace this calling.

The prophet Jonah is a prime example of the struggle. Although he delivered at least one oracle of good news that could have made him a popular preacher (2 Kings 14:25), Jonah also received an assignment that would have immediately landed him on Israel's list of least popular prophets. God called him to preach to the despised Assyrians so that they would repent and be spared (Jonah 1:2; 4:2). Israel was in the midst of a national upturn in fortunes, and the last thing anyone wanted was for their international threat from the north to be saved. Self-centered nationalism had eclipsed their divine commission.

But God stayed on course with his plan to bless the nations. In the book of Jonah, pagan sailors worship Israel's God, godless Ninevites repent of their sins, and even Assyrian livestock is covered in sackcloth and ashes—all while Jonah stews and simmers at God's border-breaking mercy.

> **JONAH**
>
> **Location**: From the town of Gath Hepher
>
> **Approx. Date**: 781 BC
>
> **Subject**: Nineveh (capital of Assyrian empire)
>
> **Main Concern**: Coming judgment upon the city
>
> **Key Verse**: 2:2—"From the depths of the grave I called for help, and you listened to my cry."

In the prophecies of Isaiah, this pattern of reaching across geographical boundaries and geopolitical divides provided a key paradigm for God's work in the last days:

> "In that day there will be a highway from Egypt to Assyria, and Assyria will come into Egypt, and Egypt into Assyria, and the Egyptians will worship with the Assyrians. In that day Israel will be the third with Egypt and Assyria, a blessing in the midst of the earth, whom the Lord of hosts has blessed, saying, 'Blessed be Egypt my people, and Assyria the work of my hands, and Israel my inheritance'" (Isaiah 19:23–25).

© Tupungato

The Israelites had an earthly hope and an international mission. The prophets announced that the glorious kingdom of God would be an earthly kingdom with blessing flowing to the surrounding peoples. The glories of heaven would blanket the landscape of earth, and even Israel's most hated enemies could drink from the overflow of God's mercy.

- *Dispensational premillennialists* believe that this international calling will be fulfilled when the millennial kingdom is established in Israel and blessings flow out to the surrounding nations.

- *Historical premillennialists* suggest that this calling is fulfilled as non-Jews turn in faith to Jesus, the perfect offspring of Abraham who will reign on earth for one thousand years.

- *Amillennialists* and *postmillennialists* believe that these promises are fulfilled by the diversity of those who have trusted in Jesus, a diversity that has been multiplying through the church for the past two thousand years.

- Despite these differences, *Christians agree that the people of the promised kingdom will be a colorful mosaic of redeemed people "from every tribe and language and people and nation," unified in worship of the Lamb (Revelation 5:9).*

THE REIGN OF THE KING

An Everlasting Kingdom

David praised the Lord because his kingdom is "an everlasting kingdom" (Psalm 145:13). Nebuchadnezzar was compelled to echo this same sentiment after he saw three Hebrew boys escape untouched from an executioner's furnace: "His kingdom is an everlasting kingdom, and his dominion endures from generation to generation" (Daniel 4:3). Later, Daniel watched as a human being received "an everlasting dominion" that "will not pass away" (7:14). When Daniel requested divine clarification on this issue, the promise got even better: "the saints of the Most High shall receive the kingdom and possess the kingdom forever, forever, and ever" (7:18, 27).

A Righteous Kingdom

Yet, as glorious as it sounds to enjoy an "everlasting kingdom," the "everlasting" is only glorious as long as the "kingdom" is good. What if Hitler or Lenin or Pol Pot enjoyed an everlasting reign? We would all be rethinking our hope for eternity. ***Remarkably, God has promised not only an eternal kingdom but also a righteous kingdom.*** From Eden to Sinai to the Sermon on the Mount, God has pointed his people toward the hope of such a kingdom. Yet, it will only be at the end of time that this promise will be completely realized.

When we hear the word "righteousness," we often conjure up a vague sense of personal and private piety. But biblical righteousness was never meant to sit in the study or hover above the ground, untouched by daily human affairs. In the Old Testament, righteousness walks on the ground, echoes around the home, and plays out in the marketplace. That's why prophetic rebukes centered so often on community concerns: exploitation of the poor, oppression, abuse, hypocrisy, and partiality to the powerful (Amos 2:6–7; 4:1, 4–5; 5:11–12, 15; 8:4–6).

The ancient Israelite faithful did not anticipate a kingdom that would skip over such earthy concerns, opting for a mystical kingdom in the clouds. They awaited justice, equity, and impartiality that would set the captives free. ***They wanted to see the evils of injustice and partiality and prejudice and oppression shattered in the storm of the Messiah's coming. They wanted the entire world along with every nook and cranny of human existence to be cleansed, reformed, and made right. They were looking for a righteous kingdom.***

The New Testament carries forward the burden of this hope: "According to his promise we are waiting for new heavens and a new earth in which righteousness dwells" (2 Peter 3:13). Regardless of your millennial view, if you're a believer in Jesus, God's promise of future righteousness compels you to look expectantly for this kingdom. Those who see that the world is dark and that Jesus is the light of the world should be those who yearn most deeply for the dawn.

© sdecoret

FOUR VIEWS OF THE KINGDOM OF GOD

	Amillennialism	Postmillennialism	Historical Premillennialism	Dispensational Premillennialism
Coming King	The heavenly kingdom already exists; Jesus still to come in person	The kingdom is growing through the spread of the gospel; Jesus still to come in person	The kingdom inaugurated in Jesus' lifetime, but the earthly kingdom still awaits	The earthly kingdom still awaits, centered in God's promises to Israel
Royal Representative	Jesus reigns now from heaven	Jesus reigns now from heaven and on earth during the millennium through the gospel	Jesus reigns already from heaven and will reign on earth during future millennium	Jesus will reign on earth during future millennium
Earthly Realm	Jesus presently reigns from heaven over the earth with saints in heaven	Jesus reigns from heaven over the earth through proclamation of the gospel	Jesus will reign on earth for 1,000 years	Jesus will reign on earth for 1,000 years
Ethnic Diversity	The multi-ethnic church united in Jesus the Messiah	The gospel spreads and the kingdom expands to all nations	The nations already worship Israel's God and Israel's Messiah; this will continue and become more fully realized during future millennium	The nations will come to worship Israel's God and Israel's Messiah during future millennium
Everlasting Kingdom	Jesus is reigning now and this everlasting kingdom will be fully established when he returns to earth	The kingdom will expand on earth and usher in the everlasting kingdom	The millennial kingdom will usher in the everlasting kingdom	The millennial kingdom will usher in the everlasting kingdom
Righteous Kingdom	Righteousness characterizes the heavenly reign of Christ and his future eternal reign	Righteousness is spreading as the gospel takes hold in cultures all over the world	Righteousness will characterize the future millennial kingdom	Righteousness will characterize the future millennial kingdom

THE BEST KING IS YET TO COME

- Amillennialism holds that the kingdom is already happening in the heavens and in the lives of God's people; when Jesus returns, the kingdom will be established on earth as well.

- Postmillennialism asserts that the kingdom is subtly expanding and that this kingdom will keep expanding until it overtakes the world.

- Premillennialism anticipates a future kingdom; in this kingdom, the ruler, the realm, and the reign will be physically present on the earth, just as the prophets expected.

*But no matter what, the Old Testament hope for a kingdom **will** be fulfilled.*

This kingdom won't be a democracy. The cherubim won't be elected, angels Michael and Gabriel won't campaign for their angelic positions, and the promised king won't be calculating electoral votes. There will be no public polls in this kingdom, because human approval will no longer matter.

With all our Western political trappings, it's easy to forget that the problem with our world's rulers is not their method of government, but the fact that they (and we) are fallen people. What we need is not a new form of government but the unconstrained reign of a holy and righteous king.

The best of God's kingdom is yet to come, because the best king is yet to return. This king's name is Jesus. His promised kingdom will rise forever and never fall. And then, nothing will ever fall apart again.

The Prophetic Perspective

THE DAY OF THE LORD, EZEKIEL'S TEMPLE, AND THE END OF THE WORLD AS WE KNOW IT

What happened this week that made you yearn for God to set the world right?

- Perhaps it was the pang of a broken relationship or the death of a dear loved one.

- Perhaps it was one more slip into a particular sin that still seems to hold you captive.

- Maybe, after all these years of praying for a child, your arms are still empty.

- Or maybe, after all those tests and procedures, the doctors still haven't discovered the cause of your pain.

> Enslaved in Egypt, "the Israelites groaned" and "their cry for help rose up to God" (Exodus 2:23). In the psalms, Israel's musicians cried, "My soul is utterly terrified; but you, O Lord, how long?" (Psalm 6:3).

- No matter who you are, there has surely been some point in the past week when you groaned for a time when sin and sorrow and death will end (see Romans 8:20–23).

You're not the first person to feel this way. Such laments are woven throughout the inspired words of Scripture.

The Old Testament prophets longed for God to make the whole world right and new. The dark experience that drove much of the prophets' groaning was the exile—Israel's separation from the land that God had promised Abraham.

- In 722 BC, the barbaric Assyrians ripped the northern Israelites from their land and dispersed them across the Assyrian Empire.

- In 586 BC, the Babylonians conquered southern Israel, destroyed the temple, and deported the best and brightest Israelites to Babylon.

- In the centuries following this exile, the very name "Babylon" became a byword to describe any earthly power that defies the living God (Revelation 14:8; 16:19; 17:5; 18:2, 10, 21). Even after they returned from exile, the Israelites never regained the entire land that they had loved and left.

The experience of exile falls like a dark shadow across the Old Testament. Every Old Testament prophet warned about exile, wrote from exile, or looked back and recalled the exile. They foretold its horrors, explained its reasons, and reviewed its lessons.

But the prophets did not wallow in the pain of exile. They provided Spirit-inspired promises that the future before them was brighter than the exile behind them. Somehow, God would set the world

NORTHERN KINGDOM

Around 930 BC, after the death of King Solomon, the ten northern tribes of Israel separated from the southern tribes; this kingdom became known as "Israel." Jeroboam was the first ruler of the northern kingdom, and Samaria was a capital city. In 722 BC, the Assyrians conquered the northern kingdom.

SOUTHERN KINGDOM

Around 930 BC, the southern tribes of the Israelite kingdom became a separate realm after a time of civil war; the southern kingdom became known as "Judah." Rehoboam was the first ruler of the southern kingdom, and Jerusalem was the capital city. In 586 BC, the Babylonians conquered the southern kingdom.

© Kamira

MULTIPLE FULFILLMENTS

"False Summits"

Have you ever heard of a "false summit"? Serious hikers probably have! A false summit is an approaching peak that reaches into the sky and looks like it might be the pinnacle of the mountain. But as you draw closer to this summit, you recognize that this was not the ultimate peak after all! The summit you were seeking still lies well ahead.

The false summit isn't "false" in the sense that it doesn't exist or that it isn't real. It's a real summit—but it is a secondary summit because the best summit is yet to come.

The fulfillment of prophecy works that way too.

It may appear at first that a prophecy referred to one single future event. Yet, as history unfolded, it became clear that the original prophecy referred to multiple events. These initial peaks of fulfillment were *not* counterfeits or false fulfillments! They were *real* fulfillments but they were *secondary*—because the best and fullest fulfillment was yet to come.

An Example of a Secondary Summit

The prophet Joel predicted that God's Spirit would cause God's people to prophesy and that cosmic wonders would fill earth and heaven (Joel 2:28–32). Centuries later, when Peter saw followers of Jesus speak God's truth at Pentecost, he proclaimed to the people, "This is what was uttered through the prophet Joel" (Acts 2:14–21). Yet, as far as we know from history, no cosmic phenomena flashed through the Jerusalem sky that day.

© Lizard

Could Peter have been referring to recent signs that accompanied the death of Jesus? (Luke 23:44–45).

Or was Peter predicting the heavenly signs that would be seen later, actual cosmic events when the Romans destroyed the Jewish temple in AD 70?[66]

Or could Peter have been referring to an ultimate fulfillment of these words that will occur nearer to the time of the second coming of Jesus? (Matthew 24:29–31; Revelation 6:12; 19:11–17).

Regardless of how you understand Joel's prophecy, one fact is clear: ***The fulfillment of this one prophecy unfolded in more than one episode.***

This is an example of "multiple fulfillment." Also known as "progressive fulfillment," "typological fulfillment," or "analogous fulfillment," this is the recognition that a single prophetic announcement can be fulfilled at one point in history and yet also be fulfilled later in a greater way.[67]

right and restore his people. These promises were more than mere predictions about the future—although they certainly *were* predictions and they *will* come true! These prophetic words were also confessions of confidence that God would not abandon his people. Before the end of time, the prophets expected that God would ...

- Act decisively on "the day of the Lord" to demonstrate that he is the true God and that he hasn't forgotten his people.
- Bring about a new temple.
- Make the world new.

1. GOD IS IN CHARGE: THE OLD TESTAMENT PROPHETS AND THE DAY OF THE LORD

The middle of the eighth century BC was a time of wealth and leisure in the northern kingdom of Israel. There were "winter houses" and "summer houses" with ivory panels and hewn stone walls (Amos 3:15; 5:11). The people sprawled on couches with bodies that were fragrant, stomachs that were full, and souls that were empty (Amos 6:4–7).

Prophet Amos, old Russian Orthodox icon

JOEL

Location: Unknown

Approx. Date: 450 BC

Subject: Judah, Jerusalem and surrounding nations

Main Concern: The great and dreadful day of the LORD

Key Verse: 3:13—"Swing the sickle, for the harvest is ripe. Come, trample the grapes, for the winepress is full and the vats overflow—so great is their wickedness."

AMOS

Location: Town of Tekoa

Approx. Date: 765–754 BC

Subject: Northern kingdom (Israel)

Main Concern: Judgment upon Israel for injustice and lack of mercy

Key Verse: 5:24— "Let justice roll on like a river, righteousness like a never failing stream!"

The northern Israelites were "at ease in Zion" (Amos 6:1). They believed that the day of the Lord would bring only good news for them. It would be a time when God would destroy other nations and pour more prosperity on Israel.

The prophet Amos disagreed. "Why would you have the day of the LORD?" Amos demanded. "It is darkness, and not light!" (Amos 5:18–20).

The day of the Lord would include bad news as well as good news. What's more, by linking the day of the Lord with an impending judgment on Israel, he revealed something else: ***"The day of the Lord" could describe any definite and decisive act of God that was dawning on the prophetic horizon.***

Every day of the Lord in the Old Testament was, however, a "secondary summit." Each of these days of the Lord pointed forward, toward the ultimate day of the Lord when God will begin to draw the curtain on his plan for the ages (Zephaniah 1:14–18; Malachi 4:1–5). *The days of the Lord in the Old Testament*

DAY OF THE LORD (also "day of God," "that day")

Any time when God clearly and decisively demonstrates his reign over the earth by vindicating those that are faithful to him or by purifying people for his glory. The day of the Lord is not one particular day but any time when God acts decisively to demonstrate his sovereignty. Each "day of the Lord" throughout human history is a type or a picture that points forward to "the last day"—to the final day of the Lord when God establishes and reveals his reign once and for all.

Characteristics of the Day of the Lord:
- Judgment (Isaiah 13:9; 1 Corinthians 5:5)
- Salvation (Joel 2:30–32; Acts 2:20–21)
- Cataclysmic wonders (Joel 2:1–3; 3:14–15; 2 Peter 3:10–12)
- Divine vengeance (Jeremiah 46:10; 2 Thessalonians 2:1–10)
- Final victory (Zephaniah 1:14–18; 2 Peter 3:13)

In some contexts, "day of the Lord" pointed to God's judgment on idol-worshipping nations or his discipline of his own people (Isaiah 13:6, 9; Jeremiah 46:10; Amos 5:18, 20; Zephaniah 1:7, 14). Joel identified a devastating locust plague as a day of the Lord (Joel 1:15). And yet, the day of the Lord was not always bad news. According to the prophet Joel, the day of the Lord would also be a day of rescue for "everyone who calls upon the name of the Lord" (Joel 2:32). A day of the Lord in the Old Testament was a time when God set some small part of his world right again.

were tiny hints of "the last day" when God will make the whole world right again. This day will include judgment and salvation, resurrection and revelation (John 6:39–54; 11:24; 12:48; 1 Corinthians 5:5).

OLD TESTAMENT PROPHETS AND THE DAY OF THE LORD

Who?	When?	What happens on the Day of the Lord?
Obadiah	845 BC	Judgment on Edom (Obadiah 1:15)
Joel	835 BC	Plague of locusts (Joel 1:15) Invasion (Joel 2:1–11) Outpouring of Spirit, signs in heavens, opportunity for salvation (Joel 2:28–32) Conflict in the End Times (Joel 3:14)
Amos	760 BC	Judgment on Israel (Amos 5:18–20)
Isaiah	739 BC	Fall of Babylon (Isaiah 13:6–9)
Zephaniah	640 BC	Judgment on Judah (Zephaniah 1:7–14)
Jeremiah	627 BC	Defeat of Egypt (Jeremiah 46:10)
Ezekiel	593 BC	Defeat of Egypt (Ezekiel 30:3)
Zechariah	520 BC	Judgment on Jerusalem, conflict in the end times (Zech. 14:1–9)
Malachi	433 BC	Judgment on Judah, end times conflict (Malachi 4:1–6)

And when exactly will this day come?

Well, no human being knows. When Jesus walked and talked on planet earth, *he* didn't even know when this event was scheduled in his Father's day-planner (Matthew 24:36; Mark 13:31–32). And so, we don't know either. What we *do* know is that the last day is yet to come and that Jesus stands at the center of God's plans for this day. The Old Testament prophets had glimpsed the return of Jesus from a distance, but they could not see clearly "what person or time the Spirit of Christ in them was indicating" (1 Peter 1:10–11). On this side of the cross and empty tomb, we know *who* will return in glory; we simply don't know *when*.

Recognizing that "the day of the Lord" doesn't necessarily mean one single day, many premillennialists see "the day of the Lord" as a time-period that includes the great tribulation and the millennial kingdom. Others take this climactic "day" to refer only to the Messiah's glorious return to earth.

Either way, this much is clear: "The day of the Lord" includes the coming of Jesus in the clouds, and that event will come "like a thief in the night" (1 Thessalonians 5:2, 9). **Before the last day of the Lord has ended, God will respond to his people's groanings and set the world right again.** He will renovate the current cosmos with fire, and a new heaven and earth will dawn (2 Peter 3:10–13).

© Fribus Ekaterina

2. WHAT ABOUT THE TEMPLE?

The question that many people have asked in the centuries since the fall of the second temple has been, *"Will a temple ever be built again?"*

The answer to this question is, "Yes!" The prophet Ezekiel clearly predicted and described a new temple (Ezekiel 40–43). Other prophets seem to suggest the same: Micah and Isaiah saw a day when people from all nations will come to "the house of the God of Jacob" (Isaiah 2:2–4; Micah 4:1–3), and Zechariah suggested that the Messiah himself would build this temple (Zechariah 6:12–13).

But the prophets' predictions raise a further question:

"What *kind* of temple were they describing?"

- Were the prophets predicting a physical temple that will be built before the end of time?

© bogdan ionescu

TIME LINE OF GOD'S PRESENCE

The tabernacle and temple were central to how the Israelites worshiped God! And no wonder: In the tabernacle and in the first temple, God had revealed his presence to his people in a cloud of splendor (Exodus 40:34–35; 1 Kings 8:10–11; 2 Chronicles 5:13–14).

- In the days of the judges and early kings, the tabernacle moved from place to place with the people before settling in Shiloh and then in Gibeon (Joshua 18:1; 19:51; 22:9; 1 Kings 3:2–4; 1 Chronicles 16:39; 21:29; 2 Chronicles 1:2–13).

- King David had made plans to build a house for God's tabernacle. However, God had already decided that David's son—not David himself—would be the builder of the temple in Jerusalem (2 Samuel 7).

- King Solomon, son of David, constructed the first temple (1 Kings 8). This temple stood until the glory of the Lord departed (Ezekiel 8:6–10:18), and the Babylonians tore the building to the ground in 586 BC (2 Kings 25:9).

- At the end of the exile, as soon as the Persian King Cyrus provided an opportunity for the people to return to Jerusalem, the Israelites began making plans for a new temple. A remnant of Israelites completed the second temple in 515 BC, very close to seventy years after the fall of the first temple (Ezra 5:2–6:18).

- When a Syrian ruler defiled this temple, a Jewish revolutionary known as Judas "the Hammer" Maccabeus defeated the Syrians and rededicated the temple to Israel's God. Today, the festival of Hanukkah still celebrates a miraculous provision of lamp oil that marked the Maccabean renewal.

- A few years before the birth of Jesus, Herod the Great began expanding the second temple into a towering masterpiece of marble and gold. According to Jewish historian Josephus, the structure was so resplendent "at the rising of the sun" that the temple courts "reflected a fiery splendor and forced all who looked to turn their eyes away."[68]

- But this temple fell as well. In AD 70, the Romans crushed a Jewish rebellion and burned the second temple to the ground. When the smoke cleared, all that remained of the temple mount was a western retaining wall and some arched entrances that once opened into a grand colonnade.[69]

Today, no Jewish temple stands on the temple mount. Instead, two Muslim structures dominate this site: the Al-Aqsa mosque and a shrine known as the Dome of the Rock.

- Or were they describing a spiritual temple?
- Could they even have been using picturesque language to describe the future people of God?

On these points, Bible-believing Christians throughout the ages have disagreed.

A Future Physical Structure

Ezekiel's description of the coming temple is highly detailed—all the way down to the dimensions of hooks and hewn stones (Ezekiel 40:42–43). All this exquisite detail has convinced many biblical scholars that Ezekiel glimpsed an actual, future structure. Many believe that this yet-to-be-constructed temple will stand as a center of Jewish worship during the thousand-year reign of Jesus on earth.

But what about the animal sacrifices that Ezekiel predicted for this temple? (Ezekiel 43:18–27). Will such bloody offerings really take place during the thousand-year reign? Some say yes, and suggest that these future sacrifices will commemorate the atoning sacrifice of Jesus.

Others are not so sure. They wonder how such sacrifices could possibly take place while Jesus, the risen sacrifice, reigns over his people. After all, didn't the death of Jesus mark the end of all sin offerings (Hebrews 10:11–14)? Wouldn't any return to animal offerings represent a redemptive U-turn, back to the Old Testament sacrificial system?[70] Such a system—even if the sacrifices were commemorative—would repudiate the sufficiency of Jesus' death on the cross. If that's the case, perhaps the sacrifices in the prophet's vision are figurative pictures of how God's people will worship in the future kingdom, couched in terms that would have made sense to Ezekiel's first readers.

A Present and Future Spiritual Reality

Still other biblical scholars suggest that what Ezekiel saw symbolized something far greater than any physical structure.

- Perhaps Ezekiel glimpsed the ideal temple of God in the heavens (Revelation 7:15; 11:19; 14:15–17; 16:1, 17); if so, it is possible that the sacrifices signify pure worship in the presence of God.

- This temple might point to the presence of God within the future New Jerusalem (Revelation 21:2, 22).

- Or perhaps Ezekiel's temple pointed forward to the church. After all, didn't the apostle Paul refer to Christians as "the temple of God"? (1 Corinthians 3:16–17; 6:19; 2 Corinthians 6:16). Jesus is the "cornerstone" of this temple (Ephesians 2:20–21). Perhaps Ezekiel's temple signified the future people of God, and the sacrifices symbolized Christians' sacrifices of obedience and praise in response to Christ's one sacrifice (Romans 12:1; Hebrews 13:15; 1 Peter 2:5). If that's the case, there is no need for a future, physical temple. The temple is the people of God, the men and women from every nation who have trusted Jesus and who now are "being built together into a dwelling place for God" (Ephesians 2:22).

> **A MILLENNIAL TEMPLE?**
>
> Dispensational premillennialists as well as many historical premillennialists expect a temple to be built by Jesus himself during his millennial reign; this temple will fulfill the prophecies in Ezekiel 40–43.

The challenge is whether such a spiritual fulfillment really reflects what Ezekiel prophesied. The prophet saw a temple, not a group of people. If God fulfills this vision by dwelling among people, wouldn't that mean that God went back on his promises?

© Joshua Haviv

Not necessarily!

Think of it this way: Suppose a father in 1900 promised to give his young son a horse and buggy whenever his son married. During the son's later childhood and adolescence, this young man might have dreamt about the precise contours of the buggy and the breed of his horse. This was truly a good promise from his father! Now, suppose that, when the son married in the 1920, the father did not give him a horse and buggy. Instead, the son and his bride received a brand-new automobile with leather seats, nickel-plated headlights, and battery ignition.

> ### A TRIBULATION TEMPLE?
>
> Some dispensational premillennialists expect a temple to be built during the great tribulation; the Antichrist will defile this temple (Daniel 9:27; Matthew 24:15; 2 Thessalonians 2:3–4; Revelation 11:1–2). Others understand Daniel 9:27 to refer to the defiling of the second temple in 167 BC or to the Roman destruction of the temple in AD 70. Matthew 24:15 and Revelation 11:1–2 might also refer to the fall of the second temple in AD 70.

Did the father break his promise to his son?

Of course not. "The essence of the father's word has remained the same: a convenient mode of transportation. What has changed is the precise form of transportation."[71] In the 1920s, new circumstances made the gift of a car far more

© Stasys Eidiejus

appropriate than the finest horse and buggy. In the same way, on this side of the cross and empty tomb, perhaps a spiritual temple represents a greater fulfillment of Ezekiel's words than the grandest physical structure.

Whatever your precise perspective on how Ezekiel's temple relates to the end times, this much is true: **God *will* fulfill his inspired Word**. Whether the fulfillment is material or spiritual, earthly or heavenly, Ezekiel's meticulously mapped picture of restoration shows that God has a glorious plan for his people's future: He will dwell among his people, they will worship him in purity, and blessings will flow from his presence. This is part of the hope that will bring humanity's exile to an end.

Tabernacle and Temple Timeline

Date	Event	Scripture	Other Sources
1446 BC	Bezalel and Oholiab oversee the construction of the tabernacle, according to the plans that God gave to Moses	Exodus 31, 35–36	
c. 1400 BC	Tabernacle set up in Shiloh	Joshua 18:1	
Before 1000 BC	Tabernacle transferred to Gibeon	1 Chronicles 16:39	
953 BC	King Solomon dedicates first temple on the Temple Mount	2 Chronicles 6:1–7:22	
586 BC	Babylonians destroy first temple	2 Chronicles 36:19	
515 BC	Second temple dedicated	Ezra 6:13–22	
167 BC	Syrian king Antiochus IV Epiphanes defiles second temple		1 Maccabees 1:55–59
165 BC	Rededication of second temple		Josephus, *Antiquitates Judaicae*, 12:7:6–7
c. 20 BC	King Herod the Great begins expansion of second temple	John 2:20	Josephus, *Antiquitates Judaicae*, 15:11:1
70 AD	Roman army destroys second temple		Josephus, *Bellum Judaicum*, 6:1–5

GOG, MAGOG, AND THE PEOPLE OF GOD

Immediately before his vision of the temple, the prophet Ezekiel experienced a far less glorious vision: God told Ezekiel to prophesy against "Gog, of the land of Magog, the prince, chief [or, Rosh], Meshech, and Tubal" (Ezekiel 38:1–2). Then, Ezekiel watched as these people and nations rose up against God's people before God himself destroyed them (Ezekiel 39:4–20).

But who are these nations? And when will this battle occur?

Pointers to Future Nations?

Some dispensational premillennialists have tried to tie each of these nations to modern regions that were unknown to Ezekiel. According to these scholars, what Ezekiel glimpsed was a physical conflict between specific nations that will occur during the Tribulation. And so, "Gog" is a future ruler, "Rosh" is Russia, "Magog" represents the Islamic former Soviet republics, while "Meshech and Tubal" refer to Muslims in Turkey and Iran.

Pointers to Perennial Earthly Powers?

Other interpreters point out that "Rosh" is simply the Hebrew word for "chief"; so, it's highly unlikely that this has anything to do with Russia. What Ezekiel seems to have been saying was that "Gog" from the land of "Magog" would the prince and chief of "Meshech and Tubal." But did Ezekiel glimpse any specific nations in this three-country confederacy of Magog, Meshech, and Tubal? And why did he join these nations a few verses later with Persia, Cush, Put, Gomer, and Togarmah? (38:5–6). Some of these names do appear elsewhere in Scripture: According to the genealogies of Genesis, Gomer was the father of Togarmah and the brother of Meshech, Tubal, and Magog (Genesis 10:2–3). But what did they mean in Ezekiel's day? By the time of Ezekiel, it's possible that these terms represented distant, almost-unknown peoples near Asia Minor. If so, the ruler Gog and these mysterious realms probably didn't imply any particular people groups; instead, these terms symbolized the far distant realms of the earth. What Ezekiel envisioned was a time near the end of time when all the earth's kingdoms, from near to far, would gather together to try to destroy God's people.

Pointers to Perennial Spiritual Powers?

Most amillennialists and postmillennialists, as well as many premillennialists, see these names not as nations but as symbolic references to demonic powers: "spiritual forces of evil in the heavenly realms" (Ephesians 6:12). After all, didn't Michael the archangel fight against a demonic "prince of the Persian kingdom"? (Daniel 10:13). If the battle in Ezekiel is a spiritual battle, these nations are symbols of dark powers in every age—spiritual powers that will seek, up to the very end of time, to destroy the people of God.

WHAT HAPPENED TO THE ARK OF THE COVENANT?

Everyone knows what happened to the ark of the covenant, right? An archaeologist from the Midwestern United States named Dr. "Indiana" Jones rediscovered the ark and saved it from the Nazis; now, it's hidden in a top-secret government warehouse—from the movie *Raiders of the Lost Ark*.

Well, that's probably not what really happened. The truth is, no one knows for certain. Here's what we do know:

- The glory of the LORD left the temple before the Babylonians sacked the structure (Ezekiel 8:6–10:18); this could mean that from this point forward people could touch the ark without being killed.

- Shishonq I of Egypt could have taken the ark of the covenant to his capital city of Tanis (1 Kings 14:25–26).

- It is possible that, when King Manasseh placed idols in the temple of God, faithful priests removed the ark of the covenant from the temple (2 Kings 21:4–7; 2 Chronicles 33:7–9).

- It's possible that the Babylonians took the ark of the covenant. This is what many Jews seem to have assumed in the centuries between the Old and New Testaments (see the non-biblical text 4 Ezra 10:19–22). According to Chronicles, "all the articles of the house of God" were "brought to Babylon" (2 Chronicles 36:18). It may be that these items included the ark. Yet, when King Cyrus returned these articles, the ark is not listed (Ezra 1:7–11). If the Babylonians did take the ark, it must have been lost or destroyed before the time of Cyrus.

- According to one Jewish tradition, the prophet Jeremiah hid the ark in a cave on Mount Nebo (mentioned in the non-biblical text 2 Maccabees 2:4–10).

- According to two other Jewish traditions, King Josiah hid the ark. A medieval rabbi named Moishe Maimonides claimed that Josiah placed the ark in a cave near the Dead Sea (*Laws of the Temple*, 4:1). Another tradition claims that Josiah buried the ark in a wooden storehouse under the Temple Mount (*Yoma* 35b). An architect named Leen Ritmeyer discovered a cut-out section of bedrock, about the size of the ark, directly beneath where the ark would have been placed in the temple. Ritmeyer suggests that the ark is hidden there.[72]

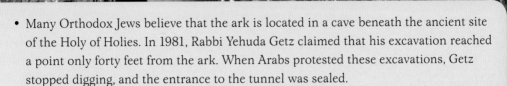

- Many Orthodox Jews believe that the ark is located in a cave beneath the ancient site of the Holy of Holies. In 1981, Rabbi Yehuda Getz claimed that his excavation reached a point only forty feet from the ark. When Arabs protested these excavations, Getz stopped digging, and the entrance to the tunnel was sealed.

- The Christians of Axum, Ethiopia, claim that a son of the Queen of Sheba acquired the ark after the queen visited King Solomon (see 1 Kings 10:1–13). Now, they say, they keep the ark hidden in the Church of St. Mary of Zion.

- When the Romans entered the temple in AD 70, there seems to have been no ark of the covenant in the temple.[73]

- John saw an ark of the covenant in his vision (Revelation 11:19). This may have been a figurative description of God's glorious presence, part of an ideal heavenly temple of God, or the actual ancient ark of the covenant taken up into the heavens.

THE TABERNACLE, TEMPLE, AND ARK IN HISTORY AND PROPHECY

(According to Premillennial Dispensational View)

Ark might have been placed beneath Holy of Holies

If hidden, the ark appeared undisturbed by Roman destruction

Tabernacle

First Temple

Second Temple

Ark is placed in the tabernacle

∴

The *shekinah* glory fills the Holy of Holies

Ark is transferred to the temple

∴

The *shekinah* glory fills the Holy of Holies

Ark might lie hidden in secret chamber

∴

Roman eagle insignia defiles sanctuary

485 Years CONQUEST & SETTLEMENT	374 Years MONARCHY	70 Years EXILE	586 Years GENTILE DOMINATION

1446 BC
EXODUS
Ark is built by Moses & Bezalel

Tabernacle constructed

ARK Captured and returned

966–960 BC
First temple built (Solomon's)

586 BC
First temple destroyed

516 BC
Second temple built (Zerubbabel's)

19 BC
Second temple enlarged (Herod's)

AD 70
Second temple destroyed

Dome of the Rock

Location of the ark unknown

Tribulation Temple

(2 Thess. 2:4; Rev. 11:1–2)

Millennial Temple

(Ezek. 40–48; Hag. 2:6–9)

Dome of the Rock	Tribulation Temple	Millennial Temple
Some argue that the ark remains hidden during church age	Ark is placed in third temple	Ark re-installed by Messiah and *shekinah* returns (Ezek. 43:4–7)
For some, the Islamic shrine defiles the Holy of Holies	Abomination of Desolation desecrates third temple	All of Jerusalem becomes God's throne (Jer. 3:16–17) and is called "Holy to the Lord" (Zech. 14:20)
	70th Week (Dan. 9:27)	

Temple site is preserved through history **CHURCH AGE**	**7 Years** **TRIBULATION**	**1000 Years** **MILLENNIAL KINGDOM**

For pre-mill dispensationalists, the search for the ark increases as the end of the church age nears and Jews re-establish their sovereignty over the Temple Mount and make preparations to rebuild temple	**First Half** Israel enters into a covenant with Antichrist, recovers the ark, and rebuilds the temple	**Second Half** Third temple is desecrated by Antichrist as he enthrones himself on the ark	Restoration of national Israel Second coming and reign of Christ on earth	New heavens and new earth (eternal state)

Chart concept and design originally by Dr. J. R. Price
Temple illustrations © Bill Latta

FOUR PERSPECTIVES ON EZEKIEL'S TEMPLE[74]

What Did Ezekiel See?	Where Is the Temple Located?	When And How Is the Temple Constructed?	Which Views of the End Times Might Take This Perspective on the Temple?
A physical structure?	Jerusalem	The temple will be a future, physical structure, built during the millennium.	Dispensational Premillennial, Historical Premillennial
A figurative ideal temple?	Heaven	The temple exists perpetually in the heavens; Ezekiel's temple was not intended to represent any physical structure.	Amillennial, Postmillennial, Historical Premillennial
A figurative ideal temple?	Blueprint	The temple represents an ideal for God's people in the mind of God; Ezekiel's temple was not intended to represent any physical structure.	Amillennial, Postmillennial, Historical Premillennial
A real heavenly temple?	In heaven, will come to earth	The temple exists in the heavens and will be revealed on earth at the end of time.	Amillennial, Postmillennial, Historical Premillennial

WHAT DO THE DETAILS OF EZEKIEL'S TEMPLE MEAN?

	If the temple is a future physical structure, then ... (Dispensational Premillennialists and some Historical Premillennialists)	If the temple symbolizes a spiritual reality, then ... (Amillennialists, Postmillennialists, and some Historical Premillennialists)
... animal sacrifices are either:	1. Commemoration, through actual animal sacrifices, of the Messiah's ultimate sacrifice 2. Figurative picture of renewed worship, presented in a way that Ezekiel and his first readers would understand	1. Symbols of eternal worship in the future 2. Portrayals of worship in the church as the sacrificed and risen Messiah reigns in heaven
... detailed measurements and materials are:	1. Prophetic prediction of actual structural details	1. Description of a heavenly temple or of the splendor of heavenly worship 2. Symbolic description of the people of God, the bride of Christ

3. SOMETHING OLD, ALL THINGS NEW: ISAIAH'S PERSPECTIVE ON GOD'S PLAN FOR THE FUTURE OF PLANET EARTH

The promise of a final day of the Lord guarantees that God will deal decisively with sin and evil—and this, by itself, should be enough to cause us to watch and wait for the appearing of Jesus in the clouds! But God's promises for the future go far beyond final judgment and salvation. **God has also promised to make all things new.**

The *new* is always exciting. A new car, a fresh start, an innovative idea. How much more when we live in a world filled with sin, soaked with tears, racked with pain, and rotting away in death. Christians, with creation itself, have an inborn longing for newness. We are filled with birth pangs of hope

> When we live in a world filled with sin, soaked with tears, racked with pain, and rotting away in death. Christians, with creation itself, have an inborn longing for newness. We are filled with birth pangs of hope (Romans 8:22–23).

(Romans 8:22–23). That's why we so deeply resonate with the words that come from the throne of God himself: "Behold, I am making all things new" (Revelation 21:5).

But we are not the first to hear or hope such things. Centuries ago, Isaiah prophesied that judgment would rain down on Israel and the nations. Yet he also relayed a kaleidoscope of hope. The second half of Isaiah (40–66) paints this hope in ever-brightening and ever–more–colorful terms. Isaiah uses the Hebrew word that means "new" ten times in these chapters.[75] Never is he referring to anything less than a grand work of God that will alter history forever. Throughout these chapters, the promises of newness grow. The climax? "Behold, I create new heavens and a new earth, and the former things shall not be remembered or come into mind" (Isaiah 65:17; see also 66:22).

The earth is not just a throwaway stage for the drama of redemption; the material world matters, and God will redeem and renew this world. According to Isaiah, houses will be built and inhabited (65:21a), vineyards will be planted and enjoyed

(65:21b), work will be happy instead of hard (65:22b), and "the wolf and the lamb shall graze together" (65:25a). "'They shall not hurt or destroy in all my holy mountain,' says the LORD" (65:25b).

Christians differ when it comes to whether some prophecies of Isaiah refer to an earthly millennium or if they are descriptions of what follows the end of time. Dispensationalists maintain that, before making all things new, God must restore Israel to the promised land and provide Israel with a physical temple. Others see these predictions as shadowy symbols of glorious realities that are fulfilled in Jesus and in the church.[76]

Despite such differences, every believer in Jesus can agree on this truth:

There will come a day when every secondary summit will pale in the shadow of the infinite peak of eternity. The ultimate day of the Lord will arrive, the glorious presence of God will descend, the final restoration will come, and everything will be new.

© Tomas Sereda

Daniel's Double Vision

WHO WAS DANIEL?

The prophet Daniel wrote the book of Daniel in the sixth century BC. The Babylonians deported Daniel to their capital city in 605 BC. Daniel was probably a teenager from the upper classes of the Israelites, perhaps even from a royal family.

Some liberal scholars have claimed that the book of Daniel was actually written in the second century BC and then falsely ascribed to Daniel. This perspective is highly unlikely because:

- A manuscript of Daniel was found in Cave 4 at Qumran, among older texts that had been copied and preserved in the second century BC. If the book of Daniel had been written only recently, in the second century, why would the book have been copied and preserved among these older texts?
- Six chapters in Daniel are written in Aramaic (Daniel 2–7). The style and vocabulary of the Aramaic sections are closer to the Aramaic of the seventh and sixth centuries BC than the second century BC.
- Nineteen Persian words appear in the book of Daniel. These words were used primarily in the fourth century and earlier, not in the second century.
- Jesus suggested that a historical figure named Daniel wrote the words ascribed to him in the book of Daniel (compare Daniel 9:27; 11:31; 12:11 with Matthew 24:15–16; Mark 13:34; Luke 21:20).

The first six chapters of the book tell about Daniel's life in the royal courts of Babylon and Medo-Persia. The last part of the book foretells the rise and fall of kings and nations as well as the rise of God's everlasting kingdom. These chapters are written in an early apocalyptic style that was important for many later writers, including the author of Revelation.[77]

HEAD OF FINE GOLD—BABYLONIA (626–539 BC)

Historical and Biblical Background of Nebuchadnezzar's Dream

- About 600 years before Jesus was born, Babylonia (Iraq today) was the most powerful and wealthy kingdom in the Middle East.

- King Nebuchadnezzar of Babylon besieged Jerusalem and took Daniel and others captive to Babylon to serve in his court. Nebuchadnezzar also took some of the sacred objects and vessels from the temple of God back to Babylon.

- One night, Nebuchadnezzar had a dream. The king threatened to kill his advisors if they could not both tell him the dream and interpret it (Daniel 2:5–11).

- Daniel asked the king for some time to interpret the dream. After Daniel prayed, God revealed the dream and its meaning to him (Daniel 2:12–23).

- The dream showed a statue with four sections. The head was gold. The chest was silver. The belly and thighs were bronze. The legs were made of iron and the feet were iron mixed with clay. A large rock struck and destroyed the statue and became a huge mountain and filled the whole earth (Daniel 2:31–35).

- Daniel told King Nebuchadnezzar the dream and interpreted it (Daniel 2:36–45). The King made Daniel ruler over Babylon.

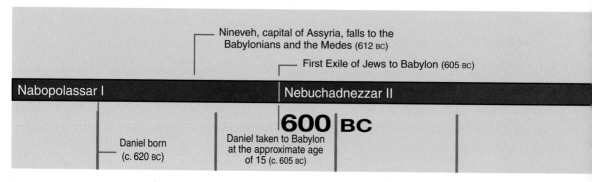

Nineveh, capital of Assyria, falls to the Babylonians and the Medes (612 BC)

First Exile of Jews to Babylon (605 BC)

Nabopolassar I

Nebuchadnezzar II

600 BC

Daniel born (c. 620 BC)

Daniel taken to Babylon at the approximate age of 15 (c. 605 BC)

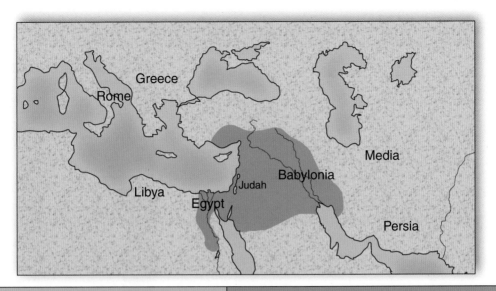

Head of the Statue (Daniel 2)	**Vision of Beasts—Lion** (Daniel 7)
• The head of the statue, made from fine gold, represented the kingdom of Babylonia, which the Lord gave King Nebuchadnezzar to rule. • The gold symbolized the superior power of Babylonia. • Eventually Babylonia would be destroyed by an inferior kingdom. • When King Nebuchadnezzar heard Daniel's interpretation, he said, "Surely your God is the God of gods and the Lord of kings and a revealer of mysteries, for you were able to reveal this mystery."	• More than 50 years after King Nebuchadnezzar's dream, Daniel had a vision about four great beasts (like a lion with eagle's wings, a bear, a leopard, and a terrifying powerful beast). • The four beasts are four kingdoms. Nebuchadnezzar of the Babylonian kingdom is compared to a lion in Jeremiah 4:7; 50:44, and to an eagle in Ezekiel 17:3, 11, 12. • Images of lions with eagle's wings were popular in Babylonia, and can be found on ancient Babylonian architecture and currency (Daniel 7:4).

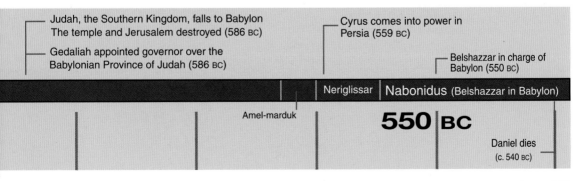

Judah, the Southern Kingdom, falls to Babylon
The temple and Jerusalem destroyed (586 BC)

Gedaliah appointed governor over the
Babylonian Province of Judah (586 BC)

Cyrus comes into power in
Persia (559 BC)

Belshazzar in charge of
Babylon (550 BC)

Neriglissar | Nabonidus (Belshazzar in Babylon)

Amel-marduk

550 BC

Daniel dies
(c. 540 BC)

CHEST AND ARMS OF SILVER—MEDO-PERSIA (539–332 BC)

Historical and Biblical Background

- In 539 BC, Darius the Mede (from Media) took Babylon without a fight.

- By 538 BC, Mesopotamia and Judah were under Persian rule. Later the Persians gained control of Egypt and Libya.

- King Cyrus and the other kings of the Persian empire developed a policy that allowed all people the freedom to worship their own gods and live their own ways.

- In 538 BC, Cyrus issued a decree ordering the restoration of the Jewish community. Jews were allowed to return to Jerusalem and rebuild the temple (Ezra 1:2–4).

- The Persians paid to rebuild the temple in Jerusalem (Ezra 6:8).

- The vessels taken by King Nebuchadnezzar of Babylon were returned to their rightful place in Jerusalem (Ezra 1:7–11).

- In 457 BC, King Artaxerxes of Persia sent Ezra to Judah for religious reform and spiritual guidance (Ezra 7:1–6).

- Nehemiah governed Judah from 444–430 BC. While in Judah, Nehemiah rebuilt the walls of Jerusalem.

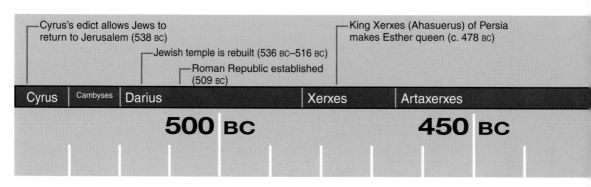

Cyrus's edict allows Jews to return to Jerusalem (538 BC)

Jewish temple is rebuilt (536 BC–516 BC)

Roman Republic established (509 BC)

King Xerxes (Ahasuerus) of Persia makes Esther queen (c. 478 BC)

| Cyrus | Cambyses | Darius | Xerxes | Artaxerxes |

500 BC   **450** BC

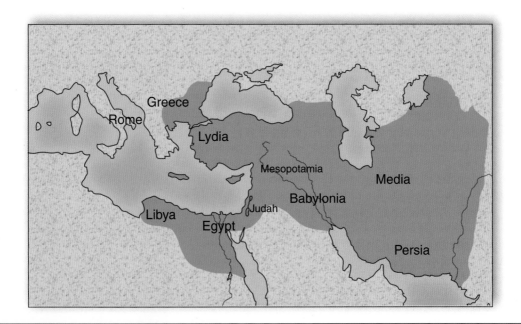

Chest and Arms of Statue (Daniel 2)	Vision of Beasts—Bear (Daniel 7)
• The chest and arms made of silver represented the kingdom of Medo-Persia, which is the second power that would rise after Babylonia. • Silver, which is of lesser value than gold, symbolized the inferior status of Medo-Persia to Babylonia. • Eventually Persia would be conquered by another kingdom.	• Daniel's vision of the beasts had shown a beast that looked like a bear. • The bear was raised on one side, which may illustrate the dominance of Persia over Media. • It had three ribs in its mouth, which may have illustrated the three major empires Persia conquered (Babylon, Egypt, and Lydia). • The bear was commanded to devour much flesh, which may have been a reference to Persia's military expansion throughout the ancient world.

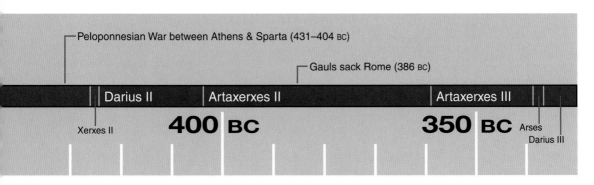

Peloponnesian War between Athens & Sparta (431–404 BC)

Gauls sack Rome (386 BC)

Darius II   Artaxerxes II   Artaxerxes III

Xerxes II

400 BC

350 BC   Arses

Darius III

BELLY AND THIGHS OF BRONZE—GREECE (332–63 BC)

Historical and Biblical Background

- In 332 BC, Alexander the Great of Greece conquered the kingdom of Persia, and expanded his kingdom as far east as the Indus river.

- Alexander the Great brought with him rapid Hellenization, the spread of Greek culture, language, and religion into the entire civilized world.

- After Alexander's death in 323 BC, his generals fought over the conquered land.

- After more than 40 years of struggles and warfare (323–280 BC), four major divisions emerged: Egypt (Ptolemies), Syria (Seleucids), Macedonia (Antigonids), and Pergamum (Attalids).

- For over 150 years, the Jews were either under the control of the Ptolemies or the Seleucids.

- From 175–163 BC, the Seleucid ruler Antiochus IV Epiphanes tried to force the Jews to abandon their law and adopt Greek culture. In 167 BC, he desecrated the Jewish temple by sacrificing a pig on an altar to the Greek god Zeus.

- In response to the desecration of the temple, a Jewish priest named Judas Maccabeus lead a revolt.

- Maccabeus won, and in 164 BC, the temple was cleansed and rededicated. This rededication is celebrated every year as Hanukkah.

— Alexander the Great conquers Egypt and Palestine, Hellenization begins (332 BC)

┌ Alexandrian Empire divided; Ptolemy rules Egypt, Seleucus rules Persia and Syria, Antigonus rules Macedonia and Greece (323 BC). The Attalids rule Pergamum.

┌ Septuagint (Scriptures translated into Greek in Alexandria) (255 BC)

Ptolemies of Egypt

Alexander the Great

300 BC

250 BC

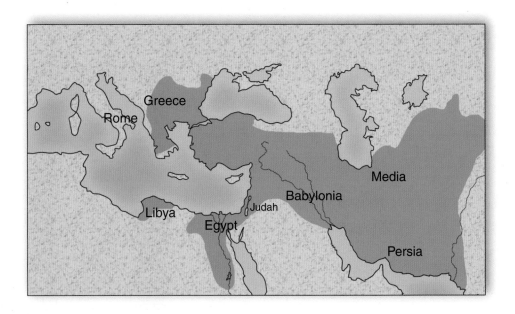

Belly and Thighs of Statue (Daniel 2)	**Vision of Beasts—Leopard** (Daniel 7)
• The belly and thighs made of bronze represent the kingdom of Greece. This third kingdom would extend throughout the known world. • Bronze, which is of lesser value than silver, symbolized the inferior status of Greece to that of Persia. • Eventually Greece would be conquered by another kingdom.	• Daniel's vision of the leopard with four heads and four wings may represent the kingdom of Greece. • The four wings may illustrate the speed of Alexander the Great's conquest. • The four heads may represent the division of Alexander's kingdom into four provinces after Alexander's death: Egypt under the Ptolemies, Syria under the Seleucids, Macedonia under the Antigonids, and Pergamum under the Attalids.

Judas Maccabeus leads Jewish revolt against the Seleucids (167 BC)

The temple in Jerusalem is defiled (167 BC)

Temple in Jerusalem rededicated (164 BC)

Seleucids of Syria	Hasmonean Dynasty

00 BC   150 BC   100 BC

LEGS OF IRON AND FEET OF IRON AND CLAY—ROME

Historical and Biblical Background

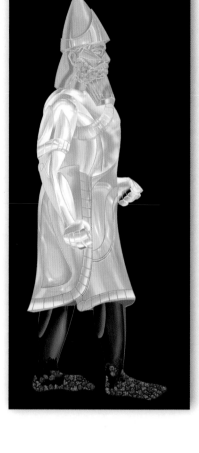

- Many scholars suggest that the fourth kingdom is the Roman empire, however the Bible does not specifically identify this kingdom as Rome.

- In 63 BC, Roman General Pompey conquered Jerusalem.

- On March 15, 44 BC, Julius Caesar was assassinated by Brutus and Cassius, who fled to the East. Two years later, Octavian and Mark Antony defeated Brutus and Cassius at the Battle of Philippi.

- In 37 BC, Herod the Great was appointed king of Judea by Octavian and Mark Antony.

- In 27 BC, Caesar Augustus (Octavian) became the first Roman Emperor.

- During his reign, Herod the Great began to refurbish the temple in Jerusalem.

- Jesus was born in Bethlehem, c. 6–4 BC.

- In AD 6, Judea became a Roman province ruled by a governor.

- Jesus Christ was crucified by the governor of Judea, Pontius Pilate. Three days after his death, Jesus rose from the dead and was seen by more than 500 people (c. AD 30).

- In AD 70, the Romans destroyed the Jewish temple and Jerusalem.

- Over time, the Roman Empire weakened due to conflict within its borders and invaders attacking from outside.

- The Roman Empire fell in AD 476.

Pompey conquers Jerusalem for Rome (63 BC)

Julius Caesar, Crassus and Pompey form the First Triumvirate (60 BC)

Jesus Born in Bethlehem (6–4 BC)

Jesus Baptized (c. AD 26)

| Julius Caesar, Crassus, and Pompey | Caesar Augustus (Octavian) | Tiberius |

50 BC   **AD 1**

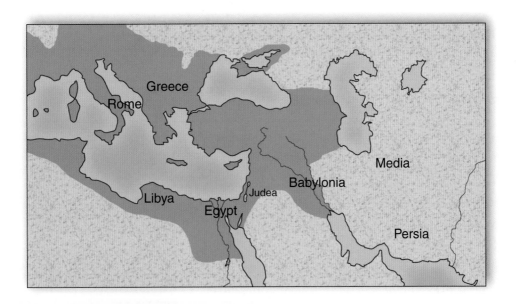

Legs and Feet of Statue (Daniel 2)	Vision of Beasts—Terrifying Beast (Daniel 7)
• The legs were made of iron and the feet were a mixture of both iron and clay. • The legs of iron suggest that this kingdom would be strong as iron and would break, smash and crush things. • This kingdom would be a divided kingdom, different from the others, both strong and weak, like iron is strong and clay is brittle. • This kingdom would have a mixture of people who would not be united (Daniel 2:41–43; 7:23).	• Daniel had a vision of a terrifying beast with ten horns and iron teeth. • The beast's ten horns are ten kings that would rise from this kingdom. • After them, another man (the "little horn" with eyes and a mouth that boasts) would speak against God and persecute God's people. Three of the first horns (kings) would be uprooted. Eventually the terrifying beast would be thrown into the blazing fire.

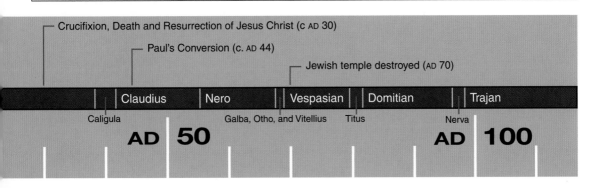

STONE CUT OUT, NOT BY HUMAN HANDS— EVERLASTING KINGDOM

Bible References & Spiritual Application

- The stone represents God's eternal kingdom that is more powerful than any other kingdom.

- At the time of Daniel, the temple in Jerusalem was in shambles and the people of Israel had been placed in captivity. The defeated captives may have feared that their God was weak and unfaithful.

- Daniel's writing demonstrates that in the midst of despair, God is still present, powerful, and in control. Kingdoms and rulers come and go, but God is ultimately in charge (Daniel 2:20–21; 7:9–14, 27).

- Despite Babylonia's wealth and power, Daniel emphasized that God's kingdom is eternal and more powerful than any earthly kingdom (Daniel 2:44).

- The book of Daniel shows that God did not forget his promises. God's promises have been fulfilled in the Son of Man (Daniel 7:13–14), who established an everlasting kingdom on earth (Daniel 2:44; 7:27).

God shall wipe away all tears from their eyes; and there shall be no more death, neither sorrow, nor crying, neither shall there be any more pain: for the former things are passed away. —Revelation 21:3, 4 (KJV)

The Son of Man – The Alpha and Omega, the be

The Rock (Daniel 2)	Vision of Beasts—The Son of Man (Daniel 7)
• A stone was cut out, not by human hands, and it struck the statue on its feet of iron and clay and broke them in pieces. Then the rest of the statue broke into pieces and what remained was carried away in the wind. Then the stone that struck the statue became a great mountain that filled the whole earth. • Daniel told the king that God will set up a kingdom that will crush all earthly kingdoms and bring them to an end. • God's kingdom will never be destroyed and will endure forever.	• After seeing the four beasts in a vision, Daniel saw one like a son of man, coming with the clouds of heaven. • The son of man [Jesus] approached the Ancient of Days [God, the Father] and was led into his presence. • The son of man was given authority, glory and sovereign power. • All peoples, nations and men of every language worshiped him. • His dominion is an everlasting dominion that will not pass away, and his kingdom will never be destroyed.

d the end, the first and the last. Revelation 22:13

THE STATUE IN THE BOOK OF DANIEL
The Kingdoms and King Nebuchadnezzar's Dream

NEBUCHADNEZZAR'S DREAM (Daniel 2)	DANIEL'S VISION (Daniel 7)	THE KINGDOMS (Dates Kingdom occupied Judah)
HEAD (FINE GOLD)	**LION** with eagle's wings	**BABYLONIA** King Nebuchadnezzar to Belshazzar (605 BC–539 BC)
CHEST AND ARMS (SILVER)	**BEAR** raised on one side; three ribs in its mouth	**MEDO-PERSIA** King Cyrus to Darius III (539 BC–332 BC)
BELLY AND THIGHS (BRONZE)	**LEOPARD** with four wings and four heads	**GREECE** Alexander the Great and the Four Divisions (332 BC–63 BC)
LEGS (IRON) & FEET (IRON AND CLAY)	**BEAST** iron teeth, ten horns; small horn with eyes and mouth	**A DIVIDED KINGDOM** Many scholars believe this kingdom to be Rome
STONE (CUT OUT, NOT BY HUMAN HANDS)	**SON OF MAN** (Jesus Christ)	**THE EVERLASTING KINGDOM OF GOD**

THE VISION OF THE RAM AND THE GOAT (DANIEL 8:1–14)

Daniel's vision of the ram and the goat in Daniel 8 left him overwhelmed, sickened, and bedridden for days. Even after his strength returned, he was appalled by what he saw (8:27). So what was it that Daniel saw around 550 BC, "in the third year of the reign of King Belshazzar"?

- As he stood on the banks of a canal in the city of Susa, Daniel saw a ram with two horns. One horn was higher than the other, and the ram was charging in every direction, dominating everyone in his path (8:2–4).

- Then a male goat approached from the distant west, hovering above the ground and having a horn between his eyes. The goat charged the ram, shattered the ram's horns, and trampled the ram. The goat became great, but soon its own horn was broken, and four other horns took its place (8:5–8).

- A little horn arose from one of the four horns. This little horn grew exponentially, even into heaven, where it pulled down and trampled some of the stars. The regular burnt offering was canceled, the sanctuary was desecrated, and some of the host of heaven joined with this little horn (8:9–12).

- Near the end of the vision, Daniel overheard two "holy ones" discussing how long these horrific desecrations would last. The answer given was "2,300 evenings and mornings" until the sanctuary was restored (8:13–14).

THE INTERPRETATION OF THE RAM AND THE GOAT (DANIEL 8:19–26)

The angel Gabriel gave Daniel a precise explanation of the vision—an explanation that history clearly confirms.

- The first two-horned goat portrayed the empire of the Medes and Persians. Under Cyrus the Great, Persia became greater than the empire of the Medes, a comparison made clear by the raised horn. Most of the military campaigns of this joint kingdom were to the west, north, and south (8:2–4).

- The male goat rushing in from the west without touching the ground was Alexander the Great, king of Greece. His swift conquest of the known world is legendary (334–331 BC). His empire was vast but short-lived (323 BC). The leopard with four wings (7:6) depicts his rapid advance.

- The four horns that replace the broken horn represent Alexander's four generals who succeeded him and ruled over his fragmented kingdom (7:6). These four horns are called by many different names due to the conflicts that occurred throughout this bloody and unstable period.

- Seleucus was one of Alexander's generals who ruled over Mesopotamia and Persia. The vile little horn was Antiochus IV Epiphanes (175–164 BC), the eighth ruler in the line that traced back to Seleucus. Antiochus IV banned sacrifices, desecrated the Jewish temple, and massacred faithful Jews, including the revered high priest Onias III in 170 BC. This vision of brutal persecution of the Jewish people is probably what devastated Daniel (8:27).

- The "2,300 evenings and mornings" may refer to 2,300 days, or a little more than six years. This period could run from 170 BC when Antiochus IV murdered the high priest Onias III to 164 BC when Judas Maccabeus rededicated the temple. Or these "2,300 evenings and mornings" might refer to the evening and morning sacrifices, totaling only 1,150 days—two sacrifices per day—or a little more than three years. This period would run from 167 BC when Antiochus IV desecrated the temple to 164 BC when the temple was rededicated.

Despite the bloody theater of future history that Daniel was compelled to watch, God had a clear purpose for pulling back the curtain on this horror show. This roller-coaster of political conflict and the atrocities of the arrogant "little horn" would threaten the resolve of God's chosen people. So, God revealed these dark days in advance to demonstrate his firm control and guiding hand even over disturbing events to come.

The Mystery of the Seventy Weeks

Suppose for a moment that you've spent the past sixty-seven years of your life in exile. In an era when few people live beyond fifty, you are approaching eighty years old. You have faithfully served king after king. Yet you remain an exile from the land that you love.

How do you think you might spend your sunset years?

Some persons would be plotting a rebellion to overthrow their rulers. Others might wallow in bitterness and anger. Still others would have forgotten the faith of their fathers and turned to the gods of their captors.

Not Daniel.

After nearly seven decades in exile, Daniel was praying and studying prophecy (Daniel 9:1–4).

© Ivonne Wierink

That's how Daniel discovered an important truth: The prophet Jeremiah had predicted that the exile would end after seventy years (Jeremiah 25:11–12; 29:10)— and Daniel recognized that the seventieth year after the exile was quickly approaching. Despite his circumstances, Daniel trusted this prophetic word and began to plead with God for the restoration of Israel.

Suddenly, Daniel's prayer was cut short—but not because of a knock on the door or the buzz of a cell phone. This was a supernatural interruption that came from God himself.

The angel Gabriel careened into the middle of Daniel's prayer "in swift flight" (9:20–23). According to Gabriel, God had sent the angel to provide Daniel with insight into the future of Israel. What the angel unpacked about Israel's future was far greater and yet far darker than anything that Daniel had yet imagined.

Byzantine icon of the angel Gabriel, 1387–1395.

HEBREW

Language in which most of the Old Testament was written. Ezra 4–6 and Daniel 2–7 were written in Aramaic instead of Hebrew.

God's response to Daniel's prayer was rare and extraordinary; the message from the angel was even more extraordinary. Part of this message centered on a difficult prophecy about "seventy weeks" that had been decreed regarding Israel and the city of Jerusalem.

WHY "SEVENTY WEEKS"?

So what were these "seventy weeks" that the angel predicted? How much time do they represent? The word translated "weeks" is the Hebrew word that also means "sevens." And so, what Gabriel predicted was "seventy sevens." But what did Gabriel mean when he spoke of this time of "seventy sevens"?

Seventy literal weeks of seven days each would equal 490 days—far too brief a time for all of the events predicted in 9:24–27 to occur![78] That's why most interpreters of this text take the "seventy sevens" as seven periods of seven years each, for a total of something like 490 years.

> **"WEEKS"**
>
> The Hebrew word translated "weeks" is simply the word "sevens," and most interpreters view each "seven" as a period of seven years (exact or rounded), or as a symbolic number emphasizing completeness.

But why did Gabriel speak in terms of "sevens"? The Western mind is trained to estimate and to calculate in fives and tens. The ancient Jewish mind was more likely to think in terms of sevens. The number "seven" symbolized completeness or perfection, stemming from God's choice to rest from his work of creation on the seventh day. But there is another reason for the emphasis on the number "seven" in this particular text:

- God had commanded Israel to work the land for six years, then to let the land rest in the seventh year (Leviticus 25:4).

- For nearly five centuries, the Israelites failed to obey these commands. As a result, God scattered them among foreign nations for seventy years, until every missed year of rest had passed (Leviticus 26:34–35; 2 Chronicles 36:20–21). The Israelites had treated God's land like a slave for centuries. God sent them into exile so they could learn a seventy-year lesson and the land could enjoy a seventy-year rest—490 years divided by 7-year cycles equals 70 years of neglected rest.

- Now, near the end of this seventy-year span of judgment, God decreed "seventy sevens" to deal with his people's sin once and for all. *The time it would take to resolve the problem of Israel's sin would be the same that it had taken to create the problem in the first place: 490 years—or, "seventy sevens."*[79]

WHEN DID THE "SEVENTY SEVENS" BEGIN?

At this point the overachievers could be reaching for a calculator while the less mathematically inclined may be reaching for a bookmark. But don't forget that this angelic announcement is the answer to a godly man's prayer! God sent this message for the good of future generations—including your generation and mine.

To estimate the endpoint of Daniel's seventy weeks, the first step is to determine when the 490 years began in the first place. According to Gabriel, the tick-tock of the prophetic clock would begin with "the going out of the word to restore and build Jerusalem" (9:25). This would be far simpler if only one decree went out to restore Jerusalem. But that's not the case. At least three public decrees went out at different times that could fit this description.[80] The decree that you connect with the command to restore Jerusalem determines how you read the rest of Gabriel's words. So let's take a careful look at the different decrees that Gabriel might have meant:

Bas-relief of Persian soldier from Persepolis, Iran (6th century BC). © Vladimir Meinik

- **The temple decree of Cyrus?** In 538 BC, the newly-enthroned Persian king Cyrus decreed that he would allow the Israelites to rebuild the Jerusalem temple (2 Chronicles 36:22–23; Ezra 1:1–4; 6:1–12). Cyrus never specifically mentioned restoring the city, but this may have been implied. What's more, God did indicate through Isaiah that Cyrus would play a crucial role in the rebuilding of Jerusalem (Isaiah 44:28; 45:13).[81] If 538 BC is the start date, 490 years takes us to 48 BC. Nothing like the events in Daniel 9:24–27 occurred around this time. So, if Gabriel meant the temple decree of 538 BC, God must have intended the numbers to be rounded rather than precise.[82]

- **The decree of Cyrus renewed by Artaxerxes?** In 458 or 457 BC, a Persian ruler named Artaxerxes repeated Cyrus' original decree (Ezra 7:12–26). If this renewal by Artaxerxes was the decree that kick-started the seventy weeks, 490 years would take us close to AD 27 (remember, there is no year "0").[83] This is very near to the time when Jesus died and rose from the dead! The year 457 also stands at the beginning of a seven-year sabbatical cycle; this connects the text to the warnings about what would happen if the Israelites refused to embrace the years of Sabbath and jubilee.[84] One potential problem with this view: Artaxerxes did not specifically command the returning Israelites to rebuild the buildings in Jerusalem. But Artaxerxes did decree rulers and judges

Cyrus the Great, allowed the Hebrews to return to Jerusalem to rebuild the temple. Jean Fouquet, 1470.

to organize the people who would live in the city; this probably implies a rebuilding of the city (Ezra 7:25–26).

- **A later decree from Artaxerxes?** In 445 BC, Artaxerxes specifically selected Nehemiah to return and to rebuild the city (Nehemiah 2:1–8). Lighting the prophetic fuse at this point requires that the 490 years be calculated as 360-day "prophetic years" to fit with later events. This is certainly possible; John seems to have used 360-day years in Revelation. According to John, forty-two months (Revelation 11:2; 13:5) equalled 1,260 days (Revelation 12:6; 11:3).[85] Still, it remains unclear whether this is what Gabriel had in mind when he spoke to Daniel. If the years were 360-day years, the first sixty-nine sevens would lead to AD 32. If the decree of Artaxerxes went out on March 14th, 445 BC, sixty-nine prophetic years would total 173,880 days and end on April 6, 32 AD—a date that some scholars believe to be the moment of the Messiah's triumphal entry into Jerusalem (Matthew 21:1–11).[86]

When Did the Seventy Weeks Begin?

What Year?	Whose Decree?	How Do The Numbers Work?
538 BC	Cyrus	Approximate, rounded, or symbolic
457 BC	Artaxerxes, renewing decree of Cyrus	Exact 365-day years
445 BC	Artaxerxes	Exact 360-day years

TRANSLATING THE SEVENTY SEVENS

"To *athnach* or not to *athnach*, that is the question"

The words of Gabriel would be difficult to interpret even if everyone agreed on how to translate the text—but, as it turns out, there are serious questions when it comes to translating one of the most significant verses in this text!

The Masoretic text is the most ancient complete text of the Jewish Scriptures. In the Masoretic text of Daniel 9:25, a tiny mark called an "*athnach*" separates the phrases "seven sevens" from "sixty-two sevens." An *athnach* goes under a Hebrew word and looks like a tiny tent with no one sleeping in it. This little tent-like mark splits the verse into two distinct parts. In Daniel 9:25, the *athnach* changes the meaning so that the "Anointed One" would arrive only 49 years after the decree to restore Jerusalem.

Marks such as the *athnach* were not, however, part of the original God-breathed text of Scripture. Jewish scholars added these marks hundreds of years later; so, it is entirely possible that the *athnach* is misplaced and that "seven sevens" and "sixty-two sevens" should not be separated after all. And, in fact, some of the most ancient Greek translations of Daniel do keep these two phrases together.

Bible translators differ on whether to separate the two phrases or to keep them together. The English Standard Version keeps the Masoretic *athnach* and separates the phrases. The New International Version—along with the King James Version and the New King James Version—ignores the *athnach*, taking an ancient Greek translation as a more accurate representation of the original Hebrew text. The result is that the two phrases are connected rather than separated. This translation seems to be the correct rendering of the text.

Translation Differences in 9:25–26a		
Version	How are the translations different?	How do the different translations change the meaning of the text?
ESV	"25 Know therefore and understand that from the going out of the word to restore and build Jerusalem to the coming of an anointed one, a prince, there shall be *seven weeks. Then for sixty-two weeks* it shall be built again with squares and moat, but in a troubled time. 26 And after the sixty-two weeks, an anointed one shall be cut off and shall have nothing."	The ESV distinguishes sharply between the first seven "weeks" and the next sixty-two "weeks." This rendering implies that the Anointed One will come after the first seven sevens (49 years from the decree to restore Jerusalem) and that Jerusalem will be rebuilt over the next sixty-two sevens (434 years).
NIV (also KJV and NKJV)	"25 From the time the word goes out to restore and rebuild Jerusalem until the Anointed One, the ruler, comes, there will be *seven 'sevens,' and sixty-two 'sevens.'* It will be rebuilt with streets and a trench, but in times of trouble. 26 After the sixty-two 'sevens,' the Anointed One will be put to death and will have nothing."	The NIV—along with the KJV and NKJV—joins the first seven "sevens" (or "weeks") with the next sixty-two "sevens." The first seven "sevens" (49 years) focus on the restoration of the city; the following sixty-two "sevens" lead to the arrival of the "Anointed One" (434 years).

Six Purposes of the Seventy Sevens

In whatever God does or allows, God has a purpose. Sometimes, God reveals his purposes to his people (Genesis 18:17–21; Daniel 2:22); other times, God's purposes remain hidden. When it comes to the "seventy sevens" or "seventy weeks," God revealed six distinct purposes through the words of the angel Gabriel. The first three are negative, and the last three are positive:[87]

Daniel 9:24	Different Perspectives on Meaning and Fulfillment	
"To finish the transgression"	The conclusion of the specific sin of Israel's rebellion that led to exile	The conclusion of God's dealings with the sin of all humanity
"To put an end to sin"	The "sealing up" of the specific sin of Israel's rebellion	The "sealing up" of the sin of all humanity
"To atone for iniquity"	The complete atonement of sin through the sacrifice of the Messiah, with an emphasis on how this sacrifice deals with Israel's sin	The complete atonement of the world's sin through the sacrifice of the Messiah
"To bring in everlasting righteousness"	The millennial kingdom and God's eternal reign that follows the millennium	The death, resurrection, and enthronement of the Messiah which inaugurated his kingdom and which brings justification to everyone who trusts in him
"To seal both vision and prophet"	This prophecy will certainly come true	All prophecy will be fulfilled in the end
"To anoint a most holy place"	Ezekiel's millennial temple or New Jerusalem temple	Zerubbabel's temple or Judas Maccabeus' rededication of the temple or Spirit on Jesus or Spirit in the church

THE "SEVENTY SEVENS" IN THREE ACTS

Have you ever attended a play that's presented in three acts? Or perhaps a symphony with three movements? Each act or movement connects to the others, and certain themes are woven throughout all three sections. Yet each act makes a distinct contribution to one overall purpose.

That's how the Gabriel presented the "seventy sevens" to Daniel. The angel segmented the seventy sevens into three sections—almost like a play with three acts or a symphony with three movements. According to Gabriel, God's plan for his people would unfold in: *Seven sevens, followed by sixty-two sevens, and one final seven.*

> **ANOINTED ONE**
>
> (translation of Hebrew *mashiakh* in Daniel 9:25–26)
>
> An individual divinely selected and empowered for a particular role related to God's people. The term could describe:
>
> - *Princes* and *kings* (1 Samuel 24:7, 11; 26:9, 11, 16, 23; 2 Samuel 1:14, 16; 19:22; 22:51; 23:1)
> - *Priests* (Leviticus 4:3, 5, 16; 16:15)
> - *Prophets* (Psalm 105:15; 1 Chronicles 16:22)
>
> This term also describes the divine Savior-King whose coming was anticipated throughout the Scriptures.
>
> *Mashiakh* is also translated "Christ" (from Greek *Christos*, "Anointed One").[88]

Act 1: The Rebuilding of Jerusalem (Daniel 9:25a)

The Babylonians had thoroughly overthrown the city of Jerusalem. During the first seven "weeks," the destroyed city would be rebuilt "with streets and a trench" (9:25). God fulfilled this part of his plan through Nehemiah (Nehemiah 2:19; 4:1–21; 6:1–14). This restoration spanned several decades—from around 445 BC to 432 BC.[89]

Act 2: Nothing to Report (Daniel 9:25b)[90]

Sixty-two sevens separate the first act of this story from the third act. After the rebuilding of Jerusalem, there is nothing to report for several centuries, at least from a prophetic perspective. These middle sixty-two weeks are simply the time between the rebuilding of Jerusalem and the arrival of the "Anointed One" (9:25).

Act 3: The Arrival of the Anointed One and the Final Seven Years (Daniel 9:25–27)

According to the words of Gabriel to Daniel, after the "seven sevens" and the "sixty-two sevens,"

- An "Anointed One" would arrive (9:25), and
- The Anointed One would be "cut off" or "put to death" (9:26).[91]

During the final "seven," someone would confirm a covenant "with many," and sacrifices would be brought to an end. An "abomination that causes desolation" would defile the temple. Amid all these dark developments, the holy place and the city would be destroyed (Daniel 9:26–27).

But who is the "Anointed One"?

And what about the "ruler" or "prince"? Is the Anointed One (9:25) the same as the prince who is yet to come? (9:26). Or are these two different people?

> ### PRINCE OR RULER
> (translation of Hebrew *nagid* in Daniel 9:25–26)
>
> Term for a broad range of positions of authority,[92] including king (1 Kings 1:35), tribal chief (1 Chronicles 12:27), military commander (2 Chronicles 11:11), palace official or temple official (2 Chronicles 28:7; 31:12), and crown prince or king-to-be (2 Chronicles 11:22).

How will sacrifices and offerings be brought to an end?

And what about the mysterious "abomination of desolations"?

On one aspect of the text, a broad range of Bible-believing scholars agree:[93] The Anointed One is Jesus, and this text predicted his death for the sins of his people (9:25–26). Beyond that bit of agreement, a wide array of perspectives have emerged.

Jesus Being Anointed while Eating Dinner with a Pharisee, by James Tissot (1886–1894).

FOUR PERSPECTIVES ON THE FINAL "SEVEN"

	Who is the "Anointed One"? (Daniel 9:25–26)	Who is the "ruler who is to come"? (Daniel 9:26)	
Jesus was both the Anointed One and the ruler yet to come	Jesus was the Anointed One and the first ruler or prince. He was "cut off but not for himself," indicating that he was a sacrifice for the sins of his people.	Jesus was the ruler or prince who was "yet to come" when Daniel wrote these words. By rejecting Jesus, the Jewish people—"the people of the ruler who is yet to come"— brought about the destruction of their temple in AD 70.	
Jesus was the Anointed One, the Roman general Titus was the ruler yet to come	Jesus was the Anointed One and the first ruler or prince. He was "cut off but not for himself," indicating that he was a sacrifice for the sins of his people.	The Roman general Titus was the ruler who was "yet to come."	
Jesus is the Anointed One, the Antichrist is the ruler yet to come—and the seventieth seven is split in two	Jesus was the Anointed One and the first ruler or prince. He was "cut off but not for himself," indicating that he was a sacrifice for the sins of his people.	The ruler "yet to come" is a future Antichrist who will appear at the end of time to deceive and to destroy.	
Jesus is the Anointed One, the Antichrist is the ruler yet to come—and the seventieth seven is a future time of tribulation	Jesus was the Anointed One and the first ruler or prince. He was "cut off but not for himself," indicating that he was a sacrifice for the sins of his people.	The ruler "yet to come" is a future Antichrist who will appear in the end times to deceive the Jewish people.	

How will "sacrifice and offering" come to an end? (Daniel 9:27)	What is the "abomination that causes desolation"? (Daniel 9:27)
Halfway through the seventieth seven (or perhaps at the end of the seventieth seven), Jesus was crucified. His perfect life and atoning death marked the end of any need for sacrifices and offerings. His death also brought about a new covenant "with many."	The Jewish religious leaders rejected Jesus, the true temple of God (see John 2:19–21). In the years following the seventieth seven, certain Jewish leaders rebelled against the Romans, fought among themselves and turned their own people against one another. All of these deeds, beginning with the abomination of rejecting Jesus, resulted in the desolating destruction of the Jewish temple.
The Roman army, under the command of Titus, ended sacrifices and offerings by destroying the temple in AD 70.	Titus and his soldiers defiled the Jewish temple, looted the treasury, and placed the Roman eagle in front of the temple.
After the first half of the seventieth seven, Jesus was crucified. His perfect life and atoning death marked the end of any need for sacrifices and offerings. The second half of the seventieth seven will occur when the Antichrist appears near the end of time.	The Antichrist will persecute God's people and deal falsely with them.
The entire seventieth seven is the time of the future "great tribulation." A "great parenthesis" of time stands between the sixty-ninth and seventieth sevens. Before or during the first part of the seventieth "week," a new temple will be built. The Antichrist will make a covenant with the nation of Israel guaranteeing safety and security. In the middle of this final "week," the Antichrist will break his pact and end sacrifices and offerings.	The Antichrist will present himself in the temple as divine.

DARE TO BE A DANIEL

Biblical scholar Edward Young dubbed the ninth chapter of Daniel "one of the most difficult in all the Old Testament" and declared that "the interpretations which have been offered are almost legion." The struggle to understand this text is not new. Fewer than four centuries after Jesus died and rose again, a man named Jerome wrote these words about Daniel's seventy weeks: "This question has been argued over in various ways by people of greatest learning."[94]

So why didn't we place these quotations at the beginning of this chapter? Because we didn't want to tempt you to skip ahead!

Yes, this is a difficult text. And yes, there's a lot of disagreement about some parts of this prophecy. Yet nearly all Bible-believing students of this text see the coming of the Messiah as the central fulfillment of Daniel's seventy weeks. The accuracy of the prophecy is astounding, and God's choice to give us a time line shows his fearlessness when it comes to putting his prophetic reputation on the line. God is clearly the architect of history, and history clearly climaxes with the death and resurrection of Jesus.

If you find yourself wearied and disoriented by all the calculations and interpretations, be encouraged and inspired by Peter's portrayal of prophets like Daniel:

> ## THE PROPHET DANIEL AND RESURRECTION FROM THE DEAD (DANIEL 12:2–4)
>
> Although a much more complete picture of the final resurrection emerges in the New Testament, resurrection is clearly foreshadowed in the Old Testament.[95]
>
> - Abraham believed that God could bring Isaac back from the grave (Hebrews 11:17–19).
> - Job hoped for a resurrection in which he would see God (Job 19:25–27).
> - Elijah raised a widow's son from the dead (1 Kings 17:17–24).
> - Daniel pictured resurrection as an awakening from sleep (12:2) and described the resurrection more comprehensively than any other Old Testament writer. Daniel's reference to "the dust of the earth" (12:2) implies a bodily resurrection. In the judgment that follows, some will receive "everlasting life" and others will experience "shame and everlasting contempt" (12:2).

"Concerning this salvation, the prophets who prophesied about the grace that was to be yours searched and inquired carefully, inquiring what person or time the Spirit of Christ in them was indicating when he predicted the sufferings of Christ and the subsequent glories. It was revealed to them that they were serving not themselves but you, in the things that have now been announced to you through those who preached the good news to you by the Holy Spirit sent from heaven, things into which angels long to look" (1 Peter 1:10–12).

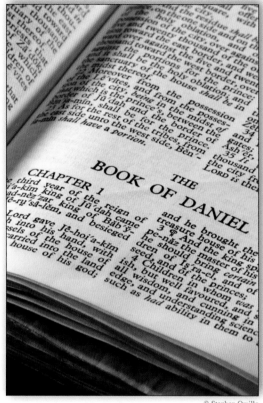

© Stephen Orsillo

You may find yourself wishing that you were in Daniel's position, receiving the vision directly from Gabriel. But Peter is telling us that Daniel and his fellow prophets were longing to know what you know.

Instead of bemoaning what you *don't* know about these "seventy weeks," celebrate what you *do* know. What you know of Christ is what the ancient prophets strained to understand and what angels still long to see. This reality should cause us to seek God's truth in God's Word from this moment until our days draw to an end—just like that eighty-year-old prophet so long ago whose reading of Jeremiah's scrolls drove him to plead with God for the restoration of his people.

THE END OF THE WORLD IN THE NEW TESTAMENT

Introduction

Which texts in the New Testament tell about the end of time?

Your first response to this question might be "Revelation" or perhaps "the letters that Paul wrote to the Thessalonians"—and you would be correct. But, in truth, *the entire New Testament tells about the end of time*, because the New Testament is all about the gospel, and the gospel is a message that has to do with God making the world new.

> **Because Jesus died and rose again, the world as we know it will not last forever.**

The gospel—the good news of Jesus—reminds us that God has not abandoned his world to sin and sickness, sorrow and death. God is redeeming his world, and this redemption is rooted in the death and resurrection of Jesus. Because Jesus died and rose again, the world as we know it will not last forever.

So, which books of the New Testament tell about the end times?

> **EPHESIANS 1:7–10**
>
> "In him we have redemption through his blood, the forgiveness of sins, in accordance with the riches of God's grace that he lavished on us. With all wisdom and understanding, he made known to us the mystery of his will according to his good pleasure, which he purposed in Christ, to be put into effect when the times reach their fulfillment—to bring unity to all things in heaven and on earth under Christ."

All of them—because all of them tell how God is making the world new through Jesus Christ.

This newness is not always clear for us, veiled as it is by the aftermath of humanity's fall. But God has promised a new world through the resurrection of Jesus, and he has sealed this promise by placing his Spirit within us (Romans 8:20–25; Ephesians 1:7–14). Every mention of the gospel in the New Testament points forward to that moment at the end of time when "every knee [will] bow, in heaven and on earth and under the earth, and every tongue acknowledge that Jesus Christ is Lord, to the glory of God the Father" (Philippians 2:10–11).

WHAT IS THE GOSPEL?

(Adapted from www.joethorn.net)

1. Gospel (from *godspel*, Old English rendering of Greek *euangelion* "good message") is the life, death, and resurrection of Jesus that accomplishes salvation and restoration for all who believe and, ultimately, for the whole creation.

- Through his **life**, Jesus fulfilled the Law of God and accomplished all righteousness on behalf of sinners who have broken God's Law at every point.

- Through his **death**, Jesus atoned for our sins, satisfying the wrath of God and obtaining forgiveness for all who believe.

- Through his **resurrection**, Jesus guaranteed victory over sin and death in him and through him. Jesus' saving work not only redeems sinners, uniting them to God, but also guarantees the future restoration of all creation.

- *This is the "good message," that God redeems a fallen world by his grace.*

2. "Gospel" may also describe one of four New Testament texts—ascribed to Matthew, Mark, Luke, and John—which provide eyewitness accounts of the life, death, and resurrection of Jesus.

CHAPTER 11
Why People Missed the Promised Messiah

The longing for a rescuer has been with us ever since sin entered the world.

In those first awful moments of blame and naked shame, God promised the mother of humanity, Eve, that one of her descendants would shatter the serpent's skull (Genesis 3:15). No wonder, then, that the desire for a savior can be found in the earliest records of nearly every nation and culture.[96]

Everyone is looking for someone to set the world right again. Thousands of years after humanity's Fall in the garden, these dreams have not faded.

- Yearnings for a rescuer are as close as the novels on your shelf, the video discs beside your television, or the movie tickets that are crumpled in your pocket. Whether you prefer science-fiction or romance, someone in nearly every fictional book or film is seeking a savior to set something right.

- This yearning for a savior is present in real life as well. For one person, it may take the form of romantic longing for that perfect partner. For someone else, it's the passionate conviction that, if only one particular political candidate is elected, that person will restore the nation's lost glory. Still others may seek out a spiritual guide who seems to possess all the answers.

We cannot escape the desire that was born in Eden, the longing for a savior to set the world right.

In Jesus' times, the Jewish people in his era even had a particular title for their long-awaited rescuer. They called this person "the Messiah."

Jesus pulls Adam and Eve out of their graves, Chora Church/Museum, Istanbul.

"WHO DO PEOPLE SAY THAT I AM?" JESUS IN THE FIRST-CENTURY OPINION POLLS

Mount Hermon loomed high in the northern sky as Jesus and his disciples made their way toward the cities around Caesarea-Philippi. These were pagan communities, devoted to the worship of deceased emperors and to the gods of the Greeks and Romans. A few decades before Jesus' times, Herod the Great had constructed a massive marble temple here for Caesar Augustus.[97]

As the disciples approached the city, they glimpsed a towering wall of sheer stone.[98] A century or two later, carved images to pagan gods would pockmark even these cliffs.

View at the remnants of the temple of Pan with Pan's grotto on a hill in Caesarea-Philippi

No faithful Jews would typically have chosen to visit this place. No self-respecting Jewish travel agents were offering their brothers special deals on vacations in Caesarea-Philippi. Here, vile and idolatrous practices tainted almost every aspect of life. Yet, it was here that Jesus clearly revealed himself as the Messiah.

"Who do people say that I am?" Jesus asked the men who walked beside him (Mark 8:27).

- "John the Baptist" was the disciples' first reply. John was already dead—executed by Antipas, son of Herod the Great, after Antipas made a drunken deal with his queen's daughter (see Matthew 14:2; Mark 6:16–32; Luke 9:7). Apparently, after hearing about the wonder-worker named Jesus, some people wondered whether John, after being beheaded, had been "re-headed" and resurrected as Jesus!

- Immediately after mentioning that possibility, the disciples spouted out several other popular options: "Elijah," "Jeremiah," "one of the prophets" (Matthew 16:14; Mark 6:15; 8:28). These Old Testament figures were, of course, dead as well; so, their presence would require resurrection too.

Each of these popular possibilities pointed to one greater possibility: *Might Jesus be the Messiah?*

How "John the Baptist" and "Elijah" pointed to the Messiah	How "Jeremiah or one of the other prophets" pointed to the Messiah
The Messiah's arrival would coincide with the coming of someone like Elijah (Malachi 4:5; Mark 9:11–13). John the Baptist was like Elijah, all the way down to the way he dressed (compare 2 Kings 1:8 with Mark 1:6). Jesus declared that John the Baptist was the Elijah-like prophet predicted in Malachi's prophecy (Matthew 17:10-12).	In the times between the Old and New Testaments, some Jewish texts were written testifying that the time of the prophets had ended. No prophecy would be given until the dawning of a new era with a "faithful prophet." (See 1 Maccabees 4:46; 9:27; 14:41.) If John or Jesus were prophets, the years of prophetic silence were over, and the new messianic era was dawning.

"WHO DO YOU SAY THAT I AM?" JESUS IN SIMON PETER'S PERSONAL POLL

Yet it wasn't enough merely to admit that—from the people's perspective—Jesus might be connected to the Messiah. Jesus pressed his disciples with one further question. "'But you, who do you say that I am?'" (Mark 8:29).

That's when Simon Peter made the crucial confession: "You are the Christ, the Son of the living God" (Matthew 16:16). Or, as it appears in other versions, "You are the Messiah!"

When Simon Peter identified Jesus as "the Messiah" or "the Christ," the fisherman-turned-disciple was recognizing Jesus as the fulfillment of a divine plan that stretched from Eden until the end of time.

Yet, precisely what did "Messiah" mean in the Jewish culture of the first century AD? What sort of leader did Peter and his fellow disciples expect their Messiah to be? And, most important for our purposes, what does the messianic kingdom have to do with the end of time?

St. Peter, by Andrea Vanni, 1390

Let's take a closer look at these expectations to understand what Peter's words meant in the minds of his first hearers—and how our perspective on the Messiah and his kingdom affects our view of the end times.

THE MEANING BEHIND ALL THAT OIL

"Anointing" typically entailed pouring oil over a person's head.

© John Said

Chances are, you haven't had any oil poured over your head lately—unless you've experienced some sort of awkward accident while maintaining your car. Pouring oil on people is not common in most churches today. As a result, "anointing with oil" can sound a little strange to us.

In biblical times, anointing with oil wasn't strange at all—and the oil didn't come from drilling deep in the earth either. The oil came from the crushing of olives, and olive oil was required for everything from skin care and hair care (Matthew 6:17) to healing (Mark 6:3; Luke 10:34). But neither glistening skin nor great hair nor perfect health was the primary point of the long-awaited "anointed one" or "Messiah"!

> **WHAT DOES THE WORD "MESSIAH" MEAN?**
>
> The term that's typically translated "Messiah" in the Bible comes from a Hebrew word that means "anointed one." In the ancient Greek translation of the Old Testament known as the Septuagint, the translators chose the Greek term *Christos* to represent the Hebrew word for "anointed one." The Greek word *Christos* comes into English as "Christ." So, the words "Christ" and "Messiah" are identical: Both terms mean "anointed one."

- In the Old Testament, pouring oil on someone or something meant that the anointed object was specially set apart for God's purposes. Not only people but also sacred pillars, priestly utensils, and physical structures could be anointed (Genesis 28:16–18; Exodus 30:25–28; Leviticus 8:19; Numbers 7:1; see also 2 Corinthians 1:21–22).

- ***Pouring oil on a person marked that individual as someone God was empowering to perform a particular task.***[99] Priests and sometimes prophets were anointed (Exodus 29:7, 21; Leviticus 4:3–16; 6:22; 1 Kings 19:16). But the primary recipients of anointing were *kings.* Through anointing, kings were set apart for the task of leading the Israelite people.

- Understood in this way, every king of Israel was an "anointed one." Even a pagan ruler such as Cyrus of Persia could receive the title "anointed one," because God appointed and empowered this king to return the Israelites to their land (Isaiah 45:1–6).

- Eventually, "Messiah" came to mean far more than a God-empowered leader. As the kingdoms of Israel and Judah were conquered and sent into exile, the Jewish people increasingly hoped for

Baptism of Jesus, by Carl Bloch, 1865–1879

one particular "Anointed One" or "Messiah" who would set the world right.

WHEN WAS JESUS ANOINTED?

If Jesus was the "anointed one," when and how was he anointed? Simon Peter answered that question when he shared the message of Jesus with a Roman centurion named Cornelius: "God anointed Jesus of Nazareth with the Holy Spirit" (Acts 10:38). When Jesus was baptized, God the Father anointed Jesus with the Holy Spirit and declared Jesus to be his royal Son (Matthew 3:16–17; Mark 1:10–11; Luke 3:21–22).

Isaiah longed for a prophet who would declare to the people, "The Spirit of the Sovereign LORD is on me, because the LORD has anointed me" (Isaiah 61:1). Later, the prophet Daniel also predicted the arrival of an Anointed One, placing his coming "seven sevens and sixty-two sevens" after the decree to rebuild Jerusalem (Daniel 9:25–26). By the time the Old Testament drew to a close, the Jewish people clearly expected a Messiah. What they didn't know was when their rescuer would arrive or what exactly he would do. In the minds of many first-century Jews, "setting the world right" would require removing the Gentiles from Jerusalem, returning all Jews to their native land, and establishing everlasting peace for God's people.

Who was anointed?	Examples of anointing in the Old Testament
Kings	"Then Samuel took a flask of olive oil and poured it on Saul's head and kissed him, saying, 'Has not the LORD anointed you ruler over his inheritance?'" (1 Samuel 10:1). See also 1 Samuel 12:3–5; 16:6; 24:6–10; 26:9–11, 16, 23; 2 Samuel 1:14–16; 19:21; 22:51; 23:1; Psalm 18:50; 20:6–9; 89:38–39, 51; 105:14–15; 132:10.
Priests	"And take some blood from the altar and some of the anointing oil and sprinkle it on Aaron and his garments and on his sons and their garments. Then he and his sons and their garments will be consecrated" (Exodus 29:21). See also Exodus 29:7; Leviticus 4:3–16; 6:22; Numbers 35:25.
Prophets	"Anoint Elisha ... to succeed you as prophet" (1 Kings 19:16).

THE MEANING OF "MESSIAH" BETWEEN THE TESTAMENTS

During the four centuries between the Old and New Testaments, the longing for an "Anointed One" or "Messiah" did not fade. In fact, among some Jewish sects, these desires deepened and multiplied. *What kind of messiah or messiahs were they anticipating?*

A Sinless Descendant of David and A Liberator of Jerusalem

A text entitled *Psalms of Solomon* was penned during this time. King Solomon did not actually write these psalms—they were written far too late in history. Still, these psalms provide invaluable insights into what sort of Messiah the Jewish people were anticipating in the decades before the coming of Jesus.

Codex Alexandrinus, AD 400–440. This ancient manuscript included Psalm of Solomon as an appendix

The author of *Psalms of Solomon* begged God to raise up a "king, the son of David" (17:21); this king would be "the Lord's Christ" or "the Lord's Messiah" (17:32).[100] This Messiah would rid Jerusalem of all non-Jews, shattering the power of the Gentiles with an iron rod (17:22–24, 28). In the end, the nations would serve "under [the Messiah's] yoke," and the tribes of Israel would receive the Promised

Land again (17:28, 30, 33–34). This document also expected the Messiah to be sinless: "He himself will be free from sin," *Psalms of Solomon* states, "in order to rule a great people" (17:35).

Prophet, Priest, and King

The Dead Sea Scrolls—ancient documents copied by a Jewish sect in the desert community of Qumran before the birth of Jesus—contain similar expectations for a Messiah. ***In documents known as 4Q458 and 4Q285, the Messiah is a war leader***.

At least a few members of the Qumran community expected something more than a war leader. They anticipated both a warrior Messiah and a priestly Messiah. One scroll, known as the Damascus Document, mentions "the Messiahs of Aaron and Israel." The "Messiah of Aaron" apparently is a priest, while the "Messiah of Israel" refers to a king.[101]

Another Dead Sea Scrolls document seems to describe the arrival of three messianic figures. These three figures were predicted to be "the Prophet and the Messiahs of Aaron and Israel"[102]—in other words, a prophet, a priest, and a king.

Still, even in these documents, an emphasis on military conflict marked expectations for the messianic era. Unrighteous persons would be "delivered up to the sword."[103]

HOW THE DISCOVERIES AT QUMRAN WERE NAMED AND NUMBERED

1QpHab? 11QPsa? 4Q285? Aren't those descriptions of protocol droids in the Star Wars movies?

No, they're descriptions of Dead Sea Scrolls!

At first, the numbering system for the Dead Sea Scrolls looks confusing—but it really isn't.

- The first number tells which cave the scroll or fragment came from.
- "Q" stands for "Qumran."
- The final letters or numbers either abbreviate the document's title or number a fragment.

So, 1QpHab indicates an interpretation (*pesher* or p) of the book of Habakkuk (Hab) discovered in Cave 1 at Qumran (1Q). 11QPsa is a psalm (Psa) found in Cave 11, and 4Q285 was the two hundred and eighty-fifth fragment identified in Cave 4 at Qumran.

WHAT WERE THE DEAD SEA SCROLLS?

Muhammad edh-Dhib had lost his sheep, and he didn't know where to find them. In his search, the young Palestinian shepherd made a discovery that would impact the world long after the wayward flock was forgotten. According to some reports, he tossed a rock into a cave to determine whether some of his animals had found shelter in the shadowed interior. If that's what happened, he probably hoped to hear the bleating of a stone-struck sheep—but that wasn't what he heard at all. What the shepherd heard instead was the shattering of pottery.

Amid the shards of a broken pottery jar, there were treasures more valuable than any lamb in Muhammad's flock. What Muhammad glimpsed when he scrambled up that stony slope in 1947 were the first of the documents that would become known as "the Dead Sea Scrolls." Each scroll had been wrapped in linen and brushed with malodorous pitch. For nearly two millennia, pottery, linen, and pitch had preserved these ancient rolls of parchment.

- In the end, portions of approximately 813 original documents were discovered in eleven caves scattered along a two-mile stretch of limestone cliffs.

- Roughly one-third of the documents represent copies of the Hebrew Scriptures, and another one-third or so are commentaries on the Scriptures.

- The remaining documents describe the rules and expectations of the group that preserved the scrolls.

The scrolls were copied sometime between the second century and the Roman conquest of Judea in AD 70. Most scholars date the scrolls to the beginning of this range, in the second and first centuries BC; they believe the copyists to have been a sect known as the "Essenes."

The copies of Old Testament texts proved that, despite hundreds of years of manual copying, the words of the Hebrew Scriptures were preserved with a remarkable accuracy. The commentaries and community rules other documents provided a glimpse into some of the expectations of at least one Jewish sect in the years leading up to the earthly ministry of Jesus.

WHY COULDN'T THE PEOPLE SEE WHO JESUS WAS?

The ancient Hebrew Scriptures clearly predicted the coming of Jesus as the Messiah.

Prophecy	Old Testament References	New Testament Fulfillment
Be born in the town of Bethlehem of Judea (Judah)	Micah 5:2–5 But you, *Bethlehem Ephratah, though you are small among the clans of Judah*, out of you will come for me one who will be ruler over Israel, whose origins are from of old, from ancient times....	Matthew 2:1–6 After Jesus was born in *Bethlehem in Judea*, during the time of King Herod, Magi from the east came to Jerusalem and asked, "Where is the one who has been born king of the Jews? ..."
Be born a king of the line of David	Isaiah 9:7 ... He will reign on *David's throne* and over his kingdom ... Jeremiah 23:5; 30:9	Matthew 1:1 A record of the genealogy of *Jesus Christ the son of David*, the son of Abraham ... Also Luke 1:32; Acts 13:22, 23
Be born of the seed of Abraham	Genesis 17:7, 8; 26:3, 4	Matthew 1:1, 17; Galatians 3:16, 29; Hebrews 2:16
Kings shall bring him gifts, fall down before him	Psalm 72:10, 11 The kings of Tarshish and of distant shores will bring tribute to him; the *kings of Sheba and Seba will present him gifts*. All kings will *bow down to him* and all nations will serve him.	Matthew 2:1–11 After Jesus was born in Bethlehem in Judea, during the time of King Herod, *Magi from the east* came to Jerusalem ... On coming to the house, they saw the child with his mother Mary, and *they bowed down* and worshipped him. Then they opened their treasures and *presented him with gifts* of gold and of incense and of myrrh.
Be a firstborn son, sanctified	Exodus 13:2; Numbers 3:13; 8:17	Luke 2:7, 23
Be called out of Egypt	Hosea 11:1 When Israel was a child, I loved him, and *out of Egypt I called my son*. ...	Matthew 2:13–15, 19–21 ... So he ... took the child and his mother during the night and left for *Egypt* ...
The King comes to Jerusalem riding on a donkey	Zechariah 9:9 ... See, your king comes to you, righteous and having salvation, gentle and *riding on a donkey, on a colt*, the foal of a donkey.	Mark 11:1–10 ... When they brought the *colt* to Jesus and threw their cloaks over it, he sat on it. ... Also Matthew 21:1–5; Luke 19:28–38; John 12:14, 15

Why, then, did the religious leaders and so many other people reject Jesus as the long-awaited Messiah? Of course, there was the spiritual truth that many people's hearts were hardened so that they could not recognize the Messiah (John 12:40; Romans 11:7; 2 Corinthians 3:14). But even in this hardening, there were human factors at work as well. Here are a few of them:

1. Many messianic pretenders had already misled the people. By the time Jesus arrived on the scene, at least three men had recently claimed to be the Messiah:

   - Around the time Jesus was born, a slave of Herod the Great named Simon of Perea led a rebellion against the Romans; he was executed.

   - Soon afterward, a shepherd named Athronges claimed to be the Messiah and rebelled against Herod Archelaus; he too was killed.

   - In AD 6, Quirinius the governor tried to take a census; Judas of Galilee

Pontius Pilate presenting a scourged Christ to the people—*Ecce homo!* (Behold the man!) by Antonio Ciseri

responded to the census by making messianic claims and by leading a rebellion (Acts 5:37). The Romans killed Judas and brutally crushed his revolt.[104]

2. Jesus repeatedly declared that he would die (Matthew 16:21; 20:18; Mark 8:31; 9:12; 10:32–34; Luke 9:22; 17:25; John 12:33). From the perspective of most of his people, Jesus could not die if he was truly the Messiah. After all, the Messiah was supposed to live forever (John 12:34).

3. Even many of Jesus' own disciples did not understand the Old Testament prophecies until later (Luke 24:25–27, 44–45).

4. Jesus made the amazing claim that he was God in human flesh (see Mark 2:5–7; John 8:58–59)—a declaration that would have been difficult to believe, especially before the resurrection.

In Jesus, God fulfilled every Old Testament prophecy about the Messiah—but what God did was very different from what the people expected. Perhaps this should remind us today that, when God fulfills his promises that have to do with the end times, God might do this in a very different way than we expected.

Role	What people expected	What people needed
Prophet	Someone to speak God's truth	Someone to be God's Word and to send his Spirit to lead his people into all truth (John 1:1–14; 15:26; 16:13)
Priest	Someone to offer sacrifices on behalf of Israel in a renewed temple	Someone to be the sacrifice who dies for his people's sins and the temple where God's presence dwells (Hebrews 10:10–14; Matthew 12:6; John 2:19–21)
King	Conqueror of the Romans, bringing political peace now	Conqueror of sin, bringing peace to his own people now and peace to the entire earth later (Matthew 21:5; 25:31; John 12:15–16; 18:36–38; 1 Corinthians 15:54–57)

WHAT KIND OF KINGDOM DID JESUS PLAN TO BRING?

After four centuries of prophetic silence, at a time when the Roman Empire ruled much of the known world, the Messiah slipped into human history as an embryo nestled in the virgin womb of a peasant girl. Several Jewish sects had clear expectations for what sort of savior their Messiah ought to be. Some of the expectations were correct—but others fell far short of what God the Father had destined Jesus to do.

- Some were seeking a prophet, a priest, and a king—though they didn't necessarily expect these three to be the same person. At least a few of the teachers at Qumran seem to have expected two or even three messianic leaders.
- Most people anticipated a royal descendant of David; this righteous ruler would lead a military conflict resulting in messianic triumph.
- This triumph was expected to launch an era of unprecedented prosperity and peace for the Jewish nation. During this era, God would restore the kingdom to Israel, and the Messiah would rule the land that God promised to Abraham.

Yet, the kingdom did not come in the way that the people expected during the time that Jesus spent on the earth. No smack-down between Jesus and the Roman army ever happened. And, a few moments before he ascended into the eastern sky, Jesus completely sidestepped his disciples' question about when he would restore Israel's kingdom (Acts 1:6–8).

The Jewish people expected something like this:

Coming of
the Messiah

Time of Promises & Prophets

Time of Fulfillment

(Present time for
Old Testament Israelites)

(Last days when God prospers
Israel & restores them to their land)

But what actually happened looks more like this:

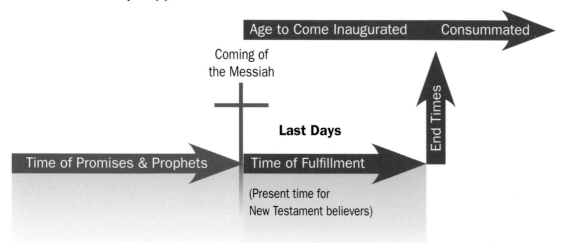

- *So why didn't Jesus do away with every evil regime during his first visit to planet earth?*
- *Why didn't Israel's kingdom come in the way that so many Jews anticipated during this era?*
- *Why is the final fulfillment of God's kingdom still in the future?*

Christians differ on the answers to those questions—and how you answer will vary depending on your view of the end times.

A Kingdom Postponed: The Dispensational View

The ministries of John the Baptist and Jesus the Messiah both began with the same message: "The kingdom of God is at hand!" (Matthew 3:2; Mark 1:14). According to dispensationalists, this announcement meant that God was offering the millennial kingdom to Israel.

- If the religious leaders had recognized Jesus as the Messiah, God the Father would not only have resurrected Jesus after his death on the cross; God would also have established Jesus as an earthly king. Jesus would have broken the power of the Roman Empire and extended his reign throughout the earth, beginning in Jerusalem.
- But the Jewish religious leaders rejected Jesus (Matthew 11–12), and so God postponed the kingdom. That's why the kingdom is still future right now.

- After this rejection, Jesus began to proclaim a new plan. This new plan centered on the church, a mixed multitude of Gentiles and Jews who receive Jesus as their Lord and Messiah. God, of course, knew that this would happen, but God never revealed this plan to the Old Testament prophets. The church was neither predicted nor expected in the Hebrew Scriptures.[105]

- After removing the church from the earth at the rapture, God will resume his work with Israel. According to dispensationalists—appealing to such texts as Hosea 5:15, Zechariah 12:9–11, and Matthew 23:39—Jesus will not return to reign on earth until the Jews repent and recognize him as their rightful Messiah.[106]

- When this happens at the end of the great tribulation, Jesus will establish his long-postponed kingdom on earth and exalt the Jewish people above the Gentiles.[107]

A Kingdom "Not of This World": The Covenantal and New Covenantal Views

Covenantalists and new covenantalists disagree with dispensationalists on this point.

- They contend that God never meant to establish a political kingdom during the earthly ministry of Jesus.

- From the very beginning, God intended his Messiah to inaugurate a kingdom that is "not of this world" (John 18:36).

- Jesus did not come to lead Israel into battle against the nations; he came to crush the serpent's power and to shatter sin's curse on the cross (Mark 10:45; John 12:23–27).

The kingdom that Jesus inaugurated was not a response to Israel's rejection. Even in the Old Testament, God revealed that his coming kingdom would include Jews and Gentiles.

- Joel predicted the outpouring of the Holy Spirit on "all flesh," a prophecy that began to be fulfilled on Pentecost and soon extended beyond the Jewish people (Joel 2:28–29; Acts 2:16–18; 10:45).

- Amos prophesied a day when Gentiles would be called by God's name (Amos 9:11–12; Acts 15:16–17).

- Paul viewed Gentile believers as the fulfillment of Hosea's prophecy that a people who were "not God's people" would become God's beloved children (Hosea 1:10; Romans 9:24–26).

- God planned this mingled kingdom "from the foundation of the world" (Matthew 25:34).

- According to *covenantalists*, the church has replaced Israel as the people of God. According to *new covenantalists*, Israel provided a temporary picture of what God planned to do through the church. But covenantalists and new covenantalists both agree that the church is not a parenthesis or a detour within God's work with Israel. The church is a living expression of God's eternal plan to bring together "all things" in Jesus (Ephesians 1:10).

The final fulfillment of the kingdom is future because that's what God intended from the beginning. The church participates here and now in a Christ-inaugurated reign that is spreading throughout the earth (Colossians 1:13; 1 Thessalonians 2:12; Hebrews 12:28; 2 Peter 1:11)—but this kingdom is only a foretaste of a fulfilled kingdom that is still to come.

COMMON VIEWS: THE MEANING OF SIMON PETER'S CONFESSION

So, is there any common ground among dispensationalists, covenantalists, and new covenantalists on this issue? Certainly! And the common ground matters far more than the differences: ***All three perspectives agree that Jesus the Messiah was a prophet, a priest, and a king who came to die for his people's sins***.

When Simon Peter recognized Jesus as the Messiah (Mark 8:29), he probably understood Jesus to be a prophet; he almost certainly expected Jesus to rise to the role of a royal warrior. Peter may even have seen Jesus as a priestly figure. What Peter simply could not stomach was the idea that his Messiah would suffer and die. That's why, when Jesus began to discuss his own death, Peter pulled him aside to rebuke him

> **MARK 8:29**
>
> "But what about you?" he asked. "Who do you say I am?" Peter answered, "You are the Messiah."

(Mark 8:31–32). After all, how could a mighty messianic king that Peter was anticipating possibly *suffer* and *die*?

But the mighty king *did* die. Through his death, he conquered an enemy far greater than Rome and its armies. Yet, he won without the swords and armies that his first followers expected.

As the ultimate Anointed One, Jesus was a king, a priest, and a prophet—and so much more.

- This Messiah was not only a Jewish king who would conquer his own people's sins but also the *King of all kings* who will one day return in glory (Revelation 19:16).
- He was not only the priestly figure anticipated in the Dead Sea Scrolls but also the final sacrifice for sin and "*the great high priest* who has passed through the heavens" (Hebrews 4:14; 10:12).
- He was not only a prophet who spoke God's words like so many prophets before him (Mark 6:15); he was also *the very Word of God enfleshed*, sent to dwell among us (John 1:1, 14).

He was not the Messiah that most people expected, but **he was precisely the Messiah that every person needs**.

CHAPTER 12

What Jesus Said About the End of the World

Jesus talked a lot about the end times—and no wonder! Don't forget: Jesus is the beginning and the end, the source and the goal of God's work in human history. *The future has a name and that name is Jesus.*

Most of what Jesus told his first followers about the end times didn't take the form of lectures or discourses, though. When talking about the end of time, Jesus mostly told parables—analogies in the form of short stories with a particular point about God's work.

Jesus told his disciples about:

- A field where weeds and wheat grew together because an evil neighbor had tossed weed seed into the field (Matthew 13:24–43);

- A net filled with every kind of seafood; some fish were saved in baskets while the rest were hurled into a raging furnace (Matthew 13:47–50);

- A king who condemned an uninvited guest for crashing the crown prince's wedding banquet (Matthew 22:1–14);

- Five bridesmaids who missed the bridegroom because they didn't bring enough olive oil with them (Matthew 25:1–13);

© DNY59

195

- Three servants who would be glorified or condemned, based on what they did with what they were given (Matthew 25:14–30);
- People from all nations who would be separated "as a shepherd separates the sheep from the goats," based on how they responded to the followers of Jesus (Matthew 25:31–46).

What do these parables teach us? Well, I suppose they could remind you to keep extra oil with you at all times, to double-check your wedding invitations, and to be careful what your neighbor tosses in your garden. But seriously: What do these teachings of Jesus tell us about

The Foolish Virgins, by James Tissot (1886–1894).

the end times? *Here are three truths about the end of time that come directly from these parables*:

1. **Jesus will return:** In the parable of the bridesmaids, the bridegroom comes back at an unexpected hour (Matthew 25:10). In the story about the sheep and the goats, the Son of Man returns "in his glory" (Matthew 25:31). At his return, he sends angels to gather the wheat and to separate the fish (Matthew 25:41–42; 13:47–50). (Jesus clearly had no problems with mixing metaphors.)

2. **No one knows when Jesus will return:** Before and after the story of the bridesmaids who ran out of oil, Jesus made it clear that no one would be able to know the time of his return (Matthew 24:36; 25:13). The angels don't know. The disciples of Jesus won't know. In fact, during his time on planet earth, not even Jesus knew when he would return!

3. **There will be a final judgment:** After separating the wheat from the weeds, angels throw the weeds into a fiery place where the condemned will

grind their teeth and cry in agony (Matthew 23:41–42). A similar fate meets the fish that weren't kept, the uninvited wedding guest, the servant who kept his master's money to himself, and the goats that reject the brothers and sisters of Jesus (Matthew 23:47–50; 22:13; 25:30, 46).

When it comes to those three points from the parables that tell us about the end times, everyone who trusts the truth of Scripture can find common ground.

WHAT JESUS SAID ON THE MOUNT OF OLIVES

There is one exception to this pattern of parables in the teachings of Jesus about the end times. Once, as Jesus left the temple courts, a few of his followers pointed out the splendor of the temple that Herod the Great had renovated. Jesus responded by predicting the unthinkable: ***The Jewish temple would be destroyed***.

When the disciples reached the Mount of Olives, Jesus revealed to them a series of events that were, for him and his first followers, still in the future. Because these words were spoken on the Mount of Olives, they are sometimes known as the "Olivet Discourse." Three of the New Testament Gospels—Matthew, Mark, and Luke—include the Olivet Discourse (Matthew 24; Mark 13; Luke 21).

The Disciples Admire the Buildings of the Temple, by James Tissot (1886-1894).

- But how far in the future were the events that Jesus described?

- Were they only a generation away? Could they have been fulfilled around AD 70, when the temple was destroyed?

- Were they far in the future, close to the time when Jesus returns to earth?

- Or might Jesus have described both events? Did his discourse predict first-century events as well as ones that will happen in the end times?

Biblical scholars differ on the answers to these questions. The differences in interpretation come down to two words that we learned earlier. Remember the terms "futurist" and "preterist" from the first section of this book? Some interpreters look at the Olivet Discourse only from a **futurist** perspective; others see both **futurist and preterist** elements in these words of Jesus.

FOUR WAYS TO READ END-TIMES TEXTS

Four Views	How Revelation Is Viewed	More About This View
Futurist	Revelation is prophecy primarily about the future end of the world.	In the futurist view, all or nearly all of Revelation is yet to occur. Revelation is a prophecy that describes the end of time and the years leading immediately to the end. Dispensational premillennialists as well as some historic premillennialists interpret Revelation in this way.
Historicist	The book of Revelation is prophecy about church history from the time of John to the end of the world.	Historicists view the events in Revelation as symbolic descriptions of historical events throughout church history. (Some futurists also understand the Seven Churches [Revelation 1–3] in a historic manner, treating each church as descriptive of a particular era of church history.)
Idealist	Revelation is a non-historical and non-prophetic drama about spiritual realities.	This perspective seems to have originated among ancient Alexandrian theologians, who frequently spiritualized and allegorized biblical texts, but this view also has contemporary followers.
Preterist	The book of Revelation is prophecy that was fulfilled primarily in the first century AD.	"Partial Preterism" views most of Revelation as prophecy fulfilled in the first century AD, though final chapters of Revelation describe future events to occur at the end of time. "Full Preterists" contend that the return of Jesus described in Revelation 19 was spiritual and occurred in AD 70. Christians throughout church history have understood full preterism to be a heresy. Preterists are typically *amillennialists* or *postmillennialists*, though some *historic premillennialists* might fit in this category.

© Igor Zh.

TWO VIEWS OF THE OLIVET DISCOURSE (Matthew 24; Mark 13; Luke 21)

VIEW 1 FULFILLMENT IN THE END TIMES ONLY: FUTURIST

How should these words of Jesus be interpreted? As a description of the end times (futurist)

Who takes this perspective?

- Dispensational premillennialists
- Some historical premillennialists

Overview

The disciples asked about

1. The destruction of the temple
2. The sign of the Messiah's return
3. The end of the age

In the Gospels According to Matthew and Mark, Jesus did not answer their first question. At most, Jesus may have described the destruction of the temple in Luke 21:20–24. Instead of addressing the destruction of the temple, Jesus taught his disciples about a future tribulation, near the end of time as we know it. His focus was on:

1. The calamities at the beginning of the tribulation
2. The Antichrist's sacrilege in the rebuilt Jewish temple
3. The return of "the Son of Man" to earth

© Vaclav Volrab

VIEW 2 PARTIAL FULFILLMENT IN THE FIRST CENTURY, COMPLETE FULFILLMENT WHEN JESUS RETURNS TO EARTH: PRETERIST AND FUTURIST

How should these words of Jesus be interpreted? As a description of the fall of Jewish temple and of the end of the age (preterist and futurist)

Who takes this perspective?

- Amillennialists
- Postmillennialists
- Some historical premillennialists

Overview

The disciples asked about

1. The destruction of the temple
2. The sign of the Messiah's return at the end of the age

Jesus *answered* both questions.

1. Jesus described the time of "distress" or "tribulation" that would begin around AD 70 when the Romans destroyed the temple (Matthew 24:4–28).

2. Jesus told his disciples about the "sign" of his coming (Matthew 24:29–31).

- Most take this "sign" to be the return of Jesus to earth at the end of time.

  - Understood in this way, the tribulation is not a seven-year event near the end of time as we know it.

  - Instead, the tribulation began in the first century and will continue until Jesus returns.

- A few identify the "sign" as an event that occurred in AD 70, when the temple was destroyed. This first-century judgment pointed forward to the judgment that will come when Jesus returns to earth.

The Siege and Destruction of Jerusalem in AD 70, by David Roberts (1850)

The Fall of the Temple, the Sign of the Son and the End of the Age

Matthew 24:1–3

As Jesus left the temple and was walking away, his disciples came up to him to call his attention to its buildings. "Do you see all these things?" he asked. "Truly I tell you, not one stone here will be left on another; every one will be thrown down." While Jesus sat on the Mount of Olives, the disciples came to him privately. "Tell us," they said, "when will this happen, and what will be the sign of your coming and of the end of the age?" (see also Mark 13:1–4; Luke 21:5–7).

VIEW 1 FULFILLMENT IN THE END TIMES ONLY: FUTURIST

"Not one stone here will be left on another"

- The religious leaders of Israel rejected Jesus as their Messiah. Had the Jewish people accepted Jesus, he would have established a millennial kingdom in the first century.

- Because God's people rejected their Messiah, God took their kingdom from them and allowed their holy place to be destroyed (Matthew 21:43; 23:33–39).

- This text was precisely fulfilled in AD 70. According to an eyewitness named Josephus, the precious metals of the burning temple melted and filled the gaps between the stones. Soldiers pried the stones apart to gain access to the gold.[108]

"When will this happen, and what will be the sign of your coming and of the end of the age?"

- The disciples were asking three separate questions, according to dispensationalists:
  - When will the temple be destroyed?
  - What will be the "sign of your coming"?
  - What is the sign of "the end of the age?"
- Jesus did not answer the first question; instead, "his answers are projected forward to the end times, or the end of world history as we know it."[109]

© arindambanerjee

VIEW 2 PARTIAL FULFILLMENT IN THE FIRST CENTURY, COMPLETE FULFILLMENT WHEN JESUS RETURNS TO EARTH: PRETERIST AND FUTURIST

"Not one stone here will be left on another"

- The religious leaders of Israel rejected Jesus, their Messiah and the true temple of God (Matthew 12:6; John 2:22).

- A generation after this rejection, several factions of Jewish revolutionaries tried to establish a kingdom for themselves. This revolt resulted in the Roman destruction of the temple (Matthew 23:29–39).

- This prediction that "not one stone" would be "left on another" was precisely fulfilled in AD 70. According to an eyewitness named Josephus, the precious metals of the burning temple melted and filled the gaps between the stones. Soldiers pried the stones apart to gain access to the gold.[110]

"When will this happen"

- The disciples' first question focused on how they could know when the temple would be destroyed.

"The sign of your coming and the end of the age"

- These are not two separate events; they are two aspects of the same future occurrence.

- In the most ancient Greek manuscripts, these two phrases share one definite article. This pattern suggests that "the sign" of the Messiah's coming and "the end of the age" will occur at the same time.

Photograph taken by Mark A. Wilson

Stones from the Western Wall of the temple Mount

Natural Disasters, Lying Prophets, and False Messiahs

Matthew 24:4–11, 23–26

Jesus answered: "Watch out that no one deceives you. For many will come in my name, claiming, 'I am the Messiah,' and will deceive many. You will hear of wars and rumors of wars, but see to it that you are not alarmed. Such things must happen, but the end is still to come. Nation will rise against nation, and kingdom against kingdom. There will be famines and earthquakes in various places. All these are the beginning of birth pains. Then you will be handed over to be persecuted and put to death, and you will be hated by all nations because of me. At that time many will turn away from the faith and will betray and hate each other, and many false prophets will appear and deceive many people. ... At that time if anyone says to you, 'Look, here is the Messiah!' or, 'There he is!' do not believe it. For false messiahs and false prophets will appear and perform great signs and wonders to deceive, if possible, even the elect. See, I have told you ahead of time. So if anyone tells you, 'There he is, out in the desert,' do not go out; or, 'Here he is, in the inner rooms,' do not believe it" (see also Mark 13:5–9, 21–23; Luke 21:8–16).

VIEW 1 FULFILLMENT IN THE END TIMES ONLY: FUTURIST

"In my name"

- "In my name" describes how false prophets and false messiahs will arise even in the church as the end times draw near.

"Wars and rumors of wars," "famine," "earthquakes," "persecuted," "false messiahs and false prophets"

- All of these events describe the era immediately before the future seven-year tribulation or during the early part of this tribulation.

- According to most dispensational premillennialists, Jesus will remove his church from the world before the tribulation.

Some dispensationalists see parallels between Matthew 24:4–9 and Revelation 6:2–11:

- Matthew 24:5 = Antichrist = Revelation 6:2
- Matthew 24:6–7 = Wars = Revelation 6:3–4
- Matthew 24:7 = Famine = Revelation 6:5–6
- Matthew 24:7–8 = Pestilence and earthquakes = Revelation 6:7–8
- Matthew 24:9 = Martyrdom = Revelation 6:9–11[111]

VIEW 2 PARTIAL FULFILLMENT IN THE FIRST CENTURY, COMPLETE FULFILLMENT WHEN JESUS RETURNS TO EARTH: PRETERIST AND FUTURIST

"In my name"

- "In my name" refers to false messiahs and false prophets who claim for themselves the status that rightly belongs only to Jesus.

"Wars and rumors of wars"

- Conflict broke out in AD 66 between the Romans and roving bands of Jewish revolutionaries: In AD 68, Emperor Nero committed suicide and—before Vespasian gained the title of emperor in 69—three other emperors rose and fell amid violent civil war. Under Vespasian and later his son Titus, Roman legions arrived in Galilee and swept southward toward Jerusalem, crushing the Jewish rebellion.

- On the shores of the Sea of Galilee, Josephus wrote, "one could see the whole lake red with blood and covered with corpses, for not a man escaped."[112]

"Famine"

- A Christian prophet predicted a famine that occurred in the late 40s during the reign of Emperor Claudius (Acts 11:28).

- In the days preceding the fall of Jerusalem in AD 70, food was so scarce that one women killed and ate her own infant.[113]

"Earthquakes"

- An earthquake rocked Pompeii and Herculaneum in AD 62. The philosopher Seneca, writing in the mid-60s, described how earthquakes had obliterated twelve cities in Asia and recently shaken communities in Achaia and Macedonia.[114]

- Josephus reported a severe quaking of the earth around Jerusalem soon before the city fell to the Romans.[115]

"You will be handed over to be persecuted"

- After a fire in Rome in AD 64, Emperor Nero viciously persecuted Christians in and around Rome.

- Simon Peter was martyred during this period of persecution.

"False messiahs and false prophets"

- Twelve years after Jesus spoke these words, a false prophet named Theudas led hundreds to their deaths (Acts 5:36). Later an unnamed Egyptian and his followers met a similar fate (Acts 21:38).

- The Jewish historian Josephus described the AD 50s and 60s as a time when "the country was filled anew with robbers and impostors. ... These impostors and deceivers persuaded many to follow them into the desert, and pretended that they would exhibit manifest wonders and signs." Even as the Jewish temple was burning, a false prophet rallied his people to renew their revolt against the Romans.[116]

Love Grows Cold and the Gospel Goes Worldwide

Matthew 24:12–14

Because of the increase of wickedness, the love of most will grow cold, but the one who stands firm to the end will be saved. And this gospel of the kingdom will be preached in the whole world as a testimony to all nations, and then the end will come (see also Mark 13:10; Luke 21:17–19).

VIEW 1 FULFILLMENT IN THE END TIMES ONLY: FUTURIST

"The whole world"

During the seven-year tribulation, the gospel will reach the entire world through those who have embraced Jesus as their Messiah.

Their message will be rejected.

VIEW 2 PARTIAL FULFILLMENT IN THE FIRST CENTURY, COMPLETE FULFILLMENT WHEN JESUS RETURNS TO EARTH: PRETERIST AND FUTURIST

"The whole world"

"The whole world" and "all nations" meant that, when these events occurred, the gospel would have been made available to people in every nation known at that time.

According to Paul, this happened no later than the late AD 50s.

When he wrote his letter to the city of Colossae around AD 57, Paul said that the gospel had already reached "the whole world" (Colossians 1:5–6; see also Romans 1:8).

So, these words were fulfilled in the first century, before the fall of the Jewish temple.

© Dejan Gileski

Daniel's Desolation in the Holy Place

Matthew 24:15–20

So when you see standing in the holy place 'the abomination that causes desolation,' spoken of through the prophet Daniel—let the reader understand—then let those who are in Judea flee to the mountains. Let no one on the housetop go down to take anything out of the house. Let no one in the field go back to get their cloak. How dreadful it will be in those days for pregnant women and nursing mothers! Pray that your flight will not take place in winter or on the Sabbath (see also Mark 13:14–18; Luke 21:20–23a).

VIEW 1 FULFILLMENT IN THE END TIMES ONLY: FUTURIST

"The holy place"

- This term refers to a future Jewish temple that will be built soon before the seven-year tribulation begins or during the first part of the tribulation.

"The abomination that causes desolation"

- The future "beast" or "Antichrist" will enter the tribulation temple and proclaim himself to be divine.

- This proclamation will occur halfway through the seven-year tribulation.

- This sacrilegious act will mark the beginning of the "great tribulation," the second half of the tribulation (2 Thess. 2:3–9; Rev. 13).

- Jesus was warning Messianic Jews in Israel during the future tribulation to flee to the hills when this event occurs. The worst of God's wrath will fall on the earth during the second half of the tribulation.

Roman Triumphal Arch showing spoils of Jerusalem temple.

VIEW 2 PARTIAL FULFILLMENT IN THE FIRST CENTURY, COMPLETE FULFILLMENT WHEN JESUS RETURNS TO EARTH: PRETERIST AND FUTURIST

"The holy place"

- This term could refer to the first-century Jewish temple or to the entire Promised Land (See 2 Maccabees 2:18, where a Jewish writer between the Old and New Testaments refers to the whole land as "the holy place").

"The abomination that causes desolation"

- Predicted in Daniel 9:27, this sacrilegious event occurs in the middle of Daniel's "seventieth seven."

- Early Christian leaders ranging from Eusebius and Athanasius to John Chrysostom and Clement of Alexandria connected the "abomination that causes desolation" with the events leading up to the destruction of the temple in AD 70.

- Viewed in the context of the first century, the "abomination" could be:

  1. The religious leaders' rejection of Jesus, the true temple of God; this abominable rejection resulted in the "desolation" of the Jewish temple and the Jewish people one generation later, in AD 70.

  2. The Jewish violation of the temple during the Roman siege. Seeking to strengthen their own position against other factions from their own people, some among the Jewish rebels made "the temple a receptacle of all wickedness so that the divine place has now become polluted by the hands of our own people." Josephus compared this sacrilege with the three-and-one-half years of desolation during the reign of the Syrian king Antiochus IV Epiphanes. Shortly before the fall of Jerusalem, the rebel leader John of Gischala "took to sacrilege" by melting down the temple vessels to enrich himself.[117]

  3. Roman violation of Judea, Jerusalem, and the Jewish temple. Throughout their conquest and siege, the Romans carried pagan ensigns or standards and sacrificed to them. In AD 70, the Roman soldiers set up their ensigns in the Jewish temple and celebrated their victory with sacrifices. Titus—general of the Roman army—entered the Holy of Holies. There, he committed fornication with a harlot atop an unrolled scroll of the Hebrew Scriptures.

- Jesus warned his followers to flee Judea when they saw signs of this coming desolation—and that's precisely what the followers of Jesus in Jerusalem and Judea did.

- The Jewish historian Josephus described how people slipped out of the besieged city, beginning in AD 66 and continuing through the weeks immediately prior to the fall of Jerusalem.

- According to several ancient sources, members of the Jerusalem church had received a divine warning before the revolt, telling them to leave the city. "The people of the church in Jerusalem had been commanded through a revelation, safeguarded to certain approved persons before the war began, to flee the city and to dwell in a certain town of Perea called Pella. Those that trusted the Messiah removed themselves from Jerusalem to that place; the saints entirely abandoned the royal city as well as the whole land of Judea. Then, divine retribution for crimes against the Messiah and his apostles overtook and destroyed a generation of evildoers from the earth."[118]

The Great Tribulation

Matthew 24:21–27

For then there will be great distress, unequaled from the beginning of the world until now—and never to be equaled again. If those days had not been cut short, no one would survive, but for the sake of the elect those days will be shortened. ... For as lightning that comes from the east is visible even in the west, so will be the coming of the Son of Man (see also Mark 13:19–20; Luke 21:23b–24).

VIEW 1 FULFILLMENT IN THE END TIMES ONLY: FUTURIST

"Great distress" or "great tribulation"

- The "forty-two months" mentioned in Revelation 11:2 represent the first half of the tribulation. The second half of the tribulation—also known as "the great tribulation"—are the "forty-two months" described in Revelation 13:5.

- The Antichrist will have made a seven-year covenant with the Jewish people.

- When he enters the tribulation temple, the Antichrist will break this covenant and end sacrifices (Daniel 9:25–27).

- After forty-two months of "great tribulation," Jesus will return personally and visibly to earth.

"As lightning...so will be the coming of the Son of Man"

- Both dispensational and historical premillennialists understand this arrival of Jesus as the time when Jesus will defeat every power of darkness in the battle of Armageddon and then establish his millennial kingdom.

© Sergej Khakimullin

VIEW 2 PARTIAL FULFILLMENT IN THE FIRST CENTURY, COMPLETE FULFILLMENT WHEN JESUS RETURNS TO EARTH: PRETERIST AND FUTURIST

"Great distress" or "great tribulation"

There are a couple of possibilities for the timing of this era of great terror:

1. **The great tribulation began and ended in the first century**: The years of great tribulation are the years leading up to the destruction of the Jewish temple. During this time, the location where God had chosen to place his name (Deuteronomy 12:5) was profaned in ways that had never happened before and will never happen again.

2. **The great tribulation began in the first century and will continue until Jesus returns to earth**: The great tribulation began with the first-century siege of Jerusalem and the destruction of the temple; the great tribulation will continue until Jesus returns. Throughout this time of great tribulation in which we now live, evil will continue to multiply until Jesus returns and destroys the dominion of the Devil.

"As lightning...so will be the coming of the Son of Man"

- The "coming" of Jesus will "cut short" the great tribulation. The imagery of "lightning" comes from the prophecies of Zechariah (9:14–17) and points to God's salvation of his people. Jesus expected this "coming" to be obvious and visible.

- With dispensationalists, historical premillennialists identify this lightning-like coming of Jesus with the battle of Armageddon and the beginning of the millennial kingdom.

- Amillennialists and postmillennialists take this "coming" as

  1. A symbolic reference to God's judgment on Israel in AD 70 or

  2. The return of Jesus to earth, immediately before time ends and eternity begins.

The Christian Martyrs' Last Prayer, by Jean-Léon Gérôme (1883)

The Carcass and the Birds

Matthew 24:28

Wherever there is a carcass, there the vultures will gather
(see also Mark 13:21–23).

VIEW 1 FULFILLMENT IN THE END TIMES ONLY: FUTURIST

"A carcass"

- The carcass represents Jews who refuse to recognize Jesus as the Messiah. They are dead in their sins.

"The vultures"

- The vultures represent the judgment that will fall on unbelieving Jews.

© Pichugin Dmitry

VIEW 2 PARTIAL FULFILLMENT IN THE FIRST CENTURY, COMPLETE FULFILLMENT WHEN JESUS RETURNS TO EARTH: PRETERIST AND FUTURIST

"A carcass"

- After Jesus became the final sacrifice for sin, the Jewish temple and the sacrifices there became nothing more than a "carcass," an expression of death with no promise of life (see Matthew 23:27).

"The vultures"

- The same Greek word means both "vultures" and "eagles." Atop every Roman military ensign was the image of an eagle, a creature that the soldiers worshiped.

- After conquering the city of Jerusalem, the soldiers placed their ensigns on the temple mount and sacrificed to them.[119]

The Destruction of the Temple at Jerusalem by Nicolas Poussin, 1639. (Notice the Roman military standard with the image of an eagle.)

When the Lights Go Out: Sun and Moon Darkened, Stars Fall from the Sky

Matthew 24:29

Immediately after the distress of those days 'the sun will be darkened, and the moon will not give its light; the stars will fall from the sky, and the heavenly bodies will be shaken' (see also Mark 13:24–25; Luke 21:25–26).

VIEW 1 FULFILLMENT IN THE END TIMES ONLY: FUTURIST

"After the distress of those days"

- Dispensational and historical premillennialists agree that this text refers to the same event that John described in Revelation 19:11–16.

- Many premillennialists—both dispensational and historical—expect real cosmic catastrophes to accompany the Messiah's coming. The difference is that dispensationalists take the rapture to have occurred seven years earlier, before the tribulation.

VIEW 2 PARTIAL FULFILLMENT IN THE FIRST CENTURY, COMPLETE FULFILLMENT WHEN JESUS RETURNS TO EARTH: PRETERIST AND FUTURIST

"After the distress of those days"

- Jesus described the time after the tribulation in terms drawn from the ancient Hebrew prophets. In the Old Testament, images of darkened or shaking celestial bodies symbolized divine judgment on a nation.

  1. Isaiah, predicting the fall of Babylon that occurred in 539 BC: "The stars ... will not give their light. The sun will be dark at rising, and the moon will not give its light" (Isaiah 13:10).

  2. Isaiah, portraying the crumbling of Egypt's power in the seventh and sixth centuries BC: "The Lord is riding on a swift cloud" (Isaiah 19:1).

  3. Ezekiel, portraying the aftermath in Egypt after the death of a pharaoh: "I will cover the heavens and make their stars dark; I will cover the sun with a cloud, and the moon will not give its light" (Ezekiel 32:7–8).

- It is unlikely that God physically flew around on a cloud in the atmosphere above Africa as Egypt's power faltered. The sun, moon, and stars clearly did not stop giving light when Babylon fell. So perhaps Jesus did not intend his words to mean that stars would someday fall on the earth or that the sun and moon would stop shining. Instead, Jesus was using the familiar language of the prophets to describe a future decisive judgment from God.

- Some students of the end times—primarily postmillennialists and amillennialists—take this prediction of divine judgment to point only to the fall of the temple in AD 70.

- Nearly all historical premillennialists, along with many amillennialists and postmillennialists, take these words of Jesus to refer to the judgment that Jesus will bring when he returns to earth. The Old Testament descriptions of judgments on the nations foreshadowed the full-fledged judgment that Jesus will bring when he returns to earth.

© Haywiremedia

The Sign of the Son of Man and the Trumpet that Calls the Chosen

Matthew 24:30–31

Then will appear the sign of the Son of Man in heaven. And then all the peoples of the earth will mourn when they see the Son of Man coming on the clouds of heaven, with power and great glory. And he will send his angels with a loud trumpet call, and they will gather his elect from the four winds, from one end of the heavens to the other (see also Mark 13:26–27; Luke 21:27–28).

VIEW 1 FULFILLMENT IN THE END TIMES ONLY: FUTURIST

"All the peoples of the earth will mourn"

- The words of Jesus translated here as "peoples of the earth" can also be rendered "tribes of the land." These words refer to the Jewish people. According to dispensational premillennialists, near the end of the seven-year tribulation, all the nations of the earth will unite against Israel.

- As these armies close in on Israel, the Jewish people will repent ("mourn") and finally recognize Jesus as their Messiah.

- The "sign of the Son of Man" will be the glorious appearing of Jesus. He will destroy the enemies of Israel and gather everyone who trusts him ("his elect from the four winds").

- Zechariah foresaw this event in the Old Testament and described his vision with these words: "On that day I will set out to destroy all the nations that attack Jerusalem. And I will pour out on the house of David and the inhabitants of Jerusalem a spirit of grace and supplication. They will look on me, the one they have pierced, and they will mourn for him as one mourns for an only child, and grieve bitterly as one grieves for a firstborn son. On that day the weeping in Jerusalem will be as great as the weeping of Hadad Rimmon in the plain of Megiddo" (Zechariah 12:9–11).

© Mark Strozier

VIEW 2 PARTIAL FULFILLMENT IN THE FIRST CENTURY, COMPLETE FULFILLMENT WHEN JESUS RETURNS TO EARTH: PRETERIST AND FUTURIST

"All the peoples of the earth will mourn"

Echoing the prophecies of Zechariah (12:9–12) and probably referring to the Jewish people, *peoples of the earth* can also be translated *tribes of the land*. But when is this time of mourning? And what is "the sign of the Son of Man"?

1. Some suggest that these moments of mourning took place in AD 70.

- If so, "the Son of Man coming on the clouds of heaven" is a metaphor for God's judgment on Israel, similar to Isaiah's description of God's judgment on Egypt (Isaiah 19:1). After Jerusalem fell, God began to "gather his elect" from among the nations. This gathering will continue until "the fullness of the Gentiles" comes to faith in Jesus (Romans 11:25). If that's the meaning of these words from Jesus, he was not talking about his return at all. He was describing the meaning of the destruction of the Jewish temple.

- But what in AD 70 could possibly have been a "coming" and a "sign" that people could see? (Matthew 24:27–30). It is true that a series of strange and miraculous signs marked the fall of the temple. Here's how Josephus described these occurrences: "I suppose this account would seem to be false except that eyewitnesses vouched for it: ... Before sunset, chariots were seen in the air over the whole land, and armored soldiers were speeding through the clouds and encircling the cities. ... As the priests were going by night into the inner court, they felt a quaking and heard a great noise. After that, they heard a sound something like a large crowd saying, 'Let us leave this place.'" The Roman historian Tacitus described how "in the sky, there appeared a vision of armies in glittering armor in conflict. Then a lightning flash from the clouds illuminated the temple! The doors of this holy place suddenly opened, a superhuman voice was heard declaring that the gods were leaving, and at the same time came the sound of a rushing tumult." In light of these reports, is it possible that a visible "sign of the Son of Man" did appear "in the clouds of heaven" in AD 70? If this interpretation is correct, God began to "gather his elect" from among the Gentiles ("from the four winds") after Jerusalem fell (Matthew 24:31); this will continue until "the fullness of the Gentiles" comes to faith in Jesus (Romans 11:25). Then Jesus will return physically to the earth.[120]

2. Another point of view is that the great tribulation began with the Roman persecution of Christians and the destruction of the temple. This great tribulation will continue until Jesus returns.

- Jesus will be revealed and will return to earth "immediately after the distress of those days," just as Jesus predicted (Matthew 24:29). The "mourning" represents the response of the Jewish people at the end of time who recognize how their ancestors rejected Israel's Messiah. Although supernatural signs were seen in the skies when the temple fell in AD 70, some argue that none of these first-century signs qualifies as the coming of the Son of Man in "power and great glory" (Matthew 24:30).

- In the teaching that's preserved in Matthew 24, Jesus—after predicting how the Roman soldiers would sacrifice to their eagle ensigns on the temple mount—shifted his focus from the disciples' first question ("When will this happen?") to their second question ("What will be the sign of your coming?"). Jesus indicated this shift in focus by mentioning "the sign of the coming," to connect his words clearly with the disciples' second question.

- Jesus provided very little in the way of signs; the only "sign" he offered was his actual arrival! That's why he emphasizes only a few verses later that his followers must always be ready. His arrival on earth will be unmistakable, like "lightning" accompanied by a "trumpet" (see 1 Corinthians 15:52; 1 Thessalonians 4:16). Many who take this perspective also anticipate a spiritual awakening among the Jewish people before Jesus returns (Zechariah 12:9–12; Romans 11:17–27).

A Lesson from the Fig Tree

Matthew 24:32–35

Now learn this lesson from the fig tree: As soon as its twigs get tender and its leaves come out, you know that summer is near. Even so, when you see all these things, you know that it is near, right at the door. Truly I tell you, this generation will certainly not pass away until all these things have happened. Heaven and earth will pass away, but my words will never pass away (see also Mark 13:28–31; Luke 21:29–3).

VIEW 1 FULFILLMENT IN THE END TIMES ONLY: FUTURIST

"This generation"

- According to some dispensational premillennialists, "this generation" refers to the generation that will be on earth during the great tribulation. If that's the meaning of "this generation," Jesus was telling the disciples was that those living during the great tribulation will be the people who see the return of Jesus to earth. Other dispensationalists see the blooming of the fig tree as a symbol of the establishment of the modern nation of Israel in 1948–or perhaps of the Six Day War in 1967. If so, the tribulation will occur in the lifetimes of people who were alive in 1948 or 1967.[121]

- What Jesus was telling the disciples was that those living during the great tribulation will be the people who see the return of Jesus to earth.[122]

"All these things"

- The generation that endures the great tribulation will be the generation that witnesses "all these things," including the return of Jesus. Or perhaps the generation that witnessed the establishment of the modern nation of Israel will be the generation that sees the tribulation and return of Jesus.

© Andrey Burmakin

VIEW 2 PARTIAL FULFILLMENT IN THE FIRST CENTURY, COMPLETE FULFILLMENT WHEN JESUS RETURNS TO EARTH: PRETERIST AND FUTURIST

"This generation"

- Some students of Scripture understand "generation" to mean only the people who were alive when Jesus spoke these words. The typical measure of a generation in Old Testament was forty years (see Numbers 14:34). Jesus spoke these words around AD 30. So, AD 70 was exactly a generation away.

- Other students see "generation" more in terms of the "chosen generation" of Christians in every age (1 Peter 2:9). This interpretation of the text has a long history: John Chrysostom, a pastor in the fourth century AD, understood "this generation" as a reference to the church age. If that was the intent of Jesus' words, what Jesus was declaring was that no persecution or tribulation would destroy the church; the church will persist until the return of Jesus, when the last of these prophecies will finally be fulfilled.[123]

"All these things"

- If "all these things" meant only the destruction of the temple, it is possible that "this generation" included only the people who were alive when Jesus spoke these words.

- If "all these things" includes the return of Jesus to earth, "this generation" meant the entire church age, from the beginning of the church until the return of Jesus to earth.

John Chrysostom (mosaic). Saint Sophia Cathedral, Kiev.

CHAPTER 13 Cast of Characters at the End of Time: The Heroes

Today, the island of Patmos is a tourist resort. Luxury liners dock daily at the port of Skala before returning to the Greek mainland. A plush hotel, fine restaurants, and plenty of shops line the shores of this island.

In the first century AD, no luxuries were to be found on Patmos.

When a Roman ruler exiled John to this sparsely-vegetated scrap of volcanic rock, there were only caves and a handful of clustered buildings. This was a place

© GoodSalt/Lars Justinen

where governors sent political exiles to prevent them from causing problems for the Roman Empire. It was rugged, isolated, and sparsely populated—not a prison colony, mind you, but certainly not the spot where you would choose to spend your family vacation.

It was in this place of exile that John was worshiping his Savior "on the Lord's day" (Revelation 1:10). Without warning, a voice like a trumpet tore through the silence. John whirled around and glimpsed the glorified Son of Man, surrounded by seven golden lampstands. The Son of Man had hair like snow, eyes like fire, and feet like bronze. One look at him was enough to cause John to fall on his face. In this moment, Jesus declared himself to be "the first and the last" (Revelation 1:17). Later, he revealed himself as "Alpha and Omega," "the beginning and the end" (22:13).

Jesus is the central character and the ultimate hero of this book. John's vision begins with Jesus and ends with Jesus (1:1–20; 22:12–21). Not only in Revelation but also in other end-times texts, there are other significant characters—righteous and unrighteous, heroes and villains—but Jesus remains central.

The Son of Man and the Seven Lamps, in Bamberg Apocalypse, Folio 3 recto, c. 1000.

In this chapter, we'll take a look at some of the heroes in God's end-times script:

- John the exile, who saw the visions that revealed "what will take place later" (1:19),

- The twenty-four elders around a heavenly throne,

- 144,000 witnesses sealed by an angel,

- The multitude that endures great tribulation,

- Two witnesses who die for their testimony to the truth of Jesus,

- And Jesus himself, the Lion who is also a Lamb, the risen Lord and the King of kings.

> **REVELATION 1:1–2**
>
> "The revelation from Jesus Christ, which God gave him to show his servants what must soon take place. He made it known by sending his angel to his servant John, who testifies to everything he saw—that is, the word of God and the testimony of Jesus Christ."

JOHN THE EXILE

How do you know who wrote the book that you're reading right now?

Perhaps you've met one of the people mentioned on the cover of this book about the end times, so you feel fairly certain who wrote these words. Maybe, if you've never heard of the alleged authors, you could study some promotional literature about this book. If you were really concerned about the authorship, you might scour the Internet to verify that the authors listed on the cover really could have written these words. You might even try to find us at our workplaces; that would come really close to stalking us, though, and we would prefer that you didn't do that.

But what if you lived in an era prior to covers and copyright pages and computer searches? Suppose books were copied by hand and the only name inscribed in your book was the author's first name. And what if that first name was the one of most common names in your part of the world?

Saint John at Patmos by Jacopo Vignali

That's precisely the situation that the first readers of Revelation faced. The book of Revelation mentions no details about the author except that he was a servant of Jesus, exiled on the island of Patmos. His name is given only as "John"—which happens to have been the fifth most frequent name for Jewish males in the first century.[124]

So how did ancient people know who wrote the book of Revelation?

Here's how: When one church provided another church with a copy of an important writing, they didn't just pass on a stack of papyrus. They also passed on a tradition about who wrote the book. These early traditions could typically be traced all the way back to their source.

For a text to be seen as authoritative in the churches, the original source had to be either an eyewitness of the risen Lord Jesus or a close associate of an eyewitness. Christians in the first and second centuries were extremely careful to trace every authoritative text back to an eyewitness or associate of an eyewitness.[125]

PAPYRUS, PAPYRI

(from Greek *papyros*)

Plant from which ancient people manufactured paper. Papyrus plants are nearly twelve feet tall and have a stem as thick as your wrist. The stems were sliced lengthwise in thin strips, then cut into shorter pieces. Two layers of slices were placed on top of each other—with the grain of the top layer running perpendicular to the one beneath it—then beaten together and dried to make paper.

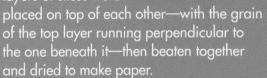

So what traditions did early Christians recite to one another about the book of Revelation?

The earliest and most reliable traditions about Revelation identified the author as John the apostle—the "beloved disciple" who left his father to follow Jesus and who wrote the Gospel According to John (Matthew 4:21–22; John 20:30–31).

WHEN DID JOHN WRITE REVELATION?

Who wrote Revelation is relatively certain. Although not everyone agrees, the most ancient evidence points to the apostle John. *When* the apostle John wrote Revelation is far less certain. Unlike books today, no one placed copyright dates in copies of biblical texts! To decide the approximate date when this biblical text was written, scholars compare what's inside the book with what was happening in the world outside the book. In the case of Revelation, that process results in two primary possibilities:

Evidence that Revelation may have been written during the reign of Emperor Nero (54–68)	Evidence that Revelation may have been written during the reign of Emperor Domitian (81–96)
An ancient ascription: A fifth-century version of Revelation in the Syriac language refers to the book as "the Revelation given by God to John the Gospel-writer, on the island of Patmos where he was banished by Emperor Nero." It is possible that this ascription preserves an earlier tradition.	**The testimony of Irenaeus**: The second-century writer Irenaeus of Lyons—a student of Polycarp, who knew the apostle John—reported that John wrote Revelation while in exile during Domitian's reign.[14]
Persecution of Christians: It seems that Christians may have been in the early stages of a time of persecution when John wrote Revelation (1:9; 2:2–3, 9–10, 13; 3:8–10). Nero instigated the first imperial persecution of Christians in AD 64; this persecution lasted until Nero's death in 68.	**Worship of the Roman emperor**: Hints can be found throughout Revelation that Christians may have been coerced to worship the emperor (13:4, 14–17; 14:9; 15:2; 16:2; 19:20; 20:4). Nero was never worshiped as divine in his lifetime. Worship of the emperor does seem to have occurred during Domitian's reign, in the AD 80s and 90s. Coins from Domitian's reign refer to Domitian as "father of the gods." An idol of Domitian may have been constructed in the city of Ephesus.
The temple in Jerusalem: If Revelation had been written in the AD 90s, it seems that John might have mentioned the fall of the Jewish temple that occurred in AD 70. The wording of Revelation 11:1–2 suggests to some scholars that the temple in Jerusalem was still standing when John wrote this book.	**The church of Laodicea**: The description of Laodicea's self-sufficiency may reflect a time in the AD 80s when the Laodiceans rebuilt their city with no outside assistance after an earthquake (Revelation 3:17).

- The Christian philosopher Justin mentioned this tradition in the mid-second century AD.

- A few years later, the church father Irenaeus of Lyons—the student of a pastor named Polycarp who had studied with the apostle John—reported the same source for Revelation.

- In the early third century, the writings of Tertullian of Carthage repeated this long-standing tradition.[126]

- It wasn't until the mid-third century AD that any writer mentioned any possible author besides the apostle John.[127]

When all the evidence is examined, the idea that anyone other than the apostle John wrote Revelation has little support. John the apostle was well known as the author of Revelation. That's the tradition that early Christians received and shared with one another, and there are no compelling reasons to forsake those ancient recollections.

If John the apostle did in fact write Revelation—and I am convinced that he did— these visions on Patmos were not the first time that he had seen Jesus. John first glimpsed Jesus along the stony shores of the Sea of Galilee. He heard the call of Jesus while washing and twining his nets amid baskets of fresh-caught fish. He ate with Jesus, he drank with Jesus, and then he saw him die. Three days later, he ran panting into an empty tomb and, that evening, he saw Jesus alive. After Jesus ascended into the skies, it was John who cared for his Messiah's mother; it was John who wrote the Gospel that described Jesus as "the Word." And now, in the visions that he narrates in Revelation, John sees Jesus once again—but this time, he does not see him as a traveling teacher, gathering a rather dubious crew of disciples. John sees Jesus

The Very Rich Hours of the Duke of Berry, "Saint John on Patmos" (1412–1416).

in his glory, and—after receiving divine messages for seven churches—John is taken through an open door into the throne room of God (Revelation 4:1).

EMPEROR NERO

Ruled the Roman Empire, AD 54–68. After a fire in Rome, a rumor circulated that Nero had started the fire. According to the ancient historian Tacitus, "To get rid of this report, Nero accused and inflicted exquisite tortures on a class hated for their abominations, the ones called Christians."[128] This persecution seems to have been limited to the regions around Rome, but it likely affected attitudes toward Christians beyond Rome.

EMPEROR DOMITIAN

Ruled the Roman Empire, AD 81–96. Domitian repeatedly declared himself to be divine during his lifetime. According to the ancient historian Suetonius, "Domitian issued an encyclical in the name of his governors that declared 'Our Master and our God bids that this be done.'"[129]

PATMOS

Island off the west coast of Asia Minor. According to Tacitus, persons who threatened the peace of the Roman Empire were sent to coastal islands such as Patmos.[130] Fourth-century church historian Eusebius reported that Emperor Domitian exiled John in AD 95; eighteen months later, after Domitian's death, John returned from the island.[131]

THE ENIGMA OF THE TWENTY-FOUR ELDERS

Four times in the book of Revelation, John saw twenty-four unnamed elders. These two dozen elders worship the living God without ceasing (Revelation 11:16; 19:4). They wear white robes and cast their golden crowns to the ground before the throne of God (Revelation 4:4–11). They carry golden bowls that are filled with the prayers of God's holy people (Revelation 5:8). But who are the twenty-four elders? John described what the elders *do*, but he never specifically said who they *are*. Here are a few possibilities:

- *An angelic council?* A council of angelic beings, perhaps the guardians of Israel and the church, that surrounds the throne of God. Scripture describes angelic beings around the divine throne (1 Kings 22:19; Psalm 89:7). White clothing is the garb of angelic creatures in other biblical books (Matthew 28:3; Acts 1:10), and "elders" can function as a title for angels (Isaiah 24:23).

- *Heavenly expression of earthly priesthood?* Heavenly reflection of the twenty-four groups of priests and Levites who praised God in the Jerusalem temple (1 Chronicles 24:4; 25:9–31).

- *God's people in glory?* Symbol of believers in Jesus from the Old and New Testaments, dwelling in eternal glory. The number "twenty-four" points symbolically to Israel's twelve patriarchs and the church's twelve apostles; according to Revelation 21:12–14, the names of the tribes of Israel and the apostles of Jesus are inscribed on the foundations of the eternal city. Throughout Revelation, white robes are the characteristic clothing of "the saints," believers in Jesus Christ (Revelation 3:4–18; 6:11; 7:9–13; 19:14).

- *The church during the tribulation?* Symbol of the raptured church dwelling in eternal glory during the future seven-year tribulation.

144,000 Virgins with Seals on Their Heads

At first, after John takes his trip through a door into the heavens, everything John sees revolves around the throne of God (Revelation 4:1–2). Then, after a series of cosmic upheavals, his attention is suddenly drawn earthward again. He sees "four angels, standing at the four corners of the earth"—perhaps representing all the powers of creation itself, under the power of God (7:1). Then, ascending on the eastern horizon, John glimpses an angel who holds "the seal of the living God" (7:2). He hears about a crowd that's 144,000 strong, and the angel with the seal declares that these people are about to receive the seal "on their foreheads" (7:4).

REVELATION 7:1–8

"After this I saw four angels standing at the four corners of the earth, holding back the four winds of the earth to prevent any wind from blowing on the land or on the sea or on any tree. Then I saw another angel coming up from the east, having the seal of the living God. He called out in a loud voice to the four angels who had been given power to harm the land and the sea: "Do not harm the land or the sea or the trees until we put a seal on the foreheads of the servants of our God." Then I heard the number of those who were sealed: 144,000 from all the tribes of Israel. From the tribe of Judah 12,000 were sealed, from the tribe of Reuben 12,000, from the tribe of Gad 12,000, from the tribe of Asher 12,000, from the tribe of Naphtali 12,000, from the tribe of Manasseh 12,000, from the tribe of Simeon 12,000, from the tribe of Levi 12,000, from the tribe of Issachar 12,000, from the tribe of Zebulun 12,000, from the tribe of Joseph 12,000, from the tribe of Benjamin 12,000."

The sealing of the 144,000

The "seal" that John saw is not a flippered creature from the coast of Canada—although placing such seals on people's foreheads could certainly have livened up the book of Revelation.

What John described as a "seal" was the imprint from a royal ruler's signet ring. In John's lifetime, whenever someone sealed a letter with a signet ring, the contents of that letter were to remain safe until the document reached the desired destination. God's imprint upon the 144,000 is God's promise that these persons will persevere until they reach God's goal for them. Later in Revelation, John revealed the precise content of the "seal": it is the name of God the Father and God the Son (Revelation 14:1).

So does this mean that the angels will be opening a tattoo parlor to ink the divine name on the foreheads of these 144,000 faithful servants? (7:3).

> ### REVELATION 14:1–5
>
> "Then I looked, and there before me was the Lamb, standing on Mount Zion, and with him 144,000 who had his name and his Father's name written on their foreheads. And I heard a sound from heaven like the roar of rushing waters and like a loud peal of thunder. The sound I heard was like that of harpists playing their harps. And they sang a new song before the throne and before the four living creatures and the elders. No one could learn the song except the 144,000 who had been redeemed from the earth. These are those who did not defile themselves with women, for they remained virgins. They follow the Lamb wherever he goes. They were purchased from among mankind and offered as firstfruits to God and the Lamb. No lie was found in their mouths; they are blameless."

The Sealing of the 144,000, by M. Gerung (1530–1532)

Most likely not.

The protective "mark" or "seal" is probably a symbol. For John's first readers, it would actually have been a fairly familiar symbol. Jewish prophecies that were penned long before the book of Revelation mentioned a symbolic "mark" to distinguish God's people. After the writing of Revelation, early Christian writers picked up on this same image.

Who mentioned a "mark" or "seal"?	What did the text say?	What did the "mark" or "seal" mean?
The prophet Ezekiel	"'Go throughout the city of Jerusalem and put a mark on the foreheads of those who grieve and lament over all the detestable things that are done in it.' As I listened, he said to the others, 'Follow him through the city and kill, without showing pity or compassion'" (Ezekiel 9:4–5).	The mark symbolized God's protection of those who were faithful to him.
Anonymous Jewish writer between the Old and New Testaments	"The mark of God is on the righteous so that they will be saved, ... but lawless people will not escape God's judgment. The mark of destruction is on their foreheads" (*Psalms of Solomon* 15:6–9)	The mark distinguished between the righteous and the lawless in anticipation of future judgment.
The apostle Paul	"Now it is God who makes both us and you stand firm in Christ. He anointed us, set his seal of ownership on us, and put his Spirit in our hearts as a deposit, guaranteeing what is to come" (2 Corinthians 1:21–22). "And you also were included in Christ when you heard the message of truth, the gospel of your salvation. When you believed, you were marked in him with a seal, the promised Holy Spirit, who is a deposit guaranteeing our inheritance until the redemption of those who are God's possession—to the praise of his glory" (Ephesians 1:13–14). "And do not grieve the Holy Spirit of God, with whom you were sealed for the day of redemption" (Ephesians 4:30).	The Holy Spirit's presence in the Christian is God's guarantee that his children will inherit everything that God has promised them through Jesus.
Second-century pastor and martyr Ignatius of Antioch	"There are two coinages. ... Each has its appropriate stamp impressed on it: Unbelievers bear the mark of this world; the faithful in love bear the mark of God."[132]	The mark represented how the life of a Christian is different from the life of a non-Christian.
Anonymous ancient Christian writer	"I recognized my people and imprinted a seal on their faces. ... They will not be deprived of my name."[133]	The seal meant that God knew the people who belonged to him and that he would not forget them.

In Jewish and Christian writings alike, the mark or seal was *not* a physical marking. The seal on God's people symbolized how God would preserve them through tribulation. When the unrighteous received a mark, it pointed to the fact that God recognized their rebellion and that he would judge them.

When it comes to John's vision of the 144,000, what this means is that the sealing is probably *not* a physical mark. The sealing symbolizes God's guarantee that these chosen witnesses will endure to the end. This does *not* mean that these persons will escape suffering. What it *does* mean is that God will sustain them, even through persecution, until they reach the destination that God has decreed for them.

This symbol may also echo God's words to the ancient Israelites. God commanded them, through Moses, to maintain the memory of their redemption like "a mark on your hand, even bound between your eyes" (Exodus 13:16). The original intent of these words was to allow God's works to shape his people's thoughts ("bound between your eyes") and actions ("a mark on your hand"). To be marked on the forehead with God's name (Revelation 7:3; 14:1) is to have a mind that is shaped by the character of God. Paul made this same point in a different way when he called Christians to "have this mind in you, which was also in Christ Jesus" (Philippians 2:5).

A hidden identity for the 144,000?

But who exactly are the "144,000 from all the tribes of Israel"?

VIRGINS

The 144,000 are "virgins" (Revelation 14:4–5). If the 144,000 are 12,000 witnesses from each tribe of Israel in a future seven-year tribulation, "virgins" could mean these individuals have never experienced sexual relations. If the 144,000 is symbolic, the imagery probably draws from prophets and apostles who described idol-worship as the spiritual counterpart of sexual sin (Jeremiah 9:2; 23:10; Ezekiel 16:28–32; Hosea 7:4; Matthew 12:39; 16:4; 2 Corinthians 11:2; James 4:4). If so, John intended these words to show that—even in times of tribulation—God's people must remain separated from every form of idolatry. In the Hebrew Scriptures, soldiers were expected to abstain from sexual relations during times of war (Deuteronomy 23:9–10; 1 Samuel 21:4–5). The reference to the 144,000 not being "with women" could represent constant readiness to engage in spiritual warfare against the powers of evil.

Dispensationalists understand the 144,000 to be Jewish believers—12,000 virgin men from each tribe listed in the text—chosen to be witnesses during the first forty-two months of the seven-year tribulation. These persons will become believers during the first months of the tribulation; they will be "sealed" and sent as evangelists. After the trauma of the rapture and the beginnings of the tribulation, many who are left behind will begin to inquire into the meaning of these events. These 144,000 Jewish evangelists will proclaim the gospel until about halfway through the tribulation. At that time, they will be killed for their faith.[134]

Other interpreters of this text see shortcomings in the dispensationalist point of view. Here's what amillennialists, postmillennialists, and most historical premillennialists point out when they read this text: **When John named the tribes that would comprise the 144,000, he seems to have placed clues in the text to suggest that he didn't intend these tribes to be taken as the twelve tribes of ethnic Israel.**

These clues have to do with the tribes that John chose to list and how he lists them.

- John was a faithful Jew; he was very familiar with the lists of Israel's tribes that appear in the Hebrew Scriptures. Yet John recorded a different list than any of the listings that appear in the Old Testament—and in a completely different order!
- His list of tribes is not the same as the list of Jacob's sons that appears in Genesis.
- Neither does John's list match the tribal territories mapped out in the prophecies of Ezekiel.
- In fact, this list doesn't match any listing anywhere else in the Bible! The tribes are different, and the order is different too.

So why did God guide John to record such a distinct listing?

Many biblical scholars take this deliberate divergence from Old Testament listings to be a Spirit-inspired clue. The purpose of this clue was to show readers that the ethnic nation of Israel is not the focus of this list. John meant his listing of tribes to be taken as a symbol of *something other than* ethnic Israel.

WHAT IS DIFFERENT ABOUT JOHN'S LIST OF TRIBES?

The Twelve Sons of Jacob (Genesis 49)	The Twelve Tribal Territories (Ezekiel 48)	The Twelve Tribes in Revelation (Revelation 7)
Reuben	Dan	Judah
Simeon	Asher	Reuben
Levi	Naphtali	Gad
Judah	Manasseh	Asher
Zebulun	Ephraim	Naphtali
Issachar	Reuben	Manasseh
Dan	Judah	Simeon
Gad	Benjamin	Levi
Asher	Simeon	Issachar
Naphtali	Issachar	Zebulun
Joseph	Zebulun	Joseph
Benjamin	Gad	Benjamin

So, if John's list does not refer to twelve ethnic tribes from the earthly nation of Israel, what might the list mean?

According to historical premillennialists, amillennialists, and many postmillennialists, *the 144,000 symbolize the followers of Jesus on the earth, the full number of those who endure tribulation.*

This could fit with descriptions of the church that appear throughout the New Testament:

- James addressed believers in Jesus as "the twelve tribes" (James 1:1); so, first-century Christians clearly understood "the twelve tribes" to be a rightful way of referring to believers in Jesus.

- Paul understood Jesus to be the fulfillment of God's work with Israel. That's why Paul could declare that God would save "all Israel" (Romans 9:6; 11:26) because the true Israel is every person—Jew or Gentile—who trusts in Jesus.

- Paul even referred to Christians as "the Israel of God" (Galatians 6:16; see also Philippians 3:3).

- Peter described Christians as "chosen people, a royal priesthood, a holy nation"—terms drawn directly from Old Testament descriptions of Israel (1 Peter 2:9; Deuteronomy 28:9; Isaiah 43:20; 61:6).

Based on texts such as these, many Christians throughout church history have understood "144,000" as a reference to believers in Jesus on the earth during times of tribulation.

This would not mean, of course, that only 144,000 people will be saved! The number 144,000 is a symbolic number. It's the number of the tribes of Israel (12) times the number of the apostles (12) multiplied by 1,000—ten to the third power!—to depict the great magnitude of God's people.

THE GREAT MULTITUDE FROM THE GREAT TRIBULATION

If the 144,000 represent the people of God on earth during tribulation, what is the "great multitude" that John sees later? (7:9). Who is this crowd "from all tribes and people and languages"? (7:9). And why did John see this great multitude in the heavenly realm, around God's throne?

REVELATION 7:9–17

"After this I looked, and there before me was a great multitude that no one could count, from every nation, tribe, people and language, standing before the throne and before the Lamb. They were wearing white robes and were holding palm branches in their hands. And they cried out in a loud voice:

"Salvation belongs to our God, who sits on the throne, and to the Lamb."

All the angels were standing around the throne and around the elders and the four living creatures. They fell down on their faces before the throne and worshiped God, saying:

"Amen! Praise and glory and wisdom and thanks and honor and power and strength be to our God for ever and ever. Amen!"

Then one of the elders asked me, "These in white robes—who are they, and where did they come from?"

I answered, "Sir, you know." And he said, "These are they who have come out of the great tribulation; they have washed their robes and made them white in the blood of the Lamb. Therefore, "they are before the throne of God and serve him day and night in his temple; and he who sits on the throne will shelter them with his presence. 'Never again will they hunger; never again will they thirst. The sun will not beat down on them,' nor any scorching heat. For the Lamb at the center of the throne will be their shepherd; 'he will lead them to springs of living water.' 'And God will wipe away every tear from their eyes.'"

If you aren't quite certain about the identity of this multitude, don't feel bad: When one of the elders asked John who they were, the apostle himself wasn't completely certain! After John failed this apocalyptic pop quiz, the elder provided him with the answer: "These are the ones coming out of the great tribulation" (7:14).

But who is it that will come "out of the great tribulation"?

Are they the people who trust Jesus during the seven-year tribulation? *Dispensationalists* take this multitude to represent the Gentiles who trust Jesus during the future tribulation. The 144,000 ethnic Jews will proclaim the truth of Jesus; the great multitude are those that choose to believe their message. These are the saints who have come out of the tribulation after having made personal commitments to Jesus Christ.[135] Despite persecution and even martyrdom, those who trust Jesus during the tribulation will endure in faith and be saved.

Or are they the 144,000, seen from a different perspective? Most *historical premillennialists*, as well as many *amillennialists* and *postmillennialists*, take a different view of the great multitude. From their perspective, the multitude is *the same group as the 144,000, described from a different point of view*. The 144,000 are God's people enduring tribulation on earth. The "great multitude ... coming out of the great tribulation" are the same people of God seen from the standpoint of eternity, after every tribulation has ended.

Remember, John saw these visions from a perspective outside time and space. So, it was entirely possible for him to hear about God's people enduring tribulation and then immediately to see the people of God triumphant after tribulation!

Paradise, by Jacopo Tintoretto (1579)

John followed the same pattern when he described Jesus at the throne of God. John heard about Jesus as the triumphant Lion (5:5) then he saw Jesus as the sacrificial Lamb (5:6). The same Savior was described from two perspectives using two different symbols. Likewise, in Revelation 7, it's possible that faithful followers of Jesus could be both the 144,000 sealed in verse 4 and the great multitude saved in verse 9. If so, John was describing the same people of God from two different points of view.

DYNAMIC DUO OF DIVINE WITNESSES

In Revelation 11:3–12, John described two witnesses who are like "two lamp-stands." It is clear that these two witnesses testify to the truth of Jesus in times of spiritual darkness—much like the "two lamp-stands" that Zechariah described in the Old Testament (Zechariah 4:3–14). Yet John never clearly declared the secret identity of this dynamic duo. Here are some suggestions about who these two might be:

1. ***Moses and Elijah?*** Some dispensational premillennialists see them as Moses and Elijah, brought back from the dead during the tribulation to testify to the truth of Jesus. They will be killed. Three-and-a-half days later, they will be raptured.

2. ***Two prophets like Moses and Elijah?*** Other dispensational premillennialists, as well as many historical premillennialists, take the two witnesses to be two people similar to Moses and Elijah. During a time of tribulation near the end of the world as we know it, God will empower them to proclaim the gospel. They will be killed, but they will not remain dead.

Moses, by Phillippe de Champaigne, 1648

The "three-and-a-half days" that precede their resurrection could symbolize the relatively brief time that will pass before God vindicates his people. Or these two witnesses could be taken physically into the heavens after three-and-a-half days.

3. **The witness of the church?** Some interpreters from other millennial viewpoints understand the two witnesses to symbolize the church's testimony during times of tribulation. These witnesses are "lamp-stands" (Revelation 11:4)—a term that John previously applied to the church (Revelation 1:20). The church's witness is symbolized by two witnesses because God's Law required two witnesses to establish testimony as true (Deuteronomy 17:6; 19:15; Numbers 35:30). Despite persecution and even martyrdom, the testimony of the church will prove true, and God will punish those who persecute his people. "Three-and-a-half days" symbolizes the fact that persecution and even martyrdom will not last forever; in the end, God will rescue his people and raise the faithful to life again. The place of their persecution is Jerusalem (Revelation 11:8), so this text may also point to God's preservation of his church in AD 70.

Elijah, by José de Ribera, 1638

4. **The Law and the Prophets?** The two witnesses could represent the testimony of the Old Testament about Jesus. First-century Jews referred to their Scriptures using the twofold title "the Law and the Prophets." The Law and the Prophets alike testified to the truth of Jesus (Luke 24:44; Acts 28:23). Religious leaders in John's lifetime rejected this testimony, reducing the laws and prophecies to meaningless rituals (Matthew 23:25–26; 2 Corinthians 3:14–16). The resurrection of the two witnesses could express John's expectation of a future time when God will breathe new life into the testimony of the Old Testament and bring spiritual awakening to the Jewish people. Or this event could point back to the resurrection of Old Testament saints that happened when Jesus died, shortly after the religious leaders in Jerusalem had rejected the testimony of the Old Testament about Jesus (Matthew 27:51–53).

Jesus, the Star of Revelation

Even with so many heroic witnesses in these texts that tell about the end of time, it is clear that Jesus remains the true hero of God's plan. Jesus is the star of Revelation—literally! According to his own words in the vision that John saw on Patmos, Jesus is "the root and descendant of David, the bright morning star" (Revelation 22:16). Every righteous character in Revelation is righteous only because of Jesus, and every heroic witness gives all glory to Jesus.

- John saw himself first and foremost as a slave and a witness of Jesus (Revelation 1:1–2).

- The twenty-four elders fall on their faces before Jesus and sing a new song that recognizes the risen Lamb as the one who is worthy of praise (Revelation 5:8–12).

- The 144,000 take their stand around Jesus, and the seal on their foreheads is the name of Jesus and his heavenly Father (Revelation 14:1).

- The men and women in the great multitude remain faithful only because they have rinsed their robes in the blood of the Lamb (Revelation 7:14). Jesus is their shepherd and their Savior, their comforter and their guide (Revelation 7:17).

- The testimony for which the two witnesses die is the testimony of "their Lord" (Revelation 11:8).

The many millennial viewpoints differ on the exact identities of the end-times heroes—but, when it comes to the central character, there is no debate. *The same Messiah who met John on Patmos is the Word by whom the cosmos was created, the teacher who called John to leave his nets, the Lamb who was slain for his people's sins, and the King who will return in triumph. Jesus is the star, and all glory belongs to him.*

Cast of Characters at the End of Time: The Villains

Not too long ago, keepers at the Bronx Zoo reported that one of their reptiles was on the lam. This slip would likely have attracted little attention except for the fact that the missing reptile was no ordinary creature. The vacant exhibit belonged to an Egyptian cobra—a creature whose venom can reduce a human being to a corpse in less than twenty minutes.

The notion of a deadly serpent slithering through the streets of the Big Apple rapidly captured people's imagination. When someone launched a social-media account under the name "Bronx Zoo's Cobra," nearly a quarter-million people were soon following the serpent's supposed movements. "Dear NYC, apples and snakes have gone together since the beginning," was one of the first alleged messages from the cobra. My favorite update was, "Holding very still in the snake exhibit in the Museum of Natural History. This is gonna be hilarious!"

© bluecrayola

All this frivolity masked a very real fear, though: *What if there's a hidden killer on the loose, waiting silently in the places where you would least expect death to strike? And what if this creature is far closer than anyone ever expected?*

The most frightening aspect of this fear is that it's no false alarm. It's true. A deadly creature really does slither unseen through streets and alleys, offices and amusement parks—and not just in New York City.

It is not an uncaged cobra from the Bronx. I am speaking of the spirit first seen by human eyes in the Garden of Eden—the fallen angel whose aliases include the Devil and the dragon, Old Scratch and Satan.

God guaranteed in the Garden of Eden that the offspring of Eve would someday grind the serpent's skull into the earth (Genesis 3:15; see also Isaiah 27:1)—and that is precisely what Jesus accomplished through the cross and empty tomb. Yet, even after this triumph, the Devil still seeks to devour people's lives; here and now, a deadly creature is on the prowl in the cosmos (1 Peter 5:8).

Here's a crucial truth that Revelation reveals about this deadly creature: he does not work alone. The dragon enlists political, religious, and economic powers to do his dirty work. In the book of Revelation, these powers take the form of a beast from the land, a beast from the sea, and a harlot seated on a scarlet steed. Through these powers, the dragon indulges those who bow before him with opulence and political power—but he can only deliver on these offers for a limited time. According to Revelation, the dragon's prowling will be cut short by God's design.

© Mark Payne

JESUS' TRIUMPH OVER SATAN

Christians disagree about how much power Satan possesses after the triumph of Jesus. Nearly every believer, however, can find common ground on these two truths: Satan is on the prowl, but his time and powers are limited.

According to *amillennialists*, the sacrificial death and triumphant resurrection of Jesus shattered Satan's power once and for all; right now, Satan is bound.	Shortly before Jesus returns physically to earth, Satan will be released. Once again, Satan will refuse to submit to Jesus. Satan will be defeated and confined forever in a fiery lake of torment (Revelation 20:7–10).
Postmillennialists see the strength of Satan crumbling gradually as the gospel takes root around the world. Some preterists believe that Satan has been bound ever since the fall of Jerusalem in AD 70.	Shortly before Jesus returns physically to earth, Satan will be released. Once again, Satan will refuse to submit to Jesus. Satan will be defeated and confined forever in a fiery lake of torment (Revelation 20:7–10).
Premillennialists (including dispensational premillennialists) expect Satan's rebellion to grow clearer as the end of time draws nearer.	After Jesus returns to earth, Satan will be bound for one thousand years (Revelation 20:1–3). When this glorious millennial kingdom draws to an end, Satan will be released. Once again, Satan will refuse to submit to Jesus. Satan will be defeated and confined forever in a fiery lake of torment (Revelation 20:7–10).

The Archangel Michael against Lucifer, ceiling fresco by Matthäus Günther (1776).

WHAT'S IN A NAME?

John saw Satan as a fierce red dragon. So does this mean that the devil really looks like a dragon? Of course not! He is a spiritual being, not a physical creature. The devil appears in Scripture in many different forms with many different names. Here are some of the devil's names:

1. **Ancient serpent** This was Satan's first guise recorded in Scripture (Genesis 3:1; 2 Corinthians 11:3; Revelation 12:7–9).

2. **Satan** This Hebrew title means "adversary" and appears more than fifty times in the Bible (1 Chronicles 21:1; Job 1:6–12; Zechariah 3:1–2; Matthew 4:10; 2 Corinthians 11:14).

3. **Devil** From the Greek *diabolos*, this title means "slanderer" (Matthew 4:1–11; John 8:44).

4. **Beelzebul, the prince of demons** "Beelzebul" comes from the Hebrew words *ba'al* ("lord") and *zebul* ("height" or "dwelling place") and means "lord of the heights." By the time of Jesus, Beelzebul had become an epithet for Satan (Matthew 10:25; 12:24–27). Originally, "Baalzebul" may have been the name of a Canaanite deity; one Spirit-inspired author of the Old Testament expressed his disgust with this false god by writing the god's name as Beelzebub, which means "lord of the flies" (2 Kings 1:2–16).

5. **Evil one** The devil is bad; no explanation required (Ephesians 6:16; 1 John 2:13–14).

6. **God of this age** As the god of this age, the devil attempts to obscure the thinking of unbelievers so that they do not see the glory of Jesus (2 Corinthians 4:4).

7. **Ruler of the kingdom of the air** "Air" points to the fact that the battle with Satan is a spiritual struggle (Ephesians 2:2).

8. **The spirit now at work among the disobedient** Satan is a spiritual being (Ephesians 2:2).

9. **Dragon** Isaiah depicted God's cosmic enemy as a dragon (Isaiah 27:1); in Revelation, John applied this imagery specifically to Satan.

10. **Deceiver of the whole world** Satan is a liar and the source of lies (Revelation 20:2; see also John 8:44).

11. **Accuser** This term has a meaning similar to "devil": "the one who slanders" (Revelation 12:10).

The Great Red Dragon and the Woman Clothed in Sun, by William Blake (1805–1810)

No Sympathy for the Devil

The works of the devil are clear throughout Revelation, but the dragon's first personal appearance is during an interlude that's central to the book.[136] In the middle of this series of Spirit-scripted visions, John sees a woman with a robe like the sun. The woman screams in pain as she bears a son—but she and her child are not alone (Revelation 12:1–2). The dragon is there as well.

The crimson creature is fierce and mighty, with seven crowned heads and ten horns. He hurls one-third of the stars to the earth and positions himself to devour the newborn king (12:3–4). At the last moment, God intervenes, and the child ascends to a heavenly throne (12:5–6). The dragon declares war on the angels of heaven, but the child has already triumphed. The dragon is thrown from the heavens and confined to the earth (12:7–12).

Knowing that his time is short, the enraged dragon persecutes the woman and her children. He makes a final stand on the sands at the edge of the sea (12:13–17). From there, he calls forth evil minions and spews evil spirits (13:1–18; 16:14), but he cannot prevail. The seed of the woman is also the Lamb of God, and the Lamb's sacrifice has already guaranteed the dragon's defeat (12:11). The dragon is unmasked as "that ancient serpent, who is the devil, or Satan"; he is the spirit that lied to the world, and his doom is assured (12:9; 20:2).

© GoodSalt/Justinen Group

The first beast of Revelation fits the description in other New Testament texts of a regime that blasphemes Christ and persecutes his people. And so, Christians throughout the ages have taken the beast from the sea to represent the Antichrist.

The beast from the sea possesses vast political power and military might (13:7). Like the dragon, the beast is red and boasts "ten horns and seven heads" (13:1; 17:3). One of the seven heads seems to have suffered a death-blow but somehow survives. Awe-struck onlookers all over the world bow before this creature who seems immortal. In fact, the only ones who don't worship the beast are those whose names have been inscribed in the "Lamb's book of life" (13:3–4, 8). The beast persecutes these resisters and declares himself to be divine (13:6)—but such blasphemies cannot last forever. After "forty-two months," the beast's blasphemies and persecutions end (13:5).

As if John's visions weren't strange enough already, another beast suddenly emerges, this time from the land! This second beast's voice echoes the dragon's roar, but his two horns look like the horns of a lamb (13:11). The second beast mimics divine miracles—he calls fire from heaven and seems to breathe life into a statue of the first beast (13:13–15). Together, the dragon, the first beast, and the second beast represent an unholy mimicry of the holy Trinity.

The Beast with Ten Horns and the Beast with Lamb Horns, by Matthias Gerung (1530–1532)

The beast from the land enforces worship of the first beast by slaughtering anyone who does not bow before the beast from the sea (13:15). To identify the beast's faithful followers, the second beast demands that people "be marked on the right hand or the forehead" (13:18). The content of the mark is the name and the number of the first beast. That number is "666."

WHO ARE THE BEASTS?[138]

THE BEASTS ARE STILL TO COME

The Beasts Will Be Future Rulers of a Revived Roman Empire

Perspective on Revelation: Futurist

View of the End Times: Dispensational premillennial

The beast from the sea (the Antichrist)

- The Antichrist will be a global political leader during the future great tribulation.

- The modern nation of Israel will welcome him as a protector and a peacemaker (Daniel 9:27).

- He will make all people worship him (Daniel 9:27–31; 2 Thessalonians 2:4).

- He will be dealt a blow that seems fatal, but he will either survive or be revived (Revelation 13:3–4).

- His worldwide reign will last 42 months (Revelation 13:5).

The beast from the earth (the false prophet)

- This beast will be a religious leader during the future tribulation.

- Halfway through the tribulation, he will begin calling people to worship the Antichrist.

- He will place a statue of the Antichrist in the Jewish temple (Daniel 9:27; Matthew 24:15–21).

- Recognizing that "the earth" or "the land" sometimes implies Israel, many dispensationalists expect the second beast to be a Jew.

THE BEASTS HAVE ALREADY BEEN

The Beasts Were Past Powers in the Ancient Roman Empire

Perspective on Revelation: Preterist

View of the End Times: Postmillennial or amillennial

The beast from the sea (the Antichrist)

- Emperor Nero was the first beast. When spelled in Hebrew letters, Nero's Greek name adds up to 666.

- Nero's persecution of Christians lasted approximately forty-two months, from autumn of AD 64 until late spring AD 68 (Revelation 13:5).

- Nero was the sixth emperor, and Galba reigned briefly after Nero's death (Revelation 17:10–11).

- Soon afterward, God's judgment fell on Jerusalem through Emperor Vespasian.

The beast from the earth (the false prophet)

- Preterists emphasize the fact that this beast comes from "the earth" or "the land"—a terminology that, in some instances, implies the land of Israel.

- This beast could be Gessius Florus; he was the Roman ruler in Judea who persecuted Jews and triggered the Jewish-Roman War.

- This beast could also represent one or more of the false prophets in the years leading up to the fall of the temple in AD 70 (Matthew 24:11, 24).

THE BEASTS ARE ALWAYS HERE

The Beasts Are Past, Present, and Future Powers that Persecute and Demand Worship from God's People

Perspective on Revelation: Idealist

View of the End Times: Postmillennial, amillennial, or historical premillennial

The beast from the sea (the Antichrist)	The beast from the earth (the false prophet)
• The Antichrist is a symbol of rulers and realms in every age that pervert God's plan for political powers (Romans 13:1–7) by persecuting God's people or by demanding absolute allegiance.	• The false prophet is a symbol of leaders in every age that try to beguile God's people with false teachings and idolatry.
• The leopard, bear, lion, ten horns, and seven heads bring together all the kingdoms from Daniel 7, showing that this "beast" is a figurative picture of oppressive political powers throughout time.	• Jesus described such persons within the community of faith as "ravenous wolves" that wear "sheep's clothing" (Matthew 7:15).
• His reign of forty-two months symbolizes times of tribulation from the resurrection of Jesus until the end of time.	• This beast may also take the form of external political, religious, or social pressures to give absolute allegiance to anyone other than Jesus.

THE BEASTS HAVE ALREADY BEEN AND THEY ARE STILL TO COME

The Beasts Were Past Powers in the Ancient Roman Empire that Pointed Forward to Present and Future Powers

Perspective on Revelation: Preterist, idealist, and futurist

View of the End Times: Historical premillennial

The beast from the sea (the Antichrist)	The beast from the earth (the false prophet)
• Emperors such as Nero and Domitian provided a prototype for the beast.	• The beast from the earth points to social, civic, and cultural powers that may pressure God's people to submit to the Antichrist.
• Nero died and many believed he would return alive (Revelation 13:3).	• In John's day, this included local governors, religious officials, and false prophets in churches who encouraged Christians to compromise their convictions and to worship the emperor.
• Domitian demanded that he be worshiped and called "Lord and God" (13:5–8).	
• Throughout history, Nero, Domitian, and other "beasts" like them have persecuted God's church (13:7).	• Most of the seven cities mentioned in Revelation 1–3 had temples and priests dedicated to Roman emperors. Priests in these temples frequently used ventriloquism and lighting to make images seem alive (Revelation 13:15).
• Before Jesus returns, a final beastly Antichrist may still arise.	
• "Forty-two months" could be a literal time span or a symbol of persecutions throughout church history.	

CANDIDATES FOR THE OFFICE OF THE ANTICHRIST

The beast and his mysterious number have led to all sorts of speculations throughout history about who the Antichrist might be. In retrospect, many of these identifications have seemed quite ridiculous—a fact that should cause us to hesitate before suggesting that someone might be the Antichrist today. A few of the many candidates have included:

1. Emperor Nero (He persecuted the church, and his name in Hebrew can add up to 666.)

2. Emperor Constantius (The fourth-century church father Athanasius made this connection when Constantius persecuted orthodox Christians and favored congregations that denied the deity of Jesus. Athanasius also seems to have expected a final, future Antichrist.)

3. Pope Leo X (Martin Luther wrote a note to Pope Leo X entitled "Against the Execrable Bull of the Antichrist." Not surprisingly, the pope did not respond positively to this missive.)

4. Napoleon Bonaparte (In Leo Tolstoy's novel War and Peace, Pierre turns "L'Empereur Napoleon" into a series of numbers that add up to 666.)

5. Adolf Hitler (If you assign the value of 100 to the letter A, then 101 to the letter B, and so on, "Hitler" adds up to 666.)

6. John F. Kennedy (He received 666 votes at the 1956 Democratic convention, and he later died of a head wound.)

7. Henry Kissinger (Kissinger was a Middle East peacemaker of Jewish ancestry; his name in Hebrew adds up to 111, 666 divided by six.)

8. Mikhail Gorbachev (He was a world leader with a mysterious birthmark on his head; maybe it looked like a six if you stared at it long enough.)

9. Pope John Paul II (He recovered from a serious gunshot wound after an assassination attempt.)

10. Ronald Wilson Reagan (He had six letters in each name, get it? Plus, he recovered from a wound that seemed fatal.)

11. Barney the Dinosaur (Write "cute purple dinosaur" in ancient Latin characters, and it becomes "CVTE PVRPLE DINOSAVR." Extract the Roman numbers, add all the numerals together [C+V+V+L+D+I+V], and the result is 666.)

12. Barack Obama (The day after the 2008 election, the Illinois Pick 3 lottery numbers were 666.)

13. Bill Gates III (None of the twisted ways of turning his name into 666 is very convincing—but, let's face it, haven't we all wondered about this one when using Control/Alt/Delete to restart a frozen computer that's running Microsoft Windows?)

14. The World Wide Web (Yes, some have claimed that the portion of Internet known as the World Wide Web is the Antichrist. The Hebrew equivalent of W is the letter *vav*, which does double-duty in Hebrew as the number six. It's been suggested that vav-vav-vav would equal 666—but it really doesn't. Hebrew gematria has no notion of "tens place" and "hundreds place." So "WWW" results in the number eighteen (6+6+6), not 666.)

The Great Red Dragon by William Blake (1803–1805)

PAUL AND THE MAN OF PERDITION

The apostle Paul described the Antichrist—but not as a beast from the sea! Around AD 50, Paul addressed these words about the Antichrist to some anxious Christians in the city of Thessalonica:

What Paul said about the Antichrist	What we can learn about the Antichrist	How other Christians have understood Paul's words
"Concerning the coming of our Lord Jesus Christ and our being gathered to him, we ask you, brothers and sisters, not to become easily unsettled or alarmed by the teaching allegedly from us—whether by a prophecy or by word of mouth or by letter—asserting that the day of the Lord has already come. Don't let anyone deceive you in any way, for that day will not come until the rebellion occurs and the man of lawlessness is revealed, the man doomed to destruction" (2 Thessalonians 2:1–3).	Paul expected a "man of lawlessness" to be revealed before the return of Jesus to earth.	"Not to know when the end is, or when the day of the end will occur, is actually a good thing. If people knew the time of the end, they might begin to ignore the present time as they waited for the end times."[139]
"He will oppose and will exalt himself over everything that is called God or is worshiped, so that he sets himself up in God's temple, proclaiming himself to be God. Don't you remember that when I was with you I used to tell you these things?" (2 Thessalonians 2:4–5).	The "temple" or "sanctuary" may be a reconstructed Jewish temple or the site of the ancient temple. Or Paul may have meant that the Antichrist would seek to be worshiped by Christians; Paul described the church as a temple in 1 Corinthians 3:16–17; 2 Corinthians 6:16; and, Ephesians 2:21.	"No one can doubt that Paul is here talking about the Antichrist. ... There is some uncertainty about the temple where he will take his seat. Is it the ruins of the temple first built by King Solomon? Or is it in a church?"[140]

What Paul said about the Antichrist	What we can learn about the Antichrist	How other Christians have understood Paul's words
"And now you know what is holding him back, so that he may be revealed at the proper time. For the secret power of lawlessness is already at work; but the one who now holds it back will continue to do so till he is taken out of the way" (2 Thessalonians 2:6–7).	What is "holding him back" is probably the law and order of human governments. In Paul's day, this was the Roman Empire. It is also possible that the Holy Spirit is the one "holding him back."	"What is it that ... holds back the Antichrist? Some say the grace of the Spirit; others say the Roman Empire. I agree with the latter position. ... 'For the mystery of lawlessness is already at work.' He speaks here of Nero, a type of the Antichrist."[141]
"And then the lawless one will be revealed, whom the Lord Jesus will overthrow with the breath of his mouth and destroy by the splendor of his coming" (2 Thessalonians 2:8).	Jesus himself will defeat and destroy the Antichrist when Jesus returns to earth.	"Antichrist ... will display a murderous, most absolute, pitiless and unstable temper toward all, but especially toward us Christians. He will act insolently for three-and-a-half years. Then he will be defeated."[142]

Nero's Torches, by Henryk Siemiradzki (1876).

SEVEN HEADS, TEN HORNS, AND OTHER FREAKISH PHYSICAL FEATURES OF THE DRAGON'S CRONIES

Here's a summary of what John saw when the first beast rose from the sea:

- "It had ten horns and seven heads, with ten crowns on its horns, and on each head a blasphemous name.

- The beast ... resembled a leopard, but had feet like those of a bear and a mouth like that of a lion.

- One of the heads of the beast seemed to have had a fatal wound, but the fatal wound had been healed" (Revelation 13:1–3).

Apocalypse: Dragon with the Seven Heads,
by Albrecht Dürer (1497–1498)

Later, an angel informed John that this beast "once was, and now is not" and that he "is an eighth king. He belongs to the seven and is going to his destruction" (Revelation 17:11). According to this same angel,

the seven heads are also "seven mountains" (17:9). The city of Rome was widely known as "the city of seven hills." During the reign of Emperor Domitian, the seven hills were celebrated in a festival known as *Septimontium.*

Ancient Roman coin, called *sestertius*, from Vespasian's reign (69–79 AD). One side shows the image of the Emperor Vespasian. The other side shows the goddess Roma seated on seven hills.

The next beast is a little bit less bizarre—but it still seems like an unlikely candidate for becoming your child's favorite stuffed animal. The second beast brings together the voice of a dragon with the two horns of a lamb (13:11).

So what did these grotesque physical features suggest to the people who first read John's writings? And what could his visions possibly mean for people today?

Regardless of what you think about these horns and heads and oppressive beasts, one truth is certain: ***No matter what political or religious powers may rise against God's people, no hellish power or human scheme ever stands beyond God's sovereign hand.***

Ten horns with crowns	**Future union of ten nations**: According to dispensationalists, the ten horns point forward to ten nations that will unite to form a revived Roman Empire. Many dispensationalists connect these ten nations with the present European Union. The Antichrist will uproot three of these nations and rule them personally (Daniel 7:8).
	The Roman Empire: Some interpreters tie these ten horns to the horns that Daniel saw in one of his visions (Daniel 7:7–8). The ten horns in Daniel's vision could represent ten emperors of the Roman Empire, beginning with Julius Caesar and extending through Vespasian (Galba, Otho, and Vitellius would be the three uprooted kings). Or Daniel's ten horns may be ten rulers of the Syrian kingdom, beginning with Alexander the Great and extending to Antiochus IV Epiphanes. It was Antiochus IV who uprooted Seleucus IV and his two sons to take the kingdom of Syria (see Daniel 7:8). Whether the ten horns in Daniel point to Syria or to Rome, John was using this image to describe the Roman Empire. Significantly, the Roman Empire was organized in ten provinces.
	Rulers that persecute God's people: Others also connect the horns to Daniel's prophecies but in a different way. These interpreters see horns in Daniel and Revelation as symbolic descriptions of rulers in every age who, like Antiochus and the Roman emperors, persecute God's people.
Seven heads	**Past and future kingdoms**: Many dispensationalists interpret the dragon's "seven heads" as a succession of kingdoms: Egypt, Assyria, Babylon, Persia, Greece, Roman Empire, and revived Roman Empire; the eighth king represents the reign of the Antichrist. The Antichrist is the wounded head. During the tribulation, he will be killed or seem to be killed, then he will recover and become the eighth king.
	Past rulers of ancient Roman Empire: Preterists see the fallen kings as the first emperors of the Roman Empire. That would make Nero the sixth king. The eighth king could be Vespasian, the emperor in AD 70 when Jerusalem fell. Vespasian brought new life to the empire that nearly fell apart after Nero's death (Revelation 13:3).
	Kingdoms like Roman Empire that persecute God's people: When all the beastly heads in Daniel 7:4–7 are added together, the total is seven heads. The "seven heads" may symbolize all the kingdoms throughout time that seek to destroy God's people. In John's day, this power was primarily centered in the Roman Empire. That's why John said that the seven heads were also "seven hills," a metaphor for the city of Rome (Revelation 17:9).
Leopard, bear, and lion	Here's how Daniel described the four kingdoms that would precede the coming of the Messiah: "The first was like a lion.... And there before me was a second beast, which looked like a bear.... After that, I looked, and there before me was another beast, one that looked like a leopard" (Daniel 7:4–6).
	This first beast in Revelation brings together all of the beasts described in this prophecy from Daniel.
Two horns	The two horns of the second beast may represent satanic parodies of God's two righteous witnesses and of the horns of the risen Lamb of God (Revelation 5:6; 11:3).
	The two horns could also point back to Daniel's vision of the ram and the goat (Daniel 8:2–4). Daniel saw a ram with two horns. The horns in Daniel's vision symbolized the kingdoms of the Medes and the Persians. This image in Revelation may have reminded readers that, just as those past oppressive powers fell, this beast would fall as well.

THE MARK OF THE BEAST

John described a time when people would be compelled "to be marked on the right hand or forehead" (Revelation 13:16). This mark would indicate an individual's allegiance to the Antichrist. Between the Old and New Testaments, some Jews were forced to be branded with the symbol of the god Dionysius; this event may provide part of the background for this text.[143] But what did the mark of the beast imply for people in the first century? And what might the mark mean for people today?

© Bruce Rolff

1. Some Bible teachers understand the mark of the beast to be some sort of physical implant or mark that will be required during the future great tribulation. Without this mark, people will not be able to buy or to sell (Revelation 13:17).

2. Other interpreters point out how, in the Old Testament, God commanded his people to place the memory of their redemption "as a mark on your hand, even bound between your eyes" (Exodus 13:16). The original intent of these words seems to have been to allow God's redemption and God's Word to mold the hearer's thoughts ("bound between your eyes") and actions ("a mark on your hand"). In the same way, a mark "on the right hand or forehead" could imply acting and thinking in accordance with this beast. In John's day, this would have meant worshiping the emperor. Cities such as Pergamum and Thyatira had well-established trade guilds that could prevent persons from conducting business if they refused to participate in the emperor cult; it is quite possible that Christians in other cities experienced similar persecution in their buying and selling (Revelation 13:17).[144]

666

The content of the mark of the beast will be "the name of the beast or the number of his name" and this number is "six hundred and sixty-six" (13:18). But what is the meaning of this beastly number? No one knows for certain, but here are some facts that may help your understanding: In some ancient languages, *letters* also functioned as *numbers*. The first letter of the alphabet might mean "one," while the second would mean "two." The eleventh letter might denote "twenty," the twelfth letter "thirty," and so on. So it was possible to add letters and come up with the number of someone's name. This process was known as *gematria*. One example of gematria can be found in the first-century ruins of Pompeii. There, archaeologists have unearthed a fragment of graffiti that reads, "I love her whose number is 545." Another example can be found in a document known as the Sibylline Oracles, where the number of Jesus' name is calculated as "888."[145] With this background in mind, let's look at the three primary possibilities for the meaning of 666!

1. ***A number that points to absolute evil and idolatry:*** By connecting 666 with the beast—each digit of 666 falling one short of seven, the number that symbolized completeness—John was describing someone or something that would fall short of God's glory in every way. King Solomon's trajectory toward idolatry began after he defied God's law by amassing 666 talents of gold (Deut. 17:17; 1 Kings 10:14–11:13); it could be that John had in mind both threefold imperfection and Solomon's idolatry.

2. ***A name in the future:*** This number could point to a physical mark during the future tribulation that will represent the name of the Antichrist. Some see this mark as something like a tattoo or a bar code that's only visible under certain forms of light. Others anticipate a tiny computer chip or radio-frequency emitter.

EMPEROR NERO

Ruler of the Roman Empire from AD 54–68. Nero was the first emperor to persecute Christians. He murdered his own family, kicked his pregnant wife to death, and allegedly murdered his mother. Apollonius of Tiana had this to say about Nero: "I know not how many heads this beast has, he who is commonly called the tyrant ... but at least you know that wild beasts would not eat their own mothers. Nero has gorged himself on just such a diet."[146] On June 8, AD 68, the Senate declared Nero an enemy of the state. The next day, Nero stabbed himself in the throat and died. After a year of civil war, Emperor Vespasian revived the empire. Later, during Domitian's reign, many believed that Nero was alive and that he was living in Parthia. One imposter almost succeeded in convincing the people that he was Nero. Christians expected that they would be forced to worship the emperor if Nero ever returned.[147]

3. **A name from the past:** Another possibility emphasizes the fact that the Greek name "Nero Caesar" can add up to 666 when written in Hebrew letters. If Nero was who John had in mind, the inspired author may have meant to identify Nero as the beast from the sea. Or he may have been describing Nero as a prototype for this beast. In one of the earliest Greek manuscripts of Revelation, the number of the beast has been written as "616." That's the number of Nero's Latin name when written in Hebrew letters.[148]

Oxyrhynchus Papyri 4499/P115. Papyrus fragment shows the number that this copy of Revelation assigns to the Beast: 616, rather than the usual 666. The number is in the third line of the fragment shown above.

ARMAGEDDON

(from Hebrew, *Har-Megiddon*, Mount Megiddo) The ancient city of Megiddo was located between the Plain of Jezreel and Israel's western coast. Deborah, Gideon, Saul, Ahaziah, and Josiah fought decisive battles near Megiddo—largely because the area around Megiddo was broad and flat, allowing chariots to be used effectively. As a result, the valley of Megiddo became the symbol of a point of decisive conflict. In Revelation, the kings of all the earth gather for war at a place known in Hebrew as "Armageddon" or "Mount Megiddo" (Revelation 16:16). Soon afterward, Babylon falls, and Jesus returns.

1. Some take this to mean that a physical battle will occur near Megiddo near the end of the great tribulation. Nations will gather against the modern nation of Israel. Faced with certain destruction, the Jewish people will repent of their rejection of Jesus, and Jesus will return to establish his millennial kingdom.

2. Others point out that there is no **Mount** Megiddo. The highest hill on the plain of Megiddo is only one hundred feet tall. So perhaps the battle of Armageddon should be seen figuratively, as a symbol of the clash between the righteousness of Jesus and the rebellion of humanity.

BABYLON ON THE BACK OF THE BEAST FROM THE SEA

Swept by the Spirit into the desert, John spies someone straddling the back of the first beast. It is a woman, and she is drunk—but her inebriation does not flow from any typical liquors. Her drink of choice is the blood of the saints. She is wrapped in a harlot's robes, and this inscription is scrawled across her forehead: "Babylon the great, the mother of prostitutes and of the abominations of the land" (Revelation 17:5). She is wealthy, and she spends her wealth on precious stones and pearls, purple silks and exotic spices (18:11–13).

An angel unravels the mystery of this woman's identity. As it turns out, this scene is not about a woman at all. The woman symbolizes a city, "the great city that rules over the kings of the earth" (Revelation 17:18). But this city's rule does not last forever. "In one day her plagues will overtake her: death, mourning, and famine, for mighty is the Lord God who judges her" (18:8).

But what city could this woman possibly be? And when does she fall? Or could it be that she has already fallen? Here are three possibilities for the city symbolized by the woman on the beast:

What city does the harlot symbolize?	When does the city fall?
Jerusalem, judged because of their rejection of Jesus as Messiah	In AD 70, when Titus besieged the city and destroyed the temple. While the defenders of Jerusalem split into three factions (Revelation 16:19), the Roman armies passed easily over the Euphrates River (16:12). During the siege, Roman catapults hurled massive white stones into the city (16:21).
Rome and any regime that, like ancient Rome, exploits and persecutes for the sake of luxury and gain	None of these powers can last forever; they collapse upon themselves (Revelation 17:16–17). When Jesus returns, he will destroy all such powers once and for all.
Babylon, rebuilt in the future along the Euphrates River in Iraq	Near the end of the future seven-year tribulation. Babylon will fall. This fall of Babylon is also described in Isaiah 13–14 and Jeremiah 50–51.

WHO'S IN CONTROL?

Two weeks after the cobra from the Bronx Zoo turned up missing, keepers found the snake in a dark corner of the reptile house. She hadn't harmed anyone and, despite her many social-media updates, she had never even left the building. A few rat-scented wood shavings were sufficient to lure the cobra back into captivity.

When Jesus deals with the "ancient serpent" for the last time, he won't be using wood shavings to lure the devil into the lake of fire. He won't need to. Neither the dragon nor his beasts nor the woman named Babylon stands outside the control of Jesus. Jesus is "King of kings and Lord of lords," and he reigns over them all (Revelation 19:11–16).

Apart from that truth, a study of Satan would be discouraging, perhaps even frightening. But, if Jesus is truly "King of kings and Lord of lords," there is an encouraging assurance in all of this: ***No serpent or beast or other unsavory spiritual enemy can do anything apart from the will of the one who "loved us, and gave himself up for us" (Ephesians 5:2).***

CHAPTER 15 Understanding the Book of Revelation

GOD ACTING IN HISTORY

Both the Old and New Testaments reveal God as Lord over history. Christians of all eras have believed that Jesus will return, but not all Christians have agreed that Revelation is all about the second coming. Whether the visions in Revelation have been, are being, or have yet to be fulfilled is a matter of debate, but calling on Jesus to come quickly is something all Christians can agree upon—"Come, Lord Jesus!" (Revelation 22:20).

Four Views	How Revelation Is Viewed	More About This View
Futurist	Revelation is prophecy primarily about the future end of the world.	In the futurist view, all or nearly all of Revelation is yet to occur. Revelation is a prophecy that describes the end of time and the years leading immediately to the end. Dispensational premillennialists as well as some historic premillennialists interpret Revelation in this way.
Historicist	The book of Revelation is prophecy about church history from the time of John to the end of the world.	Historicists view the events in Revelation as symbolic descriptions of historical events throughout church history. (Some futurists also understand the Seven Churches [Revelation 1–3] in a historic manner, treating each church as descriptive of a particular era of church history.)
Idealist	Revelation is a non-historical and non-prophetic drama about spiritual realities.	Some aspects of this perspective seem to have originated among ancient Alexandrian theologians, who frequently spiritualized and allegorized biblical texts, but this view may have had earlier proponents as well.
Preterist	The book of Revelation is prophecy that was fulfilled primarily in the first century AD.	"Partial Preterism" views most of Revelation as prophecy fulfilled in the first century AD, though final chapters of Revelation describe future events to occur at the end of time. "Full Preterists" contend that the return of Jesus was spiritual and occurred in AD 70. Preterists are typically *amillennialists* or *postmillennialists*, though some historic *premillennialists* could fit in this category.

COMPARING VIEWS ON REVELATION

Revelation	Revelation 1:1 "soon" 1:3 "near" 1:19 "what is" (Compare, 22:6, 7, 12, 20)	Revelation 2:1–3:22 The Seven Churches of Asia Minor	Revelation 4:1–3 God on His Throne
Futurist View	These words refer to the whole of the "last days" or to the quickness with which Jesus will return.	The prophecy begins with the seven churches, which were actual churches in John's day and may also symbolize the types of churches present in the last days.	God gives John a vision from his throne of the events which are to take place "after these things."
Historicist View	The prophecy began to be fulfilled close to the author's lifetime.	The prophecy begins with the seven actual churches in John's day and proceeds through history from there.	God is about to outline his rule over history: the first part of that history is revealed under the vision of the seven seals.
Idealist View	Christ is always at hand, near and quick to save his people.	The book begins with the seven churches, which symbolize tendencies in the church that can occur in every age.	God gives John the heavenly viewpoint of the important truths about his power over all things and his care for the church.
Preterist View	Near, soon, and quickly are taken literally.	The prophecy begins with the seven actual churches of Asia Minor. It then focuses on the land of Israel before AD 70.	God's courtroom in the heavenly temple is the scene. The Judge on his throne is about to hold court.

Revelation 5:1–4	Revelation 6:1–17	Revelation 7:1–8	Revelation 8:1–13
The Scroll	The Seals	The 144,000 (see p. 228–234)	The Trumpets
The scroll could be the title deed to the earth or God's prophetic message in Revelation or God's eternal will and testament.	The seals begin to describe the great tribulation, with each opened seal leading to a greater tragedy upon the earth.	The 144,000 are Jewish Christians in the last days.	The trumpets describe the events of the tribulation in the last days.
The scroll is the coming history of the church as God reveals it and is Lord over it.	The seals are the stages of church history, perhaps describing the church from the late first century AD to the late fourth century.	The 144,000 is a symbolic number that represents the entire church.	The trumpets are the stages of church history, perhaps from about AD 400 until the fifteenth century (or to the present).
The scroll is God's will and testament, revealing his salvation plan for all time.	The seals are about recurring evils throughout history and God's authority over them.	The 144,000 are the true spiritual Israel: the church on earth.	The trumpets are about the cycles of human sin, consequences, and God's salvation.
The scroll is God's bill of divorce against unfaithful Israel or God's eternal will and testament.	The seals describe the Roman war with the Jews which lead to the destruction of Jerusalem (AD 70).	The 144,000 may be the Jewish Christians who escaped the destruction of Jerusalem.	The trumpets represent a vision of the Roman war with the Jews in the first century AD and extend the seals' description in further detail.

COMPARING VIEWS ON REVELATION (continued)

Revelation	Revelation 9:13–19 The Four Angels at the Euphrates	Revelation 10:8–11 The Little Scroll	Revelation 11:1–2 The Temple
Futurist View	The four angels represent the armies of the Orient that will march against Israel in the last days. They will cross the Euphrates as a signal of war.	The little scroll represents the divine plan for the end of the ages, showing that the Word of God is both sweet and bitter to God's prophets and messengers.	The measuring of the temple refers to the nation of Israel and the temple that will be rebuilt in the last days. Israel has been restored but still awaits the rebuilding of her faith. This faith will center on the new temple and will eventually lead some Jews to faith in Christ.
Historicist View	The four angels could represent the four principalities of the Turkish empire. The Turks destroyed the last of the Roman empire in AD 1453.	The little scroll may be the Bible at the time of the Reformation. It was sweet to those starved for God's Word, but bitter to those who wanted to control its information and keep it from common people.	The measuring of the temple, the altar, and those who worship there points to God's evaluation of the church, the doctrine of justification by faith, and what constitutes true membership in the church.
Idealist View	The four angels represent the judgment of God that comes on evil when there is no more restraint, which is represented by the river Euphrates.	The little scroll is the gospel, which must and will be preached to all "peoples, nations, tongues, and kings."	The measuring of the temple and the leaving of the outer court indicates the division that has always been present between true believers and those who are Christians only in name. The trampling of the court signifies the way the unbelieving world corrupts the church, but this will only be for a short while.
Preterist View	The four angels may represent the four legions of Roman soldiers stationed in Syria that Vespasian led against the Jews (around AD 70). The colors mentioned are Roman military colors.	The little scroll is the same divorce bill as in Revelation 5:1–4 but now unsealed and empty of contents, indicating that the judgments against Israel are now occurring.	The measuring of the temple and its rooms, like the eating of the scroll in chapter 10, mirror what happens in Ezekiel 40–47. Both indicate the destruction of the temple and the separation of the faithful (symbolized by the sanctuary) from the unfaithful (symbolized by the court).

Revelation 12:13–17	Revelation 13:18	Revelation 14:14–16	Revelation 15:1–4
The Persecuted Woman	666 (see "666," p. 258–260)	The Son of Man with the Sharp Sickle	The Song of Moses and of the Lamb
The woman is Israel (sun, moon and stars, Genesis 37:9). The Child is Christ (rod of iron, Psalm 2:9). The Dragon is Satan behind the coming Antichrist. As the head of the revived "Roman Empire," the Antichrist will attack Israel.	It is the number of the future Antichrist— someone who will be like Nero back from the dead.	It is a vision of the coming harvest at the end of the age when Christ will separate the wicked for judgment.	The song of salvation from the last-days persecution of the Antichrist and resulting judgment of God. Believers may experience some persecution but they will not have to endure God's wrath.
The woman is the true church under persecution. The "third of the stars" may refer to the division of the Roman Empire under three emperors in AD 313, or it may refer to post-Reformation divisions in Europe.	It may be the number of the word *Lateinos* and so refers to the Latin or Roman Catholic pope/papacy.	It is a vision of the end of the age when Christ will come and gather his own to himself.	The song of final salvation from the slavery of the abuse of religious and political power among many of the popes.
The woman is Israel as the ideal symbol of all the faithful. The Child is Christ and the Dragon is Satan, the great persecutor of the Church in every age. The stars are the angels that fell with Satan at his rebellion. The seven heads and crowns speak of Satan's full political power and authority. The ten horns are military might.	It is the number of imperfection and human evil that leads to idol worship.	It is a vision of the last judgment and the coming of Christ at the end of the age.	The song of salvation that all the redeemed have sung throughout history and will sing anew when Christ comes again.
The woman is faithful Israel that gave birth to Christ (the Child). The Dragon, Satan, persecuted the Messianic church, but she escaped the destruction of Jerusalem by heeding Jesus' words (Luke 21:20–22) and fleeing to the desert hills (the prepared place).	It is the number that the letters in the name "Nero Caesar" add up to. **666**	It is a vision of the coming of Christ to gather and preserve his church from the judgment that was to befall Jerusalem.	The song of salvation from and victory over the ungodly religious and political persecution that Christians suffered in Israel and the Roman world.

COMPARING VIEWS ON REVELATION (continued)

Revelation	Revelation 16:10–11 The Fifth Bowl	Revelation 17: 1–12 The Great Prostitute	Revelation 18:9–24 The Fall of Babylon
Futurist View	The bowl is the coming judgment upon the revived Roman Empire that will happen in the last days.	The prostitute is the symbol of a false religious system, a new world religious order. The religious coalition will have political influence tied to the power of the Beast (Antichrist) who is the head of the alliance (ten horns) of ten nations in Europe in the last days.	The destruction of the coming world religious, political and economic system—under the control of the Antichrist and the False Prophet—will be a crash of unparalleled dimension.
Historicist View	The bowl might be the judgment upon the Roman Pope Pius VI that occurred when the French revolutionary forces stripped the Vatican and took the Pope captive in 1798. The Pope was forced to flee Rome again in 1848. This event was predicted using 1260 days as 1260 years (12:6).	The prostitute could be the corrupt Roman Catholic Church, including false "Protestant" churches that have come out of her. Her political and religious influence is carried by the beastly Roman papacy and Western European culture.	The destruction of Rome (Babylon) will be complete and utterly devastating. The consequences of preaching a false gospel, persecuting true believers and dabbling in power politics will bring her to this end. Many will mourn her loss but it will be final.
Idealist View	The bowl shows what will happen and does happen to those who steadfastly oppose God. The judgments of darkness and sores recall the plagues of Egypt.	The prostitute is all false and corrupt religion that has allied itself with political power in order to dominate. God warns that such religion shall come to an awful end when true faith triumphs.	The destruction of Babylon reveals that God's judgment is complete and final. Whether it is Nineveh, Babylon, Rome or any other economic power that opposes God, it is destined to fail.
Preterist View	The bowl is the judgment that fell upon Rome in AD 69. In that single year, Nero committed suicide, three emperors were deposed, civil war set Roman against Roman, and the temple of Jupiter *Capitoline* was burned to the ground, causing darkness during the day.	The prostitute is Jerusalem. Her political and false religious influence is carried by the Roman Empire (Beast). The seven heads are Rome and the first seven emperors, Nero (the sixth of the emperors) ruling at that time. The ten horns are the ten imperial provinces.	The destruction of Jerusalem (Babylon) is sudden and complete. The misery and the economic disaster is nearly indescribable and a source of great despair. To this day, the temple has never been rebuilt.

Revelation 19:1–10	Revelation 20:1–15	Revelation 21:1–27	Revelation 22:1–21
The Marriage of the Lamb and His Bride	The Millennium	The New Creation	The Salvation and Healing of the Nations
The entire church is the bride of Christ whose marriage is announced and celebrated. This scene refers to events near the end of the world and history.	The millennium is the future, physical reign of Jesus Christ on earth (premillennialism).	The new creation will come when Christ comes again and ushers in the age to come.	It will continue until the great tribulation when the Antichrist will temporarily prevail. Christ in his second coming will triumph and usher in the final salvation of the faithful.
The entire removal of false religion represented by Rome/Babylon will leave the faithful to accomplish the purpose for which Christ came—the evangelization of the rest of the world. All people will be invited to come into relationship (the marriage feast with God).	The millennium is viewed as Christ's present, spiritual reign in the lives of his people (amillennialism).	The new creation will come with Christ at his second coming, yet there is a real sense in which it has already arrived in the believer's heart. Christians live now as citizens of the New Jerusalem.	It is happening now and will finally be completed when Christ returns.
Ancient Jewish weddings may be a helpful metaphor. The prophets announced the wedding. Jesus comes and betroths his bride (church), paying the dowry on the cross. When Jesus comes again, he will offer his bride a wedding feast.	The millennium is viewed as Christ's present, spiritual reign in the lives of his people (amillennialism).	The new creation is something God continually does with each new day. Yet there will come a day when Christ will personally return and make all things new.	It is what God has always been doing in the world—seeking and saving the lost. Christ will bring all things right when he returns.
The entire book has been about faithfulness using the image of marriage: the divorce bill in chapter 5, the imagery of the persecuted woman and the prostitute. The book builds toward the marriage feast of Christ and his church.	In partial preterism, the millennium may be Christ's literal reign on earth (premill) or a spiritual reign (postmill and amill). In full preterism, the millennium refers to Christ's spiritual return and reign, beginning in the first century.	The new creation is now and future. Since the destruction of the old Jerusalem, Christians are building the New Jerusalem wherever the gospel is believed, as well as expecting it in full when Christ returns.	It will continue as the gospel grows and spreads throughout the world. Jesus will finalize and renew all things when he comes.

1 SEVEN MESSAGES TO CHURCHES (REVELATION 1:1–3:22)

INTRODUCTION (1:1–8)
Blessing 1
Vision of Christ

MESSAGES TO THE CHURCHES

1. EPHESUS
Praise: Hard work, perseverance
Criticism: Forgot first love
Exhortation: Repent
Reward: Authority to eat from the tree of life

2. SMYRNA
Praise: You are rich!
Criticism: None
Exhortation: Be faithful
Reward: Not hurt by second death

3. PERGAMUM
Praise: Remain faithful
Criticism: Idolatry and sexual immorality
Exhortation: Repent
Reward: A white stone with a new name

4. THYATIRA
Praise: Deeds, love and faith, and perseverance
Criticism: Idolatry and sexual immorality
Exhortation: "Hold on to what you have until I come"
Reward: The morning star

5. SARDIS
Praise: None
Criticism: "You are dead"
Exhortation: Wake up
Reward: Be dressed in white, never blotted out from the book of life

6. PHILADELPHIA
Praise: Deeds and faithfulness
Criticism: None
Exhortation: Hold on to what you have
Reward: Become a pillar of the temple

7. LAODICEA
Praise: None
Criticism: You are lukewarm
Exhortation: Be earnest and repent
Reward: Will be seated with Christ

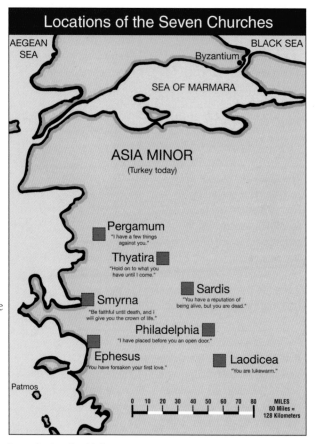

Locations of the Seven Churches

AEGEAN SEA

BLACK SEA

Byzantium

SEA OF MARMARA

ASIA MINOR
(Turkey today)

Pergamum
"I have a few things against you."

Thyatira
"Hold on to what you have until I come."

Sardis
"You have a reputation of being alive, but you are dead."

Smyrna
"Be faithful until death, and I will give you the crown of life."

Philadelphia
"I have placed before you an open door."

Ephesus
"You have forsaken your first love."

Laodicea
"You are lukewarm."

Patmos

0 10 20 30 40 50 60 70 80
MILES
80 Miles = 128 Kilometers

SEVEN SEALS
(REVELATION 4:1–8:5)

Interlude:
Vision of Heaven (4:1–11)
Scroll with Seven Seals and the Lamb (5:1–14)

Opening of Seals (6:1–8:5)
1. First Seal: White Horse—*Conqueror*
2. Second Seal: Red Horse—*No peace*
3. Third Seal: Black Horse—*Famine*
4. Fourth Seal: Pale Horse—*Pestilence*
5. Fifth Seal: Martyrs under the altar
6. Sixth Seal: Earthquake, sun black

Interlude:
144,000 sealed (7:1–8)
The Great Multitude (7:9–17)

7. The Seventh Seal:
It contains seven angels with trumpets (8:1–2)
The angel with golden censer (8:3–5)

SEVEN TRUMPETS
(REVELATION 8:2–11:19)

1. First Trumpet—Hail, fire, blood

2. Second Trumpet—Fiery mountain in sea, 1/3 of sea becomes blood

3. Third Trumpet—star falls on 1/3 of rivers

4. Fourth Trumpet—1/3 of Sun, 1/3 Moon, 1/3 Stars

Interlude: Woe! Woe! Woe! (8:13)

5. Fifth Trumpet—Demon locust from the Abyss

6. Sixth Trumpet—Two-hundred-million demonic riders from the Euphrates

Interlude (10:1–11:14):
The Little Scroll: Promise for the church

7. Seventh Trumpet—"The kingdom of the world has become the kingdom of our Lord..." (11:15)

SEVEN SYMBOLIC HISTORIES (REVELATION 12:1–14:20)

The Woman and the Dragon

SYMBOLIC HISTORIES

1. **HISTORY OF THE DRAGON**
   (12:7–12)
   Defeated
   The "ancient serpent"

2. **HISTORY OF THE WOMAN**
   (12:13–17)
   Persecuted by the dragon
   Defended by God

3. **THE SEA BEAST** (13:1–10)
   Ten horns and seven heads
   Blasphemer
   Has power to make war

4. **THE EARTH BEAST** (13:11–18)
   Two horns
   Deceiver
   666—The number of the beast

5. **THE 144,000** (14:1–5)
   Marked with God's name
   Worshippers

6. **THE ANGELIC ANNOUNCERS**
   (14:6–11)
   First angel: "Fear God"
   Second angel: "Fallen! Fallen is
      Babylon the Great"
   Third angel: Warning against
      the mark of the beast

7. **THE HARVEST** (14:14–20)

SEVEN BOWLS (REVELATION 15:1–16:21)

Commissioning of the Seven Angels with the Last Seven Plagues (15:1–8)

The Seven Bowls

1. **First Bowl**—Painful sores

2. **Second Bowl**—Turns sea into blood

3. **Third Bowl**—Turns rivers and springs of water into blood

4. **Fourth Bowl**—Sun burns people with fire

5. **Fifth Bowl**—Plunges kingdom of the beast into darkness

6. **Sixth Bowl**—Dries up the Euphrates; Armageddon

7. **Seventh Bowl**—Judgment against Babylon. "It is done!"

6

SEVEN MESSAGES OF JUDGMENT (REVELATION 17:1–19:10)

Judgment against Babylon

Description of symbolic characters

1. **First angelic message** (17:7–18)
   Explanation of the vision

2. **Second angelic message** (18:1–3)
   Announcement of the fall of Babylon

3. **Third angelic message** (18:4–8)
   Call to God's people; God's judgment on Babylon

4. **The kings of the earth** (18:9–10)
   Lament for the fall of Babylon

5. **The merchants of the earth** (18:11–17)
   Lament for the fall of Babylon

6. **The seafaring people** (18:18–19)
   Lament for the fall of Babylon
   Rejoice for God's judgment (18:20)

7. **Seventh angelic message** (18:21–24)
   Announcement of the final destruction of Babylon

7

SEVEN VISIONS (REVELATION 19:11–22:5)

1. **First Vision** (19:11–16)
   Heaven opens and the white horse rider appears

2. **Second Vision** (19:17–18)
   Angel invites birds to "the great supper of God"

3. **Third Vision** (19:19–21)
   The beast and kings ready for war

4. **Fourth Vision** (20:1–3)
   The thousand years (millennium)

5. **Fifth Vision** (20:4–10)
   Thrones with judges and Satan's doom

6. **Sixth Vision** (20:11–15)
   Judgment of the dead

7. **Seventh Vision** (21:1–22:5)
   A vision of "a new heaven and a new earth."

Epilogue (22:6–21)

Jesus is coming back: "Amen. Come, Lord Jesus."

CHAPTER 16

Kingdom Already, Kingdom Not Yet: Amillennialism

AMILLENNIALISM AND THE END TIMES

On June 5, 1944, Dwight Eisenhower rode to an airfield near the English village of Newbury. There, thousands of Allied paratroopers were preparing to plummet from airplanes above France, several miles behind Nazi lines. Eisenhower wished the troops well and watched their transports lift from the runway. When Eisenhower returned to his vehicle, it was said that his driver saw tears in his eyes. Three-fourths of these men were expected to die in the next twenty-four hours.

Even as he waved his farewell to the transports, Eisenhower carried in his pocket a note that read, "My decision to attack at this time and place was based upon the best information available…. If any blame or fault attaches to the attempt it is mine alone."[149] And indeed, during the first bloody hours of the D-Day invasion, it

seemed to some military strategists that Eisenhower might need to release this admission of failure.

Fifty days later, however, the Allies still held the beaches at Normandy. By summer's end, Nazi commanders found themselves scissored between the Allied Expeditionary Force in France and the Russian army in Eastern Europe.

U.S. Army troops landing at Omaha Beach in June 6, 1944.
The day of the Normandy landing is also known as "D-Day."

In one sense, once the Nazi armies were forced to fight on two fronts instead of only one, the war in Europe was over. The Axis Powers simply could not sustain simultaneous defenses of the east and the west.

Yet, in another sense, the victory remained far from complete! The liberation of Paris, the Battle of the Bulge, and the Berlin Strategic Offensive Operation had yet to occur. Many lives would be lost, and a final triumph would still seem uncertain at times. In the months between the summer of 1944 and VE-Day, victory in Europe was already accomplished and not yet complete.

The turning point of the war had occurred; Adolf Hitler's fall was all but inevitable. And yet, the moment of final surrender was yet to come.[150]

ALREADY AND NOT YET

So what do D-Day and VE-Day have to do with the end of time?

The time between those two days provides a great example of how a victory can be already accomplished but not yet complete! And that's how quite a few Christians from a variety of millennial views see the time between the exaltation of Jesus—his ascension to heaven—and the end of time. **Through the cross and the empty tomb, Jesus has already defeated every power of darkness—but his victory is not yet complete**.

A broad range of believers identify with the idea that the kingdom of God is "already" and "not yet." A significant number of these same persons take an *amillennial* perspective on the end of time.

Unfortunately, the tag "amillennial" isn't quite accurate—the prefix "*a-*" means "not" or "no," suggesting that amillennialists might not believe in a millennium at all.

In fact, amillennialists *do* believe in a very real millennial reign!

> ### VICTORY IN JESUS
>
> According to the book of Hebrews, Jesus, "having offered one sacrifice for sins for all time, sat down at the right hand of God" (Hebrews 10:12), suggesting that his victory is already secure. Yet, the last part of this very same sentence states that Jesus is "waiting … until his enemies are made a footstool for his feet" (Hebrews 10:13). His victory has already been accomplished, but all creation and Jesus himself still await a future day when sin and death are no more (see also Romans 8:19–24).

The difference is simply that they understand the millennial kingdom to be a *present spiritual reality* while other viewpoints treat the millennium as a *future earthly event.*

- The fifth-century church father Augustine of Hippo was an amillennialist, although some aspects of his thinking were also similar to postmillennialism.

- The same goes for the sixteenth-century reformers Martin Luther and John Calvin.

- More recently, students of Scripture ranging from J.I. Packer and Jay Adams to Herschel Hobbs, Hank Hanegraaff, and Michael Horton have embraced amillennialism.

All these amillennialists and many more throughout the church's history recognize the Bible as the final authority for their beliefs, and they have concluded that the story-line of Scripture fits best with amillennialism. With that in mind, let's take a closer look at amillennialism.

> **AMILLENNIALISM**
>
> (a- ["no"] + -mille- ["thousand"] + -annum ["year"])
>
> Eschatological perspective that does not expect a future thousand-year reign of Jesus on earth. According to amillennialists, the millennium is the present spiritual reign of Jesus with his people. This reign began when the risen Lord Jesus ascended to be exalted at his Father's side (Acts 2:33)—or perhaps when the Spirit descended on God's people during the feast of Pentecost (Acts 1:4-5; 2:1-21)—and will continue until Jesus physically returns to earth.

How much is *already* accomplished?	• Through the death and resurrection of Jesus, God has already triumphed over the curse of sin and inaugurated his eternal kingdom. Jesus defeated Satan through the cross and empty tomb.
	• According to amillennialists, ever since Jesus conquered sin and ascended to his Father, the millennial kingdom has been present in God's reign among his people.
	• The millennial kingdom of Jesus is not something that will happen in the future; the millennial kingdom is happening right now.
How much has *not yet* been fulfilled?	• At the same time, God's kingdom is not yet fully realized right now. Times of tribulation will still transpire on the earth until Jesus returns.
	• According to amillennialists, the Great Tribulation is not an event that will happen in the future.
	• The Great Tribulation happens throughout human history, whenever persecutions afflict God's people and tragedies strike God's world.
	• Even during times of tribulation, the millennial kingdom endures, particularly in God's present rule alongside the saints who already reign with him in glory.

REVELATION BY THE NUMBERS

"But wait!" someone is saying right now. "How can the millennium be a present spiritual reality that began when Jesus ascended? According to Revelation, doesn't the millennium last *one thousand years*? If Revelation says that the millennium lasts one thousand years, the millennium can't possibly stretch from the time of Jesus to the end of time. That's been almost *two thousand* years already!"

And indeed, the author of Revelation *did* describe a divine reign that lasts for one thousand years. According to John, "the souls of those who had been beheaded because of their testimony about Jesus and because of the word of God ... came to life and reigned with Christ a thousand years" (Revelation 20:4).

If almost two millennia have already passed since the resurrection of Jesus, how can the "thousand years" possibly refer to the reign of Jesus with his saints from his heavenly enthronement until his return? Are amillennialists mathematically challenged? Or do they simply not take numbers seriously?

In fact, amillennialists take biblical numbers very seriously, and they are every bit as adept at math as anyone else!

So how can an amillennialist fit two thousand years or more into the "thousand years" of Revelation 20?

It's because amillennialists see these numbers as symbols, not statistics.

© Jiri Moucka

According to amillennialists, the "thousand years" was never meant to describe a specific time span in the first place. Instead, the phrase "thousand years" symbolizes the greatness and the glorious magnitude of the Messiah's present reign in the heavens.

Like other apocalyptic authors of the first century AD and earlier, John used numbers to symbolize important concepts or ideas. And this didn't just happen when he scratched "a thousand years" on a piece of papyrus somewhere on the island of Patmos! The forty-two months of tribulation, the 144,000 sealed sons of Israel, the twelve thousand stadia span of the heavenly city, walls that are 144 cubits thick—all of these numbers in Revelation are symbols, and all of them point together toward deeper and more profound meanings than any mere numeric measurements could ever convey.

What could the numbers mean?

Number	Possible meaning	Possible examples
1,000	Great length or magnitude	Ezekiel 47:3–5; Revelation 20:1–7
42	Cleansing through tribulation	Forty-two encampments in the wilderness in Numbers 33:5–29; forty-two months in Luke 4:25; James 5:17; Revelation 11:2; 13:5
12	The people of God	Ezekiel 47:13; Revelation 12:1; 21:12–21
10	Something significant or extreme but limited	Daniel 7:7, 20–24; Revelation 2:10
7	Completeness	Ezekiel 39:9, 12, 14; Daniel 4:23; Revelation 5:6
6	Incompleteness	Revelation 13:18; perhaps Daniel 3:1

	What happens between the cross and the end of time according to amillennialism?	What Scriptures might fit with this understanding of God's plan?
Resurrection and ascension	Through the cross and empty tomb, Jesus overthrew the devil. His Father has exalted him and given him a kingdom.	John 12:30–33; Acts 5:31; Philippians 2:9; Colossians 1:13; Revelation 20:2
Reign YOU ARE HERE	Right now, Jesus is reigning with his saints in a heavenly millennial kingdom.	Ephesians 2:6; Revelation 20:3–6
Rapture and return	At the end of time, Satan will be allowed for a short time to deceive the nations again. Jesus will call every Christian—living or dead—to meet him in the clouds; then, Jesus will reveal himself on the earth, destroying every devilish resistance to his reign. All the world will see that the devil has been defeated. Jesus will judge humanity and consign to eternal torment anyone who has not already confessed Jesus as Lord.	1 Thessalonians 4:16–17; 2 Thessalonians 1:7-10; Revelation 20:7–15
Arrival of the heavenly city	After the final judgment, God will recreate the heavens and the earth; his holy city will descend from the heavens to the earth.	Isaiah 65:17; 66:22; Revelation 21:1–8

SEVEN FACETS OF A SINGLE TRUTH

So what else besides symbolic numbers makes amillennialism unique? Persons working from other millennial viewpoints sometimes treat Revelation as prophecies for the future that will occur in *the same chronological order* that they appear in the book of Revelation. Many prominent amillennialists, however, suggest that John wrote the book of Revelation in *progressive parallelisms*.[151] Progressive parallelism means that an author

> **PROGRESSIVE PARALLELISM**
>
> Literary pattern in which an author describes an event or series of events, then moves backward and retells some of these events before moving forward. A clear example of this pattern, also known as recapitulation, can be found in Genesis 1:1–2:25.

describes a series of events and then skips backward to retell some of these events again before moving forward. If God *did* guide John to write Revelation in progressive parallelisms, here's one way that the book might have been structured:

- John symbolically told and retold one inspired truth—that God will judge evil and vindicate those who trust Jesus—seven times in seven ways in seven different sections.

- John marked the end of each parallel section by mentioning eternal bliss or divine judgment.

- Each of these seven sections reveals a separate facet of one single glorious truth: Jesus has already broken the power of sin and every satanic scheme. One day, Jesus will return to earth and defeat every remnant of sin and death.

- The tribulations and judgments described in each section will *not* occur consecutively near the end of time; they are happening simultaneously throughout human history.

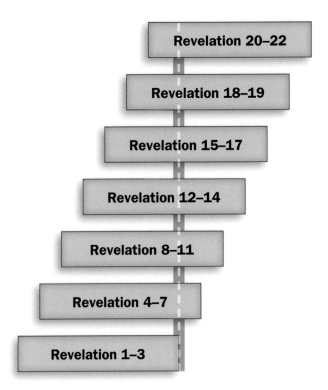

The last days

The reign of Christ from heaven that began at the time of his death, burial, resurrection, and ascension

The last day

The end of time, when the present created order gives way to new creation and Christ returns in glory

Many amillennialists maintain that these seven parallel sections are *progressive*. What that means is that each section moves forward a little further toward the end of time than the one before. The second section speaks more clearly about the end than the first, and the third section inches closer to the end than the second, and so on, until the seventh section clearly reveals God's final triumph.

Such parallelisms occur in other ancient texts too—and not just in apocalyptic texts like Revelation! In the book of Genesis, for example, the initial account of creation ends with God resting on the seventh day (Genesis 2:1–3). Then, in Genesis 2:4-25, the author of Genesis moved **backward** to the sixth day and retold the creation of humanity in more detail before moving *forward* to the temptation of humanity in Genesis 3. That's a clear biblical example of progressive parallelism.

Amillennialists suggest that God unveiled the visions of Revelation in a similar fashion. In each section of Revelation, John presented divinely-inspired depictions of tribulation and triumph. Then John backed up, retold the same truths in more detail, and moved forward—until finally, in the seventh section, John revealed the glorious end of all time, when God's final victory becomes clear and complete. In that day, God will turn the D-Day of Christ's crucifixion into a day of final victory, and the *already* will overwhelm every fragment of the *not yet*.

LIVING IN THE KINGDOM

Satan is already bound, and the saints are already reigning!

That's how amillennialists see what God accomplished through the work of Jesus on earth.

- Because Jesus has been "lifted up" on the cross, Satan has already been "cast down" (John 12:31).
- The powers of darkness have been disarmed (Colossians 2:15).
- The Son of God has gained power over death (1 Corinthians 15:56–57; Revelation 1:18; 9:1; 20:1).

This overthrow of every dark power was what Jesus was describing when he declared to his disciples, "I have been watching Satan falling like a flash from heaven. Look, I've given you authority to trample on snakes and scorpions, authority over every power of the hateful one! None of these powers—not even one—will do damage to you" (Luke 10:18–19).

The Spirit of God unveiled this truth to John by showing him a strong angel with a chain. In John's vision, this mighty messenger from God chained Satan and hurled the ancient dragon into a deep pit (Revelation 20:2). **The pit and the binding are, according to amillennialists, metaphors for the shattering of Satan's power that occurred through the earthly ministry of Jesus**. The Lord himself used a similar metaphor to describe his work when he said, "No one can enter a strong man's house … unless he first binds the strong man" (Matthew 12:29; Mark 3:27).

Satan's power is constrained because Jesus has already guaranteed his defeat.

Satan is not physically chained, of course; Satan is, after all, a spirit, a fallen angel (2 Corinthians 11:14; Revelation 12:4–9). As such, this dragonish adversary is still capable of tempting people in ways that devour their lives (1 Peter 5:8). Yet his power is constrained because Jesus has already accomplished his defeat.

So how can it be said from an amillennial perspective that Satan does not "deceive the nations any longer"? (Revelation 20:3). Through the proclamation of the gospel to non-Jews, the message of God's truth has moved beyond Israel to include "the nations" (Matthew 28:19–20; Acts 10:34–43). Since the gospel is now available to Gentiles, Satan's power over the nations is being broken; he no longer dominates the nations in the same way that he did when God's Word remained the domain of Israel.

> **GENTILE**
>
> (from Latin *gentilis*, "tribe")
>
> Anyone who is not Jewish. Also *goyim* (Hebrew, "nations") or *ethne* (Greek, "nations").

IF SATAN IS BOUND AND THE SAINTS ARE REIGNING, WHY IS LIFE SO HARD SOMETIMES?

One practical problem for amillennialism is the fact that our lives don't always feel as if the millennial kingdom is present right now. When you're singing God's praises and life is proceeding according to your plans, it's easy to imagine that Satan is bound and that Jesus is reigning alongside his saints.

- But what about the moments when you lose sight of the gospel and choose sin instead of goodness and grace?

- How about the days when there's a darkness in your soul that you just can't seem to shake?

- What about the time when you found yourself standing at the foot of a casket that was far too small? Or when you waited in the hospital with a friend who wasn't ready to die? Or when you finally admitted to yourself after all these years that your child has turned from God?

- And what about the persecution of Christians, the exploitation of children, human trafficking and hunger and sickness and death that are distorting God's good creation even as you read these words about his kingdom?

From the perspective of amillennialism, the presence of the kingdom among God's people does not preclude the presence of pain and sorrow on earth.

- How can Jesus possibly be reigning in his millennial kingdom when there is so much sin and darkness all around us?

Here's how: Even as Jesus reigns in the heavens, there is tribulation on the earth. The good and the bad will grow alongside one another until the end of time (Matthew 13:24–30, 36–43).

From the perspective of amillennialism, the presence of the kingdom among God's people does not preclude the presence of pain and sorrow on earth. Alongside the growth and development of the kingdom of God, a kingdom of darkness is present as well. Put another way, the "already" and the "not yet" are happening at the same time. Jesus is reigning with his saints in the heavens even as tribulation is unfolding on the earth.

Satan's power is restrained

Millennium

The Church Age

Tribulation

ETERNITY

Second Coming of Christ & Final Judgment

© Laurin Rinder

285

SEALS, TRUMPETS, AND BOWLS

The book of Revelation includes a series of seven seals breaking, followed by seven trumpets resounding, followed by seven bowls pouring—and then, in place of the partridge in a pear tree, you have the end of the world.

Each of these events unleashes divinely-ordained calamities on the earth. The seventh seal leads to seven trumpets, and the seventh trumpet releases the seven bowls. According to amillennialists, these tragedies are not limited to the end of time, and they don't necessarily occur in chronological sequence. The calamities that begin with the seven seals happen throughout history, beginning in the first century AD.

- **Conflict and war (Revelation 6:1–4, 7–8; 9:1–19; 16:12)**: In the AD 90s, both Messianic and non-Messianic Jews were still reeling from the ghastly days in AD 70 when the Roman army burned Jerusalem, slaughtering and enslaving its citizens. The army that follows the fifth trumpet may suggest that demonic powers stand behind some conflicts (Revelation 9:1–19).

- **Famine (Revelation 6:5–8)**: It's possible that John's first readers remembered the widespread starvation that followed a catastrophic failure of the grain harvest in AD 92. This could also refer to the shortages of food that followed the destruction of Jerusalem in AD 70.

- **Persecution (Revelation 6:9–11)**: This was another close experience for the first readers of Revelation, since both Domitian and Nero bullied Christians for their refusal to worship the emperor.

- **Natural disasters, darkness, and disease (Revelation 6:12–17; 8:7–12; 16:1–11)**: These metaphors may call to mind the great earthquakes that wracked the Roman Empire in AD 60 as well as the eruption of Mount Vesuvius in AD 79. Such events did not end in the New Testament era. Still today, war, famine, persecution, and natural disasters afflict our world. The sixth trumpet (Revelation 6:12–17) might also point to the fall of human kingdoms and empires; in the Old Testament, descriptions of shattered mountains, blackened skies, and falling stars symbolized God's judgment on nations (Isaiah 13:10–19; 34:3–5; Ezekiel 32:2–18; Jeremiah 4:23–24).

AMILLENNIALISM AND THE GREAT TRIBULATION

How, then, do amillennialists view the time of "great tribulation" described in Revelation? (Revelation 7:14).

The book of Revelation twice identifies a time of tribulation that lasts "forty-two months" (Revelation 11:2–3; 13:5). Some interpreters of Revelation understand these two references to "forty-two months" as two separate times of tribulation that will occur immediately after each other; this would result in a tome of tribulation that lasts exactly seven years.

Amillennialists disagree with this reading of Revelation.

© Michał Marcol

Amillennialists are more likely to see the "forty-two months" of the great tribulation as a symbol that draws from the forty-two encampments of Israel in the wilderness (Numbers 33:5–29) and perhaps from the forty-two months of drought during the ministry of Elijah (Luke 4:25; James 5:17). Through forty-two wilderness encampments, Israel was purified; throughout forty-two months of drought, Elijah called people to repent. Likewise, through times of tribulation, the church is continually cleansed, and non-believers are called to turn from their sin.

And so, "forty-two months" are an important symbol—but, because these months are metaphorical, they should not be expected to last exactly 1,260 days. Instead, these months symbolize the time of tribulation that began with the Messiah's victory over Satan through the cross and empty tomb (Revelation 12:5–8). This tribulation will continue until the end of time. The fact that these events originate in God's will (Revelation 5:1) and culminate in God's victory (19:1–20:15) stands as a glorious reminder that, "for those who love God, all things work together for good" (Romans 8:28).

> Amillennialism emphasizes the present reality of the millennial kingdom and the victory of Jesus through his life, death, and resurrection.

From the perspective of amillennialism, the forty-two months of the Great Tribulation are happening at the same time as the thousand years of the millennial kingdom. The millennium is the reign of Jesus in the heavens. The

great tribulation symbolizes sufferings and sorrow that have occurred and will continue to occur throughout the time between the triumph of Jesus and his glorious return. The great tribulation is not only an event that *will happen* someday *but also an event* that *has happened* and *is happening right now.*

© Suzanne Tucker

WHAT HAPPENS BETWEEN NOW AND THE END OF TIME?

Whenever Christians—including martyrs—die (Revelation 20:4), they experience "the first resurrection." Their spirits enter God's presence to reign with him as "priests of God and of Christ … for a thousand years" (Revelation 20:6; see 2 Corinthians 5:8). This "thousand years" represents the entire time until the return of Jesus. So, even though Jesus has *not yet* returned to earth, his millennial kingdom is *already* real and present in the heavens. Many amillennialists also see the millennial kingdom as present among God's people on earth here and now (Luke 17:20–21).

If amillennialism is correct, the next item on God's eschatological agenda is the moment when Jesus returns:

1. To resurrect and to judge all humanity ("the second resurrection"),
2. To reveal to the world his triumph over Satan ("he must be released for a little while"),
3. To relegate Satan to eternal torment ("the lake of fire," 20:10), and
4. To recreate his world ("a new heaven and a new earth," 21:1).

Then, faith will become sight, time will dissolve into eternity, and every tribulation will be swept away.

BELIEVING IN THE "ALREADY," LIVING IN THE "NOT YET"

© Brett Charlton

Once the Allied troops that landed in northern France on D-Day held the beaches near Normandy, there were still many battles to be fought. Yet, in one sense, VE-Day—the day of victory in Europe—became only a matter of time.

You may not accept amillennialism as the best view of the end times—and that's okay! Even if you find yourself embracing some other viewpoint, amillennialism reminds Christians of an important theme in Scripture: ***Jesus has already won***. To be sure, there are still trials and struggles and tribulations. Yet—through his perfect life, sacrificial death, and glorious resurrection—Jesus the Messiah has shattered Satan's power and won a kingdom for God's glory. Final victory is only a matter of time.

AUGUSTINE

The young man staggered through the park, a dismal and restless void gnawing at his innermost self. He dropped his book on a bench and stumbled on. "Lord," he sobbed, "how long? How long?" Suddenly, he heard a child singing, "Pick up, read! Pick up, read!" He rushed back to the bench. When he opened his book, one passage seized his eyes: "Let us walk properly, as in the day, not in revelry and drunkenness … Put on the Lord Jesus Christ, and make no provisions for the flesh" (Romans 13:13–14). "Instantly," the young man later wrote, "light … entered my heart." The man's name? Augustine.

Longing to grow closer to his newfound Savior, Augustine fled to the desert. His retreat was short-lived. When he visited a church at Hippo, the congregation ordained him as an elder. (No, no, no, this wasn't a church in a zoo; Hippo was a city in North Africa.) Six years later, Augustine became the overseer of Hippo.

In Hippo, Augustine became one of the most influential theologians in the history of Christianity. As a new believer, Augustine embraced "Millennnarianism"—the expectation of a future, earthly millennium that Christians today refer to as "premillennialism." Later, Augustine became convinced that amillennialism represented a more faithful reading of the biblical text. Here is what Augustine had to say about amillennialism and premillennialism:

> "John … spoke about two resurrections in the book which is called Revelation. Yet he spoke in such a way that some Christians do not understand the first of the two; these Christians contort the passage into ridiculous fantasies…. Some, on the basis of this passage, have suspected that the first resurrection is future and bodily…. This opinion would not be so objectionable, if it were believed that the joys of the saints in that time of rest would be spiritual and content with the presence of God. I myself, too, once held this opinion! But here is what they say: Those who rise again will enjoy leisure in intemperate fleshly banquets…. Such claims can be believed only by those that are fleshly…. Those who are spiritual call these persons … 'Millennarians.'"

> "The angel … 'laid hold … on the dragon, that old serpent, which is called the devil and Satan, and bound him a thousand years.' This is to say: the angel bridled and restrained Satan's power so that he could not seduce and possess those who were to be redeemed. … [John] used the thousand years as an equivalent for the whole duration of this age, employing the number of perfection to mark the fullness of time. For a thousand is the cube of ten."[152]

Augustine in Contemplation, by S. Botticelli (c. 1480)

CHAPTER 17 Building a Better World: Postmillennialism

Have you ever found yourself in awe at the power of the gospel?

- Perhaps it was in a worship service where a friend unexpectedly trusted in Jesus.
- Maybe it was in a small group where you watched as the gospel shattered the stranglehold of addiction in someone's life.
- Perhaps it was in your own life when you saw how the cross of Jesus calls you to trade your bitterness for God's forgiveness.

Whatever the setting, what you witnessed was the life-transforming power of the good news of Jesus. You caught a glimpse of good news that is powerful beyond all human imagination. According to the apostle Paul, the gospel is the "power of God" that restores wholeness in the lives of those who trust Jesus (Romans 1:16). This power-filled good news is not only how God rescues people from future condemnation but also how God grows and changes his people throughout their lives.

© Bassittart

WATCHING FOR THE WORLD TO CHANGE

At its best, postmillennialism is a perspective on the end times that highlights the power of the gospel. The postmillennial position emphasizes the capacity of the gospel to transform not only individuals but also entire communities, cultures, even the world.

According to postmillennialists:

- There will come a time when worldwide acceptance of the gospel ushers in the millennial kingdom.

- Jesus will not be physically present on earth during this millennium. Instead, Jesus will reign spiritually through the power and proclamation of the gospel.

- Nearly everyone throughout the world will trust in Jesus during this time. At some point after the vast majority of Gentiles turn to Jesus, the Jewish people in particular will recognize Jesus as their long-awaited Messiah (Romans 11:13–25).

> "Postmillennialism expects that eventually the vast majority of people will be saved. Increasing gospel success will gradually produce a time in history prior to Christ's return in which faith, righteousness, peace, and prosperity will prevail in the affairs of men and of nations. Jews and Gentiles will be converted leading to the 'reconciliation of the world' (Romans 11:15). After an extensive era of such conditions the Lord will return visibly, bodily, and gloriously, to end history with the general resurrection and the final judgment after which the eternal order follows."[153]
>
> Kenneth Gentry

- Entire countries and civilizations will change as citizens and leaders alike embrace the good news of Jesus. Satan will be restrained, war will give way to peace, and the saints of God will rule the nations (Revelation 20:2–6).

- According to postmillennialists, the "first resurrection" in Revelation 20:5 is not a physical restoration from the dead; it is the spiritual regeneration that occurs in the life of every follower of Jesus (Ephesians 2:6).

- Postmillennialists are, with few exceptions, covenantalists.

From a postmillennial perspective, the church has superseded ethnic Israel as the recipient of God's covenant blessings (Matthew 8:10–12; 21:19, 43; Luke 20:9–16; Galatians 6:16). God will fulfill the Old Testament promises of universal peace and triumph through the growth of his church. Jesus himself declared that the kingdom was like a seed growing into a tree or like yeast permeating dough (Matthew 13:31–33). ***What this suggests to postmillennialists is that the millennial kingdom will emerge slowly and then expand to fill the entire world***. At the end of this glorious time-period, God will allow Satan to deceive the nations for a very brief time (Revelation 20:7–9). In that moment when the Satan-inspired armies of the earth have arrayed themselves against the reign of God, Jesus will return to earth to defeat Satan once and for all (Revelation 20:10–15).

Some postmillennialists understand this glorious time-period still to be in the future. In their perspective, the great tribulation is taking place in the present, or this time may still be future. After the great tribulation, the millennial kingdom will begin to dawn.

> "The Millennium to which the postmillennialist looks forward is ... a golden age of spiritual prosperity. ... It is an indefinitely long period of time, perhaps much longer than a literal one thousand years. The changed character of individuals will be reflected in an uplifted social, economic, political and cultural life of mankind. The world at large will then enjoy a state of righteousness. ... This does not mean that there ever will be a time on this earth when every person will be a Christian, or that all sin will be abolished. But it does mean that evil in all its many forms eventually will be reduced to negligible proportions, that Christian principles will be the rule, not the exception, and that Christ will return to a truly Christianized world."[154]
>
> Loraine Boettner

Other postmillennialists take the millennium to be a present reality. These postmillennialists place the dawning of the millennial kingdom in the first century AD—perhaps around AD 30 at the ascension of Jesus, or in AD 70 with the destruction of the Jewish temple. This perspective expects a continual expansion of the gospel throughout this period, until the spiritual reign of Jesus through the gospel fills the entire earth.

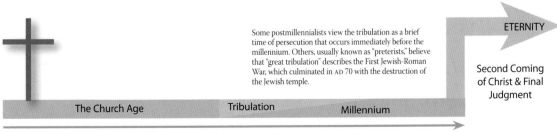

Some postmillennialists view the tribulation as a brief time of persecution that occurs immediately before the millennium. Others, usually known as "preterists," believe that "great tribulation" describes the First Jewish-Roman War, which culminated in AD 70 with the destruction of the Jewish temple.

ETERNITY

Second Coming of Christ & Final Judgment

The Church Age

Tribulation

Millennium

Society gradually improves

WHERE DID POSTMILLENNIALISM COME FROM ANYWAY?

Hints of postmillennialism can be found in a few writings from ancient and medieval times.

- Some beliefs of the third-century theologian Origen of Alexandria and of Augustine of Hippo a century later were similar to postmillennialism.

- A twelfth-century monk named Joachim of Fiore expected an "Age of the Holy Spirit"—a worldwide millennial kingdom wherein Jesus would reign spiritually through the church—to begin around AD 1260. So, postmillennialism isn't a new idea.

Joachim of Fiore

The biblical studies of an eighteenth-century English theologian named Daniel Whitby popularized postmillennialism in more modern times. As he read Scripture, Whitby became convinced that

1. A time would come when the entire world would turn to Jesus.

2. The Jews would return to the Holy Land and Muslim nations would be defeated.

3. All of this would mark the beginning of a thousand years of peace, righteousness, and happiness.

4. Jesus would not, however, return physically until this time came to a close.

THEONOMIST POSTMILLENNIALISM

Belief that, as part of the movement toward a millennial kingdom, the church should work to bring civil powers into submission to Old Testament Law. Some Charismatic Christians embrace a form of theonomist postmillennialism known as "dominion theology." Also known as "reconstructionist postmillennialism."

When the time that a series of revivals broke out in the American colonies in the 1730s and early 1800s, Whitby's postmillennial views caught the attention of a pastor in Northampton, Massachusetts. These revivals would become known among later generations as "the Great Awakening."

And what was the Massachusetts pastor's name? It was Jonathan Edwards.

Jonathan Edwards, engraved by R Babson & J Andrews, 1855.

Jonathan Edwards understood the Great Awakening revivals as God's preparation of his people for the millennial kingdom. "God seems now to be hastily gathering in his elect from all parts of the land," Edwards declared in his famous evangelistic sermon "Sinners in the Hands of an Angry God." Edwards eagerly anticipated the "future promised advancement of the kingdom of Christ" during the millennium as an event unspeakably happy and glorious. ... It is represented as a time of vast increase of knowledge and understanding, ... a time wherein religion and true Christianity shall in every respect be uppermost, ... a time wherein vital piety shall take possession of thrones and palaces, and those that are in most exalted stations shall be eminent in holiness, ... a time of wonderful union ... wherein the nations *shall beat their swords into plowshares* ... and God will *cause, wars to cease to the ends of the earth* (Isaiah 2; 32–33) ... a time wherein all heresies and false doctrines shall be exploded, and the church of God shall not be rent with a variety of jarring opinions, ... a time wherein the whole earth shall be united as one holy city, one heavenly family.[155]

Scriptures that may point to postmillennialism	
Genesis 22:17	God promised Abraham that his seed would "possess the gate" or take control of God's enemies; those who trust in Jesus are the true seed of Abraham (Galatians 3:29). According to many postmillennialists, this text promises that the church will someday have dominion over all the nations of the earth.
Isaiah 2:2–4	Isaiah prophesied that, in the latter days, all nations would come to the mountain of the LORD. According to Hebrews 12:22, the church has become this mountain. During the millennial kingdom, all nations will learn justice and peace through the church.
Matthew 13:31–33	The kingdom will expand slowly and imperceptibly—like a plant or like yeast—until it fills the whole world.
Romans 11:26–27	Before the end of time, all ethnic Israelites will come to faith in Jesus as their Messiah.

LONGING FOR THE "NOONDAY BRIGHT": POSTMILLENNIAL HISTORY AND MISSIONARY HYMNS

In the eighteenth and nineteenth centuries, postmillennialism became a particularly popular perspective among persons who were passionate about cross-cultural evangelism. Proclaiming the gospel to every nation was essential to the dawning of the millennial kingdom, so postmillennialism fit hand-in-hand with enthusiasm for missions. Many of the missionary hymns of the nineteenth century even proclaimed postmillennial eschatology. Perhaps you've sung these postmillennial lyrics at some point without even thinking about the eschatology behind them:

> *"We've a song to be sung to the nations, that shall lift their hearts to the Lord,*
> *a song that shall conquer evil, and shatter the spear and sword,*
> *and shatter the spear and sword.*

> *"For the darkness shall turn to dawning, and the dawning to noonday bright;*
> *and Christ's great kingdom shall come on earth, the kingdom of love and light."*
>
> —H. Ernest Nichol, "We've a Story to Tell to the Nations"

Inspired in part by postmillennial expectations of a time when the millennial kingdom would begin on earth, William Carey launched the Baptist Missionary Society and served as a missionary among the people of India. David Brainerd proclaimed the gospel among Native Americans in New England. John A. Broadus inspired missionary zeal in a young woman named Lottie Moon, who declared the good news of Jesus in northern China.

William Carey

WHAT ABOUT THE GREAT TRIBULATION?

From a postmillennialist perspective, the outlook for the future is bright! As the gospel penetrates the world, every civilization and culture will grow in goodness:

- Once the millennial kingdom is underway, wars will fade into a distant memory.

- Diseases will be destroyed.

- All humanity will live long and prosper.

What about the great tribulation?

Where can this time of suffering and trials fit into such an optimistic view of the end times?

Postmillennialists do understand the great tribulation to be an event that precedes the millennial kingdom—but postmillennialists differ on exactly when and how the tribulation takes place.

Jonathan Edwards, for example, speculated that "1,260 days" (Revelation 12:6) might symbolize 1,260 years from the time when the bishop of the city of Rome began to dominate the church. And so, according to Edwards, the years of the great tribulation "began in the year 606, when the pope was first seated in his chair and was made universal bishop. They will therefore, end about 1866."[156] That's why Edwards, living in the mid-1700s, saw the Great Awakening as the precursor of a postmillennial glory that was soon to come.

Other postmillennialists are *preterists* and take a completely different perspective on the great tribulation. The word "preterist" comes from the Latin *praeteritus* ("past" or "bygone") and suggests that some (or all) of the great tribulation occurred in the first century AD, around the time that the Romans destroyed the Jewish temple in AD 70. Theologian R.C. Sproul is probably the best-known orthodox preterist postmillennialist.

PRETERISM

(From Latin *praeteritus*, "past" or "bygone")

View of New Testament prophecy that understands most events described in apocalyptic texts as predictions that were fulfilled in the first century AD. Many contemporary postmillennialists are also preterists.

RADICAL PRETERISM

Belief that all biblical prophecies were fulfilled in the first century AD and that Jesus will never physically return to earth. Orthodox preterists recognize radical preterism as a heresy that must be rejected. Also known as "hyper-preterism."

POSTMILLENNIALISM AND AMILLENNIALISM: IS THERE REALLY ANY DIFFERENCE?

At this point, some might be thinking, "spiritual millennium? And Jesus returns to earth *after* the millennial kingdom? Isn't that the same as amillennialism?"

If that's what you're thinking, you're partly correct: Postmillennialism *is* similar to amillennialism. In fact, prior to the eighteenth century, Christian theologians didn't distinguish between *amillennialism* and *postmillennialism.* That's why you might see—for example—Martin Luther, John Calvin, and sometimes even Augustine of Hippo identified as amillennialists in one place and as postmillennialists somewhere else!

Here's why the two perspectives are sometimes confused: Both in amillennialism and in postmillennialism, the millennial kingdom is a *spiritual reign* instead of a physical reign. Also, in both perspectives, Jesus returns *at the end of the millennium* rather than at the beginning.

Even with these similarities, however, amillennialism and postmillennialism are far from identical!

Here are two key differences between these two views of the end times:

Resurrection of Christ, by Carl Bloch (1875).

1. According to amillennialists, the millennial kingdom and the great tribulation occur *at the same time.* Even though postmillennialists disagree about the timing of the great tribulation, most agree that the millennium takes place *after the great tribulation.*

2. According to amillennialists, Jesus is reigning *spiritually with his saints in the heavens* whereas postmillennialists believe that Jesus will reign *spiritually through the gospel on earth.*

NEVER UNDERESTIMATE THE POWER OF THE LIGHT

Despite their positive perspective on the future, orthodox postmillennialists don't believe that the spiritual reign of Jesus through the gospel is enough. They, like amillennialists and premillennialists, know that Jesus will someday return to earth. When that time comes, "the dead in Christ will rise first. Then we who are alive, who are left, will be caught up together with them in the clouds to meet the Lord in the air" (1 Thessalonians 4:17–18; see also Acts 1:9–11; 1 Corinthians 15:51–52). According to postmillennialists, this will occur after a long period of earthly peace. In the meantime, if you are a postmillennialist, your task is to proclaim the gospel to all people in preparation for the dawning of a millennial kingdom!

And what if you're *not* a postmillennialist?

Perhaps you've concluded that postmillennialists fall far short in their interpretations of Scripture. If that's the case, don't despair! You can still learn much from their perspective. The postmillennial emphasis on the power of the gospel should remind every Christian to be more passionate about proclaiming how the gospel can transform people's lives.

Regardless of your millennial perspective, it is possible to embrace the belief that the gospel really can change the world. And, by "gospel," I mean far more than the initial statement that helps someone understand how to confess Jesus as the risen Lord—although such statements are certainly important! *What I also mean is the constant awareness that, in every moment of my life, I desperately need what God has provided in the crucified and risen Christ.* The gospel is my constant

> "Postmillennialism is the belief that Christ, with his coming, his atonement, and his continuing regenerative power in those whom he calls, creates in his redeemed people a force for the reconquest of all things. The dominion that Adam first received and then lost by his fall will be restored to redeemed man. God's people will then have a long reign over the entire earth, after which, when all enemies have been put under Christ's feet, the end shall come, and the last enemy, death, will be destroyed."[157]
>
> Rousas John Rushdoony

reminder that any good that I may do is only because of the grace that God has lavished on me in Jesus Christ. Whatever problem I may face in life, the gospel forms the foundation for God's solution; if the gospel is not foundational to the solution, either I don't understand the problem or I don't understand the gospel. That's the true power of the gospel. And, even if you're not a postmillennialist, that's good news.

© Subbotina Anna

CHAPTER 18 Rapture Ready? Dispensational Premillennialism

Chances are, you're already familiar with dispensational premillennialism—even if you've never heard the phrase until you picked up this book!

- Have you ever read a novel with the title *Left Behind* embossed on the cover?

- Or how about one of the bestselling books of the twentieth century, *The Late, Great Planet Earth*?

- Maybe you've glanced through the *Scofield Reference Bible* or *Ryrie Study Bible* at some point.

- Perhaps you've even watched a movie with a title like *A Thief in the Night* or *Prodigal Planet*.

> **DISPENSATIONAL PREMILLENNIALISM**
>
> The belief that God will "rapture" Christians from the world before the earth endures God's wrath during the tribulation; Jesus will return to earth after the tribulation, before ("pre-") the millennium described in Revelation 20.

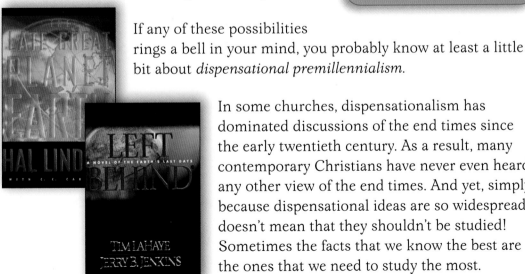

If any of these possibilities rings a bell in your mind, you probably know at least a little bit about *dispensational premillennialism.*

In some churches, dispensationalism has dominated discussions of the end times since the early twentieth century. As a result, many contemporary Christians have never even heard any other view of the end times. And yet, simply because dispensational ideas are so widespread doesn't mean that they shouldn't be studied! Sometimes the facts that we know the best are the ones that we need to study the most.

With that in mind, let's take a look at what will transpire in the end times from the perspective of dispensational premillennialism.

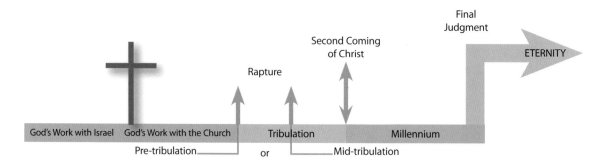

WHAT IS "THE RAPTURE"?

Someday, Jesus will return and his people will be caught up to meet him in the air.

On this point, everyone who trusts the teachings of Scripture finds common ground. This is precisely what the apostle Paul predicted in his letter to the Thessalonians: "For the Lord himself will come down from heaven, with a loud command, with the voice of the archangel and with the trumpet call of God, and the dead in Christ will rise first. After that, we who are still alive and are left will be caught up together with them in the clouds to meet the Lord in the air. And so we will be with the Lord forever" (1 Thessalonians 4:16–17).

This event is known as "the rapture."

Mural from Voroneţ Monastery, Romania (1488)

The word "rapture" does not appear in most English translations of the New Testament. Still, "rapture" is a thoroughly biblical term. In Latin translations of 1 Thessalonians 4:17, the term rendered "caught up" or "taken up" in English versions is the verb *rapiemur*, from the noun *raptus*. The word "rapture" simply comes from Paul's own words in the Latin Bible and means "being caught up."

RAPTURE

(from Latin *raptus*, "catching up")

The meeting of Jesus and his people in the air, described in 1 Thessalonians 4:13–18.

- Most dispensational premillennialists understand the rapture as an event that will occur *before* the Tribulation.
- A few dispensationalists treat the rapture as an event that happens *during* the Tribulation, either halfway through the Tribulation or immediately before the final outpouring of God's wrath.
- Dispensational premillennialists understand the rapture of the church and the return of Jesus to earth *to occur at different times.*
- Other views of the end times see that the rapture and return *happen at the same time.*

Even if you disagree with the dispensationalist view of the end times, there's no reason to avoid using the word "rapture." It's a biblical term that expresses a biblical idea.

So, if every view of the end times agrees that a rapture is coming, what's so different about dispensationalism? Here's the key difference when it comes to the rapture of the church: **Dispensational premillennialists expect the return of Jesus to occur *some time after* the rapture of the church; all other views of the end times expect Jesus to make his appearance on planet earth *immediately after* the rapture.**

Every view of the end times agrees that the rapture of the church and the return of Jesus are distinguishable events. After all, the apostle Paul himself distinguished them in his letter to Titus: Paul described the Christian life as a life of "waiting for our **blessed hope** and for **the appearing of the glory** of our great God and Savior Jesus Christ" (Titus 2:13).

- "Our blessed hope" is the confident expectation that Jesus will catch up every believer—living and dead—and transform their bodies at the rapture.
- "The appearing of the glory" points to the moment when Jesus returns to earth and reveals his royal splendor to all humanity.

© imagedepotpro

So, the question isn't whether these two events are distinguishable. The question is how much time separates the "blessed hope" of the rapture from the "appearing of the glory" when Jesus returns to earth.

- Amillennialists, postmillennialists, and historical premillennialists see that the rapture and the return *happen immediately after one another.*

- Dispensational premillennialists take the "blessed hope" and the "appearing of the glory" to *occur at different times.* According to most dispensationalists, seven years or more may separate the rapture of the church from the return of Jesus.

THREE VIEWS OF RAPTURE AND RETURN

Dispensational Premillennialism	Amillennialism and Postmillennialism	Historical Premillennialism
The rapture of the church and the return of Jesus to earth occur at different times. They are separated by 7 years or more.	The rapture of the church and the return of Jesus to earth happen together. This event will occur at the end of the millennium.	The rapture of the church and the return of Jesus to earth happen together. This event will occur immediately before the millennium.
• The return of Jesus to earth will occur some time after the rapture of the church. • Most dispensationalists place the rapture before the tribulation and the return at the end of the tribulation, immediately before the millennium. • The church will be caught up to meet Jesus (1 Thessalonians 4:13–18; Revelation 4:1–2); the church will return to earth after the tribulation as part of the Messiah's royal retinue (Revelation 19:14).	• The return of Jesus to earth will occur immediately after the rapture of the church. • The rapture will occur at the end of the millennium. • The church will be caught up to meet Jesus (1 Thessalonians 4:13–18; Revelation 19:7–9) and will then immediately return to earth as part of the Messiah's royal retinue (Revelation 19:14).	• The return of Jesus to earth will occur immediately after the rapture of the church. • The rapture will occur after the tribulation and before the millennium. • The church will be caught up to meet Jesus (1 Thessalonians 4:13–18; Revelation 19:7–9) and will then immediately return to earth as part of the Messiah's royal retinue (Revelation 19:14).

RAPTURE AND RETURN IN DISPENSATIONAL PREMILLENNIALISM

RAPTURE OF THE CHURCH	JESUS' RETURN TO EARTH
The rapture will occur at an unexpected time (1 Thessalonians 5:2; Matthew 24:44).	Jesus will return to earth after the seven-year tribulation (Matthew 24:29).
Jesus will return for his church (1 Thessalonians 4:13–18).	Jesus will return with his church (Revelation 19:14).
Believers will be taken into God's presence (John 14:3).	Believers will come to earth (Matthew 24:30).
Believers will experience the rapture (1 Corinthians 15:52).	Every eye will see Jesus as the returning king (Matthew 24:30; Revelation 1:7; 19:11–16).
No battle with Satan is mentioned in connection with the rapture.	Satan is bound (Revelation 20:1–3).
No judgment of the earth is mentioned in connection with the rapture.	The earth is judged (Revelation 20:4–5).
The rapture is a mystery (1 Corinthians 15:51).	The return of Jesus was foretold in the Old Testament (Daniel 12:1–3; Zechariah 12:10; 14:4).

TWO PURPOSES, TWO PEOPLES

The separation of the rapture of the church from the glorious return isn't the only distinguishing mark of dispensational premillennialism. In fact, this division of the rapture from the return is actually the result of a much deeper distinction.

The most important difference between dispensational premillennialism and other viewpoints has to do with how dispensationalists separate *God's work with Israel* from *God's work with the church.*

Of course, every view of the end times recognizes *some* distinction between the nation of Israel and the church. But other viewpoints treat God's work with the nation of Israel as:

1. A **picture** of what God would do through Jesus or
2. A **preparation** for the fulfillment of God's promises through the church.

According to dispensational premillennialism, God has always had **two purposes with two distinct peoples**: the church and the nation of Israel.

Lewis Sperry Chafer put it this way: "The dispensationalist believes that throughout the ages God is pursuing two distinct purposes: one related to the earth with earthly people and earthly objectives involved, which is Judaism; while the other is related to heaven with heavenly people and heavenly objectives involved, which is Christianity."[158]

Early dispensationalists separated the rapture from the return because they believed that God had to remove his heavenly people from the world before he could resume his work with his earthly people.

© Mikhail Levit

	The Nation of Israel	The Church
Dispensationalism	• God has purposed to work with two different groups of people—Israel and the church—in different ways during different "dispensations." • It is through the modern nation of Israel that God will fulfill his promises of land and blessings to the patriarchs and to the Jewish people.	• The church is a spiritual work separate from God's earthly work with the political nation of Israel. • Through this spiritual work, God is bringing Jews and Gentiles into relationship with himself through Jesus. • During the tribulation, God will remove the church from the world and resume his work with the nation of Israel.
Covenantalism	• God has always had one plan and one people. • All God's work with the nation of Israel was preparatory for his revelation of himself through Jesus and for his work through the church. • Many persons with a covenantal perspective expect that a great spiritual awakening will bring many Jewish persons to faith in Jesus as their Messiah before the end of time.	• Through the church, God is fulfilling the promises that he made to the patriarchs and to the people of Israel. • In the Old Testament and the New, God has had one covenant of grace with every person who trusts Jesus as the Messiah.
New covenantalism	• God has always had one plan that he has put in place through multiple covenants. • God's work with Israel was a temporary picture of what he had already purposed to do through Jesus in the new covenant. • Many persons with a new covenantal perspective expect that a great spiritual awakening will bring many Jewish persons to faith in Jesus as their Messiah before the end of time.	• God will fulfill his promises to the patriarchs and to Israel through the one seed of Abraham, Jesus the Messiah. • In the Old Testament and the New, God's purpose has always been to redeem every person who would trust in the Messiah.

DEFINING "DISPENSATIONAL"

The word "premillennial" is easy to define. The word points to the expectation that Jesus will return to earth before (*pre-*) the millennial kingdom. The word "dispensational" is a bit more difficult. "Dispensation" translates a Greek term that can also be rendered "stewardship" or "administration."

Paul used forms of this word in his letters to the Christians in Ephesus and Colossae: Paul described a present dispensation (Ephesians 3:2, 6) and Paul pointed forward to a future dispensation (Ephesians 1:10).

Dispensationalists see several distinct dispensations in God's master plan. In each dispensation, God governs the world differently and places different responsibilities on humanity.

But what exactly is a "dispensation"?

- Lewis Sperry Chafer wrote that a dispensation is a *period which is identified by its relation to some particular purpose of God—a purpose accomplished within that period.*[159]
- C.I. Scofield, in the notes for his study Bible, defined a dispensation as *a period of time during which man is tested in respect [to] obedience to some specific revelation of the will of God.*[160]
- According to dispensational theologian Charles Ryrie, a dispensation is *a distinguishable economy in the outworking of God's purpose.*[161]
- Here's another definition of "dispensation"—one that gets to the central point in a simpler way: *A dispensation describes the unique expectations and purposes that God has for a particular group of people during a divinely designated period of time.*

HOW MANY DISPENSATIONS?

So how many dispensations are included in God's plan?
That depends on who you ask!

- John Nelson Darby saw six dispensations in Scripture.
- C.I. Scofield found seven.

Cyrus I. Scofield.

- Clarence Larkin worked eight dispensations into his popular dispensational charts.

Even though dispensationalists may differ on the precise number of dispensations, all dispensational premillennialists agree that God has worked in particular and distinguishable ways with different groups of people throughout history.

Darby's Six Dispensations (J.N. Darby, *Apostasy of the Successive Generations*)	Scofield's Seven Dispensations (C.I. Scofield, *The Scofield Reference Bible*)
	Age of Innocence (Gen. 1–2) *Test*: Do not eat of the fruit of the tree of knowledge. *Outcome*: Exile from Eden
	Age of Conscience (Gen. 3:7) *Test*: Do what is known to be good and express sorrow for sin through animal sacrifice. *Outcome*: Rebellion and flood
Dispensation of Noah From the covenant with Noah until the calling of Abraham	**Age of Human Government (Gen. 8:15)** *Test*: Rule righteously. *Outcome*: Corrupt cultures and governments
Dispensation of Abraham From the calling of Abraham until the Law of Moses	**Age of Promise (Gen. 12:1)** *Test*: Trust God. *Outcome*: Those who blessed Abraham were blessed
Dispensation of Israel From Law of Moses to exile, resumes during the tribulation	**Age of Law (Exod. 19:1)** *Test*: Obey divine law. *Outcome*: Israel disobeyed the law and experienced exile.
Dispensation of the Gentiles From the exile of Judah to the coming of Jesus	
Dispensation of the Church From the establishment of the church until the rapture	**Age of the Church (Acts 2:1)** *Test*: Believe Jesus, make disciples of all nations. *Outcome*: Gospel spreads around the world; God removes the church at the rapture and resumes his work with Israel
Dispensation of the Millennium After the great tribulation	**Age of the Kingdom (Rev. 20:4–7)** *Test*: Be faithful to Jesus, the king of the millennial kingdom. *Outcome*: When Satan is released at the end of the millennium, some will rebel; Jesus will defeat them.

BIBLICAL HISTORY DIVIDED INTO DISPENSATIONS
(Pre-Millennial Dispensationalist View)

	NAMES OF DISPENSATIONS				
	Innocence	**Conscience**	**Human Government**	**Promise**	**Law**
	Creation	Fall	Flood	Babel	Exodus
Eternity Past					
Biblical People	Adam	Adam to Noah	Noah to Abraham	Abraham to Moses	Moses to Christ
Dispensations		Adamic	Noahic	Abrahamic	Mosaic
Sign		Curses	Rainbow	Circumcision	Sabbath
Covenants			Between God & Creation	Between God & Abraham's Seed	Between God & Israel
Responsibilities	Obey God *Gen. 1:26-28; 2:15-17*	Do Good, Blood Sacrifice *Gen. 3:5, 7, 22; 4:4*	Scatter and Multiply *Gen. 8:15–9:7*	Dwell in Canaan *Gen. 12:1-7*	Keep the Whole Law *Ex. 19:3-8*
Failure	Disobedience *Gen. 3:1-6*	Wickedness *Gen. 6:5-6, 11-12*	Did Not Scatter *Gen. 11:1-4*	Dwelt in Egypt *Gen. 12:10; 46:6*	Broke Law *2 Kings 17:7-20; Matt. 27:1-25*
Judgement	Curse and Death *Gen. 3:7-19*	Flood *Gen. 6:7, 13; 7:11-14*	Confusion of Languages *Gen. 11:5-9*	Egyptian Bondage *Ex. 1:8-14*	Worldwide Dispersion *Deut. 28:63-66; Lk. 21:20-24*
To Whom Does Covenant Apply?			All Humankind		Israel and Those Who Join Her
Redemption			Animal Sacrifices Pointed Forward to Christ's Sacrifice		

NAMES OF DISPENSATIONS

Grace	Tribulation	Messianic	White Throne	
Church Age	Daniel's 70th Week	1,000 Year Millennium	New Heaven and Earth	Eternity Future
Christ to Antichrist		Christ as King		
Davidic	Mosaic (resumes)	Messianic	New Heaven and Earth	
A Son	2nd Coming	A King	New World	
Between God & His Son's Seed		Jews Return to God & Add Faith in Christ to Their Obedience to the Covenants		
Faith in Jesus, Keep Doctrine Pure John 1:12; Rom. 8:1-4; Eph. 2:8-9		Obey and Worship Jesus Isa. 11:3-5; Zech. 14:9, 16		
Impure Doctrine John 5:39-40; 2 Tim. 3:1-7		Final Rebellion Rev. 20:7-9		
Apostasy, False Doctrine 2 Thess. 2:3; 2 Tim. 4:3		Satan Loosed, Eternal Hell Rev. 20:11-15		
Jesus & Gentiles who believe in Christ		All Those Who Believe in Christ		
	Atonement through Christ's Sacrifice			

Despite these differences, there's far more agreement than disagreement among dispensationalists when it comes to the dispensations. Virtually every dispensationalist agrees on at least three primary dispensations:

- During the **dispensation of Israel**, God worked primarily with the physical descendants of Abraham; the focus of this dispensation was earthly and political, centered on the Promised Land. Even though God's primary work was with ethnic Israel, salvation was available only through faith in the Messiah who was yet to come. God will resume this dispensation after the rapture of the church.

- When the leaders of Israel rejected Jesus as the Messiah, God postponed the promised kingdom and instituted a **dispensation of the church**. During this dispensation, God is drawing believing Jews and Gentiles together into one body. The focus of this new dispensation is spiritual. Dispensationalists see this dispensation depicted in Ephesians 3:1–6 and Colossians 1:24–25.

- In the future, Jesus will reign over all earth with ethnic Israelites in his millennial kingdom. Paul was describing this **millennial dispensation** in Ephesians 1:10.

The precise number of dispensations is not of great significance. *The most important aspect of dispensationalism is the distinction that the dispensations make between God's work with the nation of Israel and God's work with the church.* This separation between Israel and the church is "the most basic theological test of whether or not a person is a dispensationalist, and it is undoubtedly the most practical and conclusive."[162]

DISPENSATIONALISM AND THE END OF TIME

So, what is it that dispensational premillennialists expect to happen near the end of time? Of course, there are differences even among dispensationalists, but most would agree on these expectations:

1 The Antichrist and the Temple

- Many nations—described in the prophecies of Ezekiel as Gog and Magog, Meshech and Tubal—will rise against the modern state of Israel (Ezekiel 38–39).
- The Israelis will sign a treaty with a world leader who is "the beast" and "the Antichrist" (Revelation 11:7; 13:1–8; 1 John 2:18). This treaty is, from the perspective of dispensational premillennialists, the "strong covenant" revealed here to the prophet Daniel.
- The Antichrist will assist in rebuilding a new Jewish sanctuary on the Temple Mount in Jerusalem. Sacrifices and offerings will resume.

2 The Rapture and the Tribulation

- The ratification of the "strong covenant" will mark the beginning of the seven-year Tribulation (Daniel 9:27).
- The overwhelming majority of dispensational premillennialists expect that, sometime before the Tribulation begins, God will remove his church from the world through the rapture.
- These seven years of the tribulation are Daniel's "seventieth seven" (Daniel 9:24). According to dispensational premillennialists, these seven terrible years are what John envisioned in the middle chapters of Revelation (Revelation 4–19).
- Near the beginning of the tribulation, God will designate 144,000 Jewish believers in Jesus to proclaim the gospel during this time of trouble (Revelation 7:1–8). Through their testimony, a great multitude from every nation will trust Jesus (Revelation 7:9–17).

3 The Great Tribulation and Armageddon

- Halfway through the tribulation, the Antichrist will break his treaty with the Israelis and desecrate the very temple that he helped to build. In the words of the prophet Daniel, "he shall put an end to sacrifice and offering" (Daniel 9:27).
- The final forty-two months of the tribulation will be the time of "great tribulation" that Jesus described to his disciples on the Mount of Olives (Matthew 24:21). Tragedies will be unleashed on the earth like never before.
- In the end, the armies of the earth will array themselves against the Jewish people at a place known as "Armageddon" (Revelation 16:16).

4 The Repentance of Israel and the Return of Jesus

- When all hope will seem to have failed, the nation of Israel will repent and recognize Jesus as their Messiah (Hosea 5:15–6:3).
- Jesus the Messiah will return to earth and defeat his enemies with the mere words of his mouth (Revelation 19).
- For one thousand years, Jesus will reign from Jerusalem, and Satan will be bound.
- At the end of this peaceful millennium, Satan will be released, defeated, and—along with every enemy of the living God—forever consigned to "the lake of fire" (Revelation 20:7–15).

WHY DOES THE RAPTURE HAVE TO HAPPEN FIRST?

Most dispensational premillennialists believe that the rapture of the church will take place before the tribulation. The rapture might occur immediately before the tribulation. Or it could happen a few months or years before the tribulation. Either way, the tribulation will not begin until Jesus has removed his church from the world.

Why is a pre-tribulation rapture so important in the Dispensational view?

- **So that God can resume his work with the nation of Israel**: God will rapture his church from the world to resume his work with the earthly nation of Israel. In Genesis 15:18, God promised the seed of Abraham all the land from the Nile River to the Euphrates River. Dispensationalists see the establishment of the modern state of Israel in 1948 as a crucial piece of the prophetic puzzle that will culminate in the Israelis controlling not only Palestine but also every piece of land from Egypt to Iraq.

- **So that Christians will be rescued from the tribulation**: This desire to fulfill his plan for Israel isn't the only reason why God must remove the church from the world, however. It's also because the great tribulation will be a time when terrible tragedies will be experienced throughout the earth. According to the apostle Paul, Jesus will deliver his people "from the wrath to come" (1 Thessalonians 1:10). Believers in Jesus Christ are "not destined … for wrath, but to obtain salvation" (1 Thessalonians 5:9). Dispensational premillennialists take these verses to mean that God must remove Christians from the world before he unleashes his wrath during the tribulation.

© Chameleons-Eye

Where Did Dispensational Premillennialism Come From?

Pre-tribulation premillennialism is a relatively recent view of the end times. In fact, the earliest hint in church history of a pre-tribulation rapture is found in an obscure Latin text known as *Apocalypse of Pseudo-Ephraem*.

Ephraem was a Christian theologian who lived in the fourth century AD. Here's what this apocalypse has to say about the end of time: "All the saints and elect of God are gathered before the tribulation, which is to come, and are taken to the Lord."

Medieval Icon of Ephraem the Syrian

There are some serious difficulties with reading too much into this text, though.

- This document wasn't actually written by the fourth-century theologian named Ephraem. It was falsely written in Ephraem's name nearly three hundred years after Ephraem died. That's why the document is attributed to *pseudo*-Ephraem.

- Even though the text was originally written in Greek, this pre-tribulational portion appears only in a Latin translation from the eighth or ninth century AD.[163] So it's safest not to make too much of this reference.

An anonymous fourteenth-century text about an Italian preacher named Dolcino suggested that Dolcino and his followers would be "translated into Paradise" before a time of tribulation—but it is unclear whether this single line refers to the rapture of all Christians.[164]

The notion of a pre-tribulation rapture doesn't show up in any clear and consistent way until the eighteenth century. In 1744, a ministry student named Morgan Edwards speculated in a term paper that Christians could be removed from the world during or before the tribulation. Almost a century later in the 1830s, John Nelson Darby began to proclaim a pre-tribulational schema that emphasized dispensational distinctions between Israel and the church. Darby described the church age as "a great parenthesis of prophetic time" between sixty-ninth and seventieth weeks of Daniel's prophecies.[165]

Irish evangelist John Nelson Darby gave up his career as a lawyer to become a pastor.

Throughout the mid-nineteenth century, Darby developed and taught a detailed dispensational system. During this era, the influences of American transcendentalism and German higher criticism were turning seminaries throughout North America toward theological liberalism. Darby and others like him avoided these increasingly liberal institutions. Instead, Darby proclaimed dispensational premillennialism at Bible conferences and among Bible-believing pastors in large evangelical churches. As a result, by the early twentieth century, dispensational premillennialism became synonymous in many denominations with taking a stand against theological liberalism.

WHY DISPENSATIONAL PREMILLENNIALISM MATTERS

You may not agree with the dispensational perspective. However, even if you would never consider sticking an "In Case of Rapture, This Car Will Be Unoccupied" decal on your rear bumper, there's much that you can appreciate about dispensationalism.

1. **Dispensational premillennialists take Scripture seriously**. Virtually without exception, dispensationalists believe the Bible to constitute unfailing truth without any mixture of error. That's why teachers like Tim LaHaye declare, "The best guide to Bible study is 'The Golden Rule of Biblical Interpretation': When the plain sense of Scripture makes common sense, seek no other sense, but take every word at its primary, literal meaning unless the facts of the immediate context clearly indicate otherwise."[167] Most dispensationalists are driven to that perspective because they truly want to trust and to obey what the text of Scripture says.

> "All conservative evangelicals ... owe a debt to pre-tribulational premillennialists who held tenaciously to orthodox Christianity when few others did. It is difficult to think of anyone in the history of the church who held to a pre-tribulational rapture and yet denied a central tenet of the Christian faith."[166]
>
> Russell Moore

2. **Dispensational premillennialism strongly emphasizes the need to proclaim the gospel *now*.** Christians could be removed from the world at any moment; so the time to speak the gospel into the lives of people around us is now. "Now is the favorable time; behold, now is the day of salvation" (2 Corinthians 6:2).

Regardless of what millennial viewpoint happens to be correct, none of the successes or possessions that surround you at this present moment will last into eternity. But the souls that embrace the truth of Jesus? Those will shine like stars forever and ever (Daniel 12:3).

THREE SHADES OF DISPENSATIONALISM

Not all dispensationalists are identical in their beliefs! In fact, there are at least three forms of dispensational premillennialism:

- **Classic dispensationalists** see the church as God's heavenly people and Israel as God's earthly people. These two groups will remain separate even in eternity. The church will be in heaven. Israel will be on the earth.
  (John Nelson Darby, Lewis Sperry Chafer, Cyrus I. Scofield)

- **Revised dispensationalists** still see the church and Israel as distinct. At the same time, they expect the saved from both groups to coexist in eternity in glorified and resurrected bodies. Ethnic Israel is the physical seed of Abraham; prior to the end of time, the nation of Israel will still receive the land that God promised. God temporarily set aside the unbelieving nation of Israel so that he could bring together believing Gentiles with a remnant of believing Jews in the church. The church is the spiritual seed of Abraham and includes believing Jews and Gentiles.
  (John Walvoord, Charles Caldwell Ryrie, J. Dwight Pentecost)

- **Progressive dispensationalists** are similar in many ways to new covenantalists. According to progressive dispensationalists, God has had one plan that he has unfolded from the beginning of time to the present. Each dispensation has simply emphasized a different aspect of this one plan. Jesus inaugurated a kingdom during his earthly ministry, and he will bring this kingdom to fruition in a future millennium. The nation of Israel will still receive the land that God promised to Abraham, and Jesus will govern Jews and Gentiles according to their separate nationalities during the millennium. The plan of God will, however, ultimately culminate with one people, joined together in the presence of God for all eternity.
  (Craig Blaising, Darrell Bock, Bruce Ware)

JESUS AND PAUL ON THE END TIMES FROM A DISPENSATIONAL PERSPECTIVE

JESUS' TEACHINGS ABOUT THE END OF TIMES

Jesus promised his disciples that he would come again. Before his return there would be:

"Birth Pains" (Events before the "signs" of the end)

- Many will claim to be the Messiah.
- People will be deceived by these messiahs.
- Wars, famine, earthquakes, pestilence.
- Believers in Christ persecuted and killed.
- Believers will be witnesses of Jesus to kings.
- Many will turn away from the faith.
- Betrayals by parents, brothers, and friends.
- Increase in wickedness.
- Fearful events and signs from heaven.

"The Signs" of the End

- Jerusalem surrounded by armies.
- The "abomination of desolation."
- Great tribulation like never before.
- Jerusalem will be trampled on by Gentiles.
- False prophets perform signs, miracles.
- Sun darkens, moon doesn't shine, stars fall.
- Severe ocean activity disturbs the nations.
- People will faint with terror.
- Jesus will appear in the sky.
- The trumpet will sound.
- Angels will gather God's elect.

(Matthew 24–25; Mark 13; Luke 21)

PAUL'S TEACHINGS ABOUT THE END OF TIMES

1. The Lord will descend.
2. The dead in Christ will rise first.
3. The living will be caught up with them in the clouds to meet the Lord and be with him forever.
4. Don't believe those who say the Day of the Lord has already come.
5. The Day of the Lord will be preceded by:
   - Rebellion
   - The revelation of the man of lawlessness who will:
     - Oppose and exalt himself over God
     - Set himself up in God's temple
     - Proclaim to be God
     - Be revealed when the one holding him back is taken out of the way
     - Be accompanied by satanic, counterfeit miracles
     - Deceive those who do not love the truth
6. When Jesus comes, the man of lawlessness will be overthrown and destroyed.

(1 Thessalonians 4:17; 2 Thessalonians 2)

CHAPTER 19

Through Tribulation to Everlasting Life: Historical Premillennialism

Heroes of the fictional variety never seem to reach final victory without enduring trials and tribulations.

Perhaps you've read C. S. Lewis' classic series *The Chronicles of Narnia.* If so, do you recall the final chapters of *The Last Battle*? Before finding themselves in the everlasting beauty of Aslan's country, those who still believe in the reality of Aslan endure intense suffering at the hands of cruel Calormene soldiers. And it isn't just in Narnia that this principle holds true. It's woven throughout all of our most familiar fictional tales.

Before Luke Skywalker saves the galaxy, he loses his hand in a duel with his father and endures excruciating torture at the hands of an evil emperor. Before Dorothy reduces the Wicked Witch to a puddle on the floor, she endures a

© Larry Jacobsen

perilous pilgrimage, a mob of flying monkeys, and imprisonment in the witch's castle. Before the prince defeats the sorceress and kisses Sleeping Beauty, he battles a dragon and a hedge of thorns. The righteous heroes always endure tribulation before they reach the final victory.

According to historical premillennialists, it isn't only our fictional story lines that unfold in this way. That's how God's story line works as well.

The tribulation is not just for non-believers. Tribulation is for Christians too.

© Clint Cearley

AGREEMENTS AND DISAGREEMENTS

Agreements with Dispensationalism
• The biblical writers expected a future physical kingdom
• Jesus will reign personally over all the earth, and no creature will ever be predator or prey again.
• Before Jesus returns, demonic deceptions will multiply, and spiritual conditions throughout the world will worsen (1 Timothy 4:1–5; 2 Timothy 3:1–9).
Disagreements with Dispensationalism
Historical premillennialists differ from dispensationalists on the timing of the rapture. Dispensationalists expect the church to make a secret exit off the face of planet earth before the worst trials and tribulations fall on the earth. Historical premillennialists expect the rapture to happen after the great tribulation, immediately before Jesus returns to earth to establish his millennial kingdom.

HOW HISTORICAL PREMILLENNIALISTS EXPECT THE WORLD TO END

So why on earth would anyone want to believe that Christians will endure the tribulation?

Well, it's not because historical premillennialists enjoy calamity! Historical premillennialists would prefer to avoid trials and tragedies every bit as much as anyone else. Historical premillennialist Russell Moore makes this point most picturesquely when he writes, "This author certainly hopes he is wrong about the timing of the rapture and will gladly concede this point to his pretribulational friends while flying through the atmosphere."[168]

Why, then, have historical premillennialists concluded that the church will remain on earth during the tribulation?

Just like proponents of other perspectives on the end of time, historical premillennialists have taken their position because that's what they understand Scripture to teach. So what in Scripture compels historical premillennialists to take this perspective? Let's take a look at some key Scriptures that suggest to historical premillennialists that Christians will endure the tribulation.

1. The rapture of the church and the return of Jesus to earth are not separated in Paul's letters.

The apostle Paul urged persecuted Christians to watch for the coming of Jesus—but what Paul expected to happen at this coming seems to have been far more than a removal of the church from planet earth! (2 Thessalonians 1:5–10). At his coming, Jesus will:

1. "Give relief" to his church (2 Thessalonians 1:7).
2. Destroy "the lawless one" (2 Thessalonians 2:8).
3. Be "revealed from heaven in blazing fire with his powerful angels" (2 Thessalonians 1:7).
4. "Punish those who do not know God and who do not obey the gospel of our Lord Jesus" (2 Thessalonians 1:8).

Paul did not separate the "relief" that God's people will experience at the rapture from the judgment that Jesus will bring when he returns to earth. Paul seems to have seen rapture and return as two parts of one glorious "coming of our Lord Jesus Christ" (2 Thessalonians 2:1).

Later in his ministry, Paul told a pastor named Titus to look for "the blessed hope, the appearing of the glory of our great God and Savior, Jesus Christ"—with no hint that seven years of tribulation might separate "the blessed hope" from "the appearing of the glory" (Titus 2:13). *These texts suggest to historical premillennialists that the apostle Paul expected Jesus to return to earth immediately after the rapture*.

© Benjamin Haas

2. According to Revelation, the saints are on the earth during the tribulation.

According to historical premillennialists, Revelation 4:1 isn't about the rapture at all. "The voice I had first heard speaking to me like a trumpet said, 'Come up here, and I will show you what must take place after this'" (4:1). *It simply represents a shift in John's vision from an earthly viewpoint to a heavenly viewpoint.*

So, if the church isn't removed from the earth in the fourth chapter of Revelation, where *is* the church in the chapters of Revelation that tell about the tribulation? (4–19). **According to historical premillennialists, the church remains on the earth throughout the tribulation.**

The text of Revelation refers repeatedly to "saints" or "holy ones" on the earth during the tribulation (Revelation 13:7–10; 14:12). Throughout the New Testament, the term "saints" or "holy ones" points to the church (1 Corinthians 1:2; 2 Corinthians 1:1; Ephesians 1:1; 2:19; 4:12; Philippians 1:1; Colossians 1:2–4, 12, 26; Philemon 1:5–7). If the word "saints" conveys the same meaning in Revelation that it carries throughout the rest of the New Testament, the church will remain on the earth during the tribulation.

3. According to Revelation, there will be only two resurrections—one before the millennium and one afterward.

In his vision of the end of time, John foresaw the souls of believers who had remained faithful throughout the tribulation. These believers "came to life and reigned with Christ a thousand years. ... This is the first resurrection" (Revelation 20:4–5).

Now, if the rapture happened all the way back in the fourth chapter of Revelation, it would seem that this resurrection after the tribulation would be a *second* resurrection—not the first. But John repeatedly refers to this resurrection at the end of the tribulation as "the first resurrection" (Revelation 20:5–6). And so, according to historical premillennialists, John must not have expected a pre-tribulation rapture accompanied by a resurrection of the righteous dead. Instead, John anticipated only two resurrections:

1. The "first resurrection" of the righteous will take place between the tribulation and the millennium (Revelation 20:4–6).

2. Then, after the millennium has ended, the unrighteous dead will be raised to receive their eternal sentence from the earthly throne of Jesus (Revelation 20:5, 11–15).

> **HISTORICAL PREMILLENNIALISM**
>
> The belief that, after a time of tribulation, Jesus will physically return to earth and establish the millennial kingdom described in Revelation 20.

If historical premillennialists are correct, "the first resurrection" in Revelation 20 is identical to the resurrection and rapture that Paul anticipated in his letters to Corinth and Thessalonica (1 Corinthians 15:50–58; 1 Thessalonians 4:16–18). This moment of resurrection, rapture, and return will take place as the tribulation ends and the millennium begins.

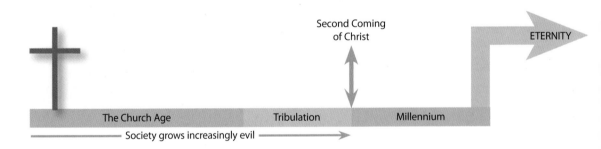

WHAT'S SO "HISTORICAL" ABOUT HISTORICAL PREMILLENNIALISM?

So why is historical premillennialism "historical"?

The word "historical" refers to the fact that this expectation is very ancient. In fact, as far as anyone can tell, historical premillennialism is the oldest Christian view of the end times. Here's what some of the earliest Christians after the apostles had to say about the end of time:

Church Fathers' Views On the Millennium	
Papias • Born before AD 70 • Disciple of the Apostle John	• **"After the resurrection of the dead, there will be a Millennium,** when the personal reign of the Messiah will be established on this earth. ... All animals, feeding only on what the earth itself produces, will become peaceable and harmonious, submitting themselves to humanity."[169] • Papias did not expect deceased Christians to be raised from the dead by means of a pre-tribulation rapture; he expected the resurrection to take place immediately before the millennium, after every tribulation ends.
Justin Martyr • Born around AD 103 • Christian philosopher and apologist	• "The man of apostasy, who speaks strange things against the Most High, will venture to do **unlawful deeds on the earth against us, the Christians**. ... I and others—who are right-minded Christians on all points—are assured that there will be **a resurrection of the dead, and one thousand years in Jerusalem,** which will at that time be built, adorned, and enlarged."[170] • Justin expected "us, the Christians" to be on earth during the great tribulation.
Irenaeus of Lyons • Born in the AD 100's • Student of Polycarp, who was a disciple of the Apostle John.	• "Ten kings shall give their kingdom to the beast and **cause the church to flee**. ... After the Antichrist has devastated all things in this world, he will reign for three years and six months."[171] • Irenaeus was certain that the church would be on the earth during the forty-two months of tribulation described by John in Revelation (11:2; 13:5). • He also clearly anticipated an earthly millennial kingdom. Irenaeus recorded this tradition that he received through Polycarp from the apostle John: "In those days, vines will grow with ten thousand branches. In each true twig will be ten thousand shoots, and in each cluster will be ten thousand grapes. Every pressed grape will produce twenty-five measures of wine. **When any of the holy ones takes hold of a cluster, another will cry out,** 'I am a better cluster, take me! Bless the Lord through me.'"[172] Although the idea of talking grape vines is a little strange—to be fair, it's almost certainly symbolic language—it is clear that, for Irenaeus, the millennium was future and physical.
Tertullian of Carthage • Born in AD 160 • Christian theologian and apologist	• A generation after Irenaeus, Tertullian of Carthage declared that, near the end of time, "the beast antichrist will wage war **on the church of God**. ... We agree that **a kingdom is promised to us on earth**, before heaven."[173] • According to Tertullian, the Antichrist would persecute the church prior to an earthly millennial kingdom.

Historical premillennialism may or may not be the correct view of the end times—but it seems to be the most ancient view. Each of these ancient church leaders expected the return of Jesus and the resurrection of the righteous to occur together, immediately before an earthly millennium. What's more, they also seem to have expected the church to endure the tribulation. Later historical premillennialists have included Charles H. Spurgeon,[174] Oswald J. Smith, Harold Ockenga, Carl F.H. Henry, George Eldon Ladd, Craig Blomberg, R. Albert Mohler, Russell Moore, Wayne Grudem, and David Dockery.

ONE PLAN: WHAT'S MOST DISTINCTIVE ABOUT HISTORICAL PREMILLENNIALISM

The timing of the rapture is *not*, however, the only difference between the historical and dispensational views. The deepest divergence between dispensational and historical premillennialists has to do with how each group views *the relationship between the nation of Israel and the church.*

Dispensational premillennialists organize God's work into "dispensations." In each dispensation, God works in a particular way with a particular people. God's activities with Israel and with the church occur—according to dispensationalists—as parts of two different dispensations.

Historical premillennialists take a very different viewpoint on God's work with Israel and the church. From a historical premillennial perspective, God's plan has always been to create one people for his glory through the death and resurrection of Jesus (Ephesians 2:15). ***All of God's work with the nation of Israel in the Hebrew Scriptures was a preparation or a picture of what he had already purposed to do through Jesus.***

Both in the New Testament and in the Old, it was only through faith in Jesus that anyone entered into a right relationship with God. God's true people in every age have been those who live by faith in Jesus as the divine Messiah-King. Before Jesus arrived on earth, people trusted in Jesus by looking expectantly for a Messiah who was yet to come (Hebrews 11:13, 39–40). Today, God makes sinners right with himself by guiding them to trust in Jesus, the crucified and risen Messiah (Romans 10:9–10). God's intent has always been to create one people through faith in Jesus.

	Historical Premillennialism	Dispensational Premillennialism
The Nation of Israel	• God has always had one plan. • God's work with the nation of Israel was a temporary picture of what God had already purposed to do through Jesus and through the church.	• God has purposed to work with two different groups of people—Israel and the church—in different ways in distinct "dispensations." • God will fulfill his promises to the patriarchs and to the people of Israel through the modern nation of Israel.
The Church	• Through Jesus, God is fulfilling the promises that he made to Israel. • In the Old Testament and the New, God's plan has always been to redeem every person who trusts in God's Messiah. • Jesus came to accomplish this redemption through his death and resurrection.	• God offered an earthly kingdom to Israel. Since Israel's religious leaders rejected this kingdom, God formed a spiritual kingdom that included Gentiles. In the Old and the New Testaments, God's plan has always been to redeem every person who trusts in God's Messiah. • During the great tribulation, God will remove the church from the world and resume his work with the nation of Israel.

HOW LONG WILL THE TRIBULATION LAST?

After pronouncing woe after woe upon the Pharisees in the temple courts, Jesus cried out, "all this will come on this generation. Jerusalem, Jerusalem" (Matthew 23:36–37).

As Jesus turned to leave the temple, his disciples looked around them and declared, "What massive stones! What magnificent buildings!" (Mark 13:1). They seemed to think that this temple would last forever.

Their teacher's reply was dark and foreboding, "Not one stone here will be left on another; every one will be thrown down." Once the disciples reached the Mount of Olives, Jesus told them about a future time of tribulation "unequaled from the beginning of the world until now" (Matthew 24:2; 21).

Historical premillennialists believe that the church remains on earth during the great tribulation. But when is this time of trials and troubles? How long will the tribulation last?

Some historical premillennialists understand the tribulation to be *a relatively brief period* that will occur near the end of time. If the "forty-two months" in Revelation 11:2 refers to the same period as the forty-two months in 13:5, the tribulation will last only three-and-one-half years. If these two periods are different, the span of the tribulation will be seven years.

Other historical premillennialists take the forty-two months as a symbolic reference that draws from the encampments of Israel in the wilderness (Numbers 33:5–29) and the months of drought during the ministry of Elijah (Luke 4:25; James 5:17). If the forty-two months are symbolic, the tribulation could be *a long time-period* that began in the first century AD and continues until the end of time.

Despite this difference, historical premillennialists do agree on one central affirmation: *Even in times of tribulation, God preserves and protects the souls of those who truly belong to him.*

THE TRIBULATION: A SHORT AND A LONG VIEW

	The Short View	**The Long View**
What is "the abomination of desolations" that Jesus predicted? (Matthew 24:15)	A future blasphemous act, committed by the Antichrist against Israel or against the church. The Antichrist may be a specific political ruler who governs during the tribulation.	The defilement of the Jewish temple, when Roman soldiers entered Jerusalem in AD 70 then burned and pillaged the temple. Antichrist includes the rulers in every age—beginning with the Roman emperors who demanded worship for themselves—that war against the power, purposes, and people of God.
Who was Jesus warning when he said "let those who are in Judea flee to the mountains"? (Matthew 24:16)	Future believers during the tribulation	Believers who were living near Jerusalem when Jesus spoke these words, who could have been caught in the terrible wrath of the Roman army.

	The Short View	The Long View
How does the tribulation described by Jesus relate to the "forty-two months" of tribulation described by John in Revelation? (Matthew 24:21; Revelation 11:2; 13:5)	The tribulation described by Jesus is the same as the time of tribulation described in Revelation. "Forty-two months" refers to three-and-a-half years (if the two references in Revelation refer to the same time-period) or to seven years (if the two references in Revelation refer to two time-periods that occur immediately after one another). This future tribulation may also be the "seventieth week" described in Daniel 9:24–27. For believers today, the tribulation is yet to come.	The tribulation described by Jesus is the same as the time of tribulation described in Revelation. "Forty-two months" refers symbolically to a long period of tribulation. The number is probably drawn from the forty-two encampments of Israel in the wilderness (Numbers 33:5–29) and the forty-two months of drought during the ministry of Elijah (Luke 4:25; James 5:17). The tribulation began with the Jewish-Roman War (AD 66–73) that resulted from the religious leaders' rejection of Jesus. The "seventieth week" described in Daniel 9:24–27 was fulfilled during these events in the first century. Believers today are living in the tribulation. The tribulation will continue and worsen until Jesus returns. Near the end of time, a final Antichrist will arise and declare himself to be divine (1 Thessalonians 2:3–8).
Where is the church during the tribulation? (Matthew 24:21–31)	The church is "the elect" (Matthew 24:22–31; compare 2 Timothy 2:10). During the tribulation, the church will endure persecution on the earth but God will protect his people from falling away.	The church is "the elect" (Matthew 24:22–31; compare 2 Timothy 2:10). During the tribulation, the church is enduring persecution on the earth but God protects his people from falling away.
What will happen at the end of the tribulation? (Matthew 24:29–31)	Immediately after the tribulation, cosmic upheavals will accompany the return of Jesus. Just as citizens in ancient times ran out to meet their king as he approached their city, the church will be caught up in the rapture to meet Jesus in the air and will then immediately return with him to the earth.	Immediately after the tribulation, cosmic upheavals will accompany the return of Jesus. Just as citizens in ancient times ran out to meet their king as he approached their city, the church will be caught up in the rapture to meet Jesus in the air and will then immediately return with him to the earth.

WHAT ABOUT GOD'S PROMISE TO ABRAHAM?

At this point, you may be asking some quite good questions about historical premillennialism:

- Didn't God choose the offspring of Abraham for a special purpose?
- If God has always had one plan and one people, what about God's promises of land to Abraham?
- Has God rejected the Jewish people?

Nearly every historical premillennialist would respond that God has **not** rejected the Jewish people. The Jews are, after all, beloved by God "for the sake of their forefathers"! (Romans 11:28).

At the same time, historical premillennialists **do** understand God's fulfillment of his promises to Israel in a slightly different way than dispensationalists:

- Historical premillennialists are **covenantalists** or **new covenantalists** when it comes to how God will fulfill his promises to Abraham and to Israel.

- God's primary purpose when he chose Abraham was for the children of Abraham to be the people through whom Jesus would come into the world.

- Even then, God intended his promises to Abraham and to the Israelites to find their fulfillment in Jesus (see chapter 4).

God's Promises to Abraham, by Tissot (1896–1902)

- During the millennial kingdom, Jesus will reign from Jerusalem not only over the land promised to Abraham but also over the whole earth. And so, during the millennium, Jesus will fulfill every promise of God. Abraham's "offspring" will rule the land from the Nile to the Euphrates and so much more. "Dispensationalists are right that only ethnic Jews receive the promised future restoration, but Paul makes clear that the 'seed of Abraham' is singular, not plural (Gal. 3:16). ... Does this promise apply to ethnic Jews? Yes, one ethnic Jew whose name is Jesus."[175]

This too was what many of the earliest church leaders taught. It's what Irenaeus of Lyons was getting at when he said that God's material promises to Abraham would be fulfilled through Jesus and the church. Irenaeus even declared that "the church is the seed of Abraham."[176] Justin Martyr defined Christians as the new Israel.[177]

© GWImages

Does this mean that ethnic Jews no longer have any special place in God's plan? Certainly not! The preservation of the Jewish people to this present time is a miraculous sign of God's continuing presence in the world. There are, as novelist Walker Percy has pointed out, "no Hittites walking about on the streets of New York"—but there are millions of descendants of the ancient Israelites.[178]

What, then, does the future hold for ethnic Jews?

At some point before the return of Jesus, many historical premillennialists anticipate a widespread spiritual awakening among the Jewish people. Jews throughout the world will turn to Jesus as their Messiah, Savior, and God. That's what Paul was predicting when he wrote that Israel would remain resistant to the gospel only "until the fullness of the Gentiles has come in" (Rom. 11:25). For historical premillennialists, the primary focus of God's promises is not the physical land of Israel but the divine person of Jesus. And so, what historical premillennialists anticipate for the Jewish people is not *the restoration of the modern nation of Israel to their land* but *a turning of Jewish people to Jesus.* Because of this expectation, there is every reason to proclaim the good news about Jesus "to the Jew first" (Romans 1:16).

> "The current secular state of Israel is not the fulfillment of God's promise to Abraham; Jesus is. Nonetheless, the state of Israel is the guardian of post-Holocaust world Judaism. This does not necessitate that we support every political decision of the Israeli government. It does mean that we stand with Israel against every form of anti-Semitic violence because we know that these are the kinsmen according to the flesh of our Messiah."[179]
>
> Russell Moore

What Matters Most about Historical Premillennialism

Even if you don't believe that the church endures the tribulation, historical premillennialism reminds us how God constantly uses day-by-day trials to move his people toward maturity.

> Historical premillennialism emphasizes God's preservation of his people through suffering and tribulation.

According to the apostle Paul, Christians must not merely tolerate the tribulations of this life; Christians must see tribulations as opportunities for God to purify and to transform his people (Romans 5:3–5; 12:12; 2 Corinthians 6:4–5). Barnabas and Paul testified together that it is only "through many tribulations that we enter God's kingdom" (Acts 14:22). Paul even declared that Christians are "destined" for tribulation (1 Thessalonians 3:3). Jesus predicted that believers would endure tribulation (John 16:21–22) and made it clear that his followers would be "in the world" during at least some times of tribulation (John 16:33).

The End Is Near

And so, with this survey of historical premillennialism, our exploration of the end times is near the end. Perhaps you've arrived at a different perspective on the end times than you had when you began this book. Or maybe you're convinced even more strongly of the viewpoint you've always held. It could be that you're looking forward to engaging in deeper study as you reconsider what you believe about the end times.

Regardless of how you see the end times right now, I want to leave you with the same simple truth that the Spirit inspired John to write at the end of Revelation: "May the grace of our Lord Jesus Christ be with you all" (22:21).

If your reading has led you to worry about details of the end times or to criticize Christians who hold different viewpoints, you have wasted your time. The closing verses of Revelation call us to "***grace***," not self-righteousness. A God-centered study of the end times should lead you closer to "our Lord Jesus Christ" and deeper into fellowship with other believers ("with you all")—even if those believers disagree with you when it comes to the details of how God will end the world! Jesus is, after all, the goal and the endpoint of God's work in history, and Jesus calls us to live in community with everyone who trusts in him.

What's more, all four views of the end times unite around these essential truths:

- Jesus is returning.
- Jesus will judge all humanity.
- God will resurrect all humanity—some to eternal life, and others to eternal death.

Which leaves us with this crucial question: Where do you stand with Jesus? If you are uncertain whether you have truly trusted Jesus, search your innermost desires. Do you despise your sin? Do you want to love God above all other things? Do you long to be obedient to Jesus? Trust Jesus now as the Master of your life and as the Living Lord of all Creation. Recognize his suffering on the cross as God's substitute for the punishment that you deserve. And then, cry out with the author of Revelation, "Even so, come, Lord Jesus!" (Revelation 22:20).

CHAPTER
20

A Quick Guide to Four Views of the End Times

AMILLENNIALISM

What is amillennialism?

In amillennialism, the millennium is the spiritual reign of Jesus in the hearts of his followers. The "first resurrection" in Revelation 20:5 is not a physical restoration from the dead. It is either:

1. The spiritual resurrection also known as regeneration
2. The life that believers experience with God between their deaths and their final resurrection.

Christ's triumph over Satan through his death and resurrection around AD 30 restrained the power of Satan on the earth (Revelation 20:1–3). Persecution of Christians (tribulation) will occur until Jesus comes again, as will the expansion of God's kingdom (the millennium).

When Christ returns, he will immediately defeat the powers of evil, resurrect the saved and the unsaved, judge them, and deliver them to their eternal destinies.

What do amillennialists emphasize?

Many amillennialists believe that the book of Revelation consists of seven sections. Instead of dealing with successive time-periods, these seven sections use apocalyptic language to describe the entire time from Jesus' first coming until his second coming in seven different ways.

Amillennialists tend to emphasize the historical context of Revelation and what the book meant to first-century readers.

According to amillennialists

- The great tribulation represents disasters, wars, and persecutions that have occurred throughout church history.
- Most references to "Israel" in Revelation are symbolic references to the people of God on earth (compare Romans 9:6–8 and Galatians 6:16).
- In apocalyptic literature, numbers represent concepts, not literal statistics. For example, six symbolizes incompleteness, seven represents completeness, ten indicates something that is extreme but limited, twelve represents the

perfection of God's people, and 1,000 symbolizes a great amount or long period of time.

What Scriptures seem to support amillennialism?

- The Bible frequently uses the number 1,000 figuratively (Psalm 50:10; 90:4; 105:8; 2 Peter 3:8).

- The first resurrection (Revelation 20:4) could refer to the spiritual resurrection (the regeneration or new birth) of persons who trust Christ (Romans 11:13–15; Ephesians 2:1–4). The first resurrection could also refer to a Christian's life with Jesus after death (2 Corinthians 5:6–8).

- The second coming of Christ and the resurrection of the saved and the unsaved will occur at the same time (Daniel 12:2–3; John 5:28–29).

- The saints are on earth during the tribulation (Revelation 13:7).

When has amillennialism been popular?

Amillennialism became popular in the fifth century. Amillennialism has remained widespread throughout church history.

Prominent amillennialists include:

The Protestant reformers Martin Luther and John Calvin as well as evangelical theologians such as E.Y. Mullins, Abraham Kuyper, G.C. Berkouwer, Herschel Hobbs, Stanley Grenz, and J. I. Packer. Many students of church history believe that the church father Augustine of Hippo (354–430) was an early amillennialist.

> Augustine of Hippo wrote in The City of God, "During the thousand years when the devil is bound, the saints also reign for a thousand years. Without any doubt, these two time-periods are identical and point to the time between the first and second coming of Christ."[180]

Satan's power is restrained — Millennium — The Church Age — Tribulation — ETERNITY — Second Coming of Christ & Final Judgment

POSTMILLENNIALISM

What is postmillennialism?

This view believes that the second coming of Christ will occur after the millennium. The millennial reign described in Revelation 20:1–6 represents a long time period when, through the preaching of the gospel, most of the world will submit to Jesus Christ. During this time, Satan will have no power over the earth, and evil regimes will collapse (Revelation 19:19–20:3). A period of great tribulation may precede the millennium. Some charismatic Christians embrace *dominion postmillennialism.* This teaches that through the contemporary charismatic movement God has been binding Satan. When the church recognizes the fullness of its power through the Holy Spirit, the church will establish God's kingdom on earth and usher in the millennium, a golden age.

What do postmillennialists emphasize?

Postmillennialists place great confidence in the preaching of the gospel; they contend that the gospel will eventually spread in such a way that nearly everyone in the world will turn to Jesus Christ. One Scripture cited in favor of this view is Mark 3:27. Augustine understood this verse to mean that before Jesus can claim his kingdom, those that are lost (the "possessions" of Satan, "the strong man") must come under the control of Jesus. Postmillennialists believe that this golden age is described in such Scriptures as Psalm 2:8, Isaiah 2:2–4, Jeremiah 31:34, Daniel 2:35, and Micah 4:1–4. Postmillennialists tend to emphasize the power of the gospel to transform societies and individual lives.

According to postmillennialists

- During the millennium, Christ will rule the earth through the gospel, through his Spirit, and through the church. He will not, however, be physically present on the earth.

- The resurrection depicted in Revelation 20:4 represents the spiritual regeneration of people who trust Jesus Christ.

- The second coming of Christ, the final conflict between good and

Loraine Boettner described postmillennialism as "that view of the last things which holds that the kingdom of God is now being extended in the world through the preaching of the gospel and the saving work of the Holy Spirit in the hearts of individuals, that the world is eventually to be Christianized, and that the return of Christ is to occur at the end of a long period of righteousness and peace, commonly called 'the millennium.'"[181]

evil, the defeat of Satan, the physical resurrection of all people, and the final judgment will occur together, immediately after the millennium (Revelation 20:7–15).

Which Scriptures seem to support postmillennialism?

- Every ethnic group will receive the gospel before the second coming (Matthew 24:14; Mark 13:10).

- The first resurrection (Revelation 20:4) could refer to the spiritual resurrection (the regeneration or new birth) of persons who trust Christ (Romans 11:13–15; Ephesians 2:1–4).

- The second coming of Christ and the resurrection of all people, saved and unsaved, will occur at the same time (Daniel 12:2–3; John 5:28–29).

When has postmillennialism been popular?

The earliest writer who was clearly postmillennialist was Joachim of Fiore (1135–1202), although many historians believe that earlier church leaders such as Eusebius of Caesarea, Athanasius of Alexandria, and Augustine of Hippo leaned toward postmillennialism.

During the 1800s, postmillennialism increased in popularity. Some Christians even believed that the increased work of missionaries throughout the world represented the beginning of the millennium.

During the early 1900s, a world war and an economic depression raised questions in many people's minds about whether the world was actually becoming a better place, and postmillennialism diminished in popularity.

Prominent postmillennialists include:

Famous preacher Jonathan Edwards as well as theologians such as B.B. Warfield, Augustus H. Strong, Charles Hodge, R.L. Dabney, Loraine Boettner, and R.C. Sproul.

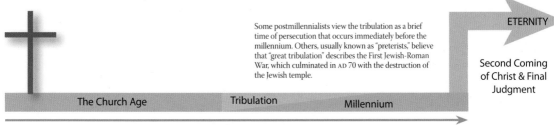

Some postmillennialists view the tribulation as a brief time of persecution that occurs immediately before the millennium. Others, usually known as "preterists," believe that "great tribulation" describes the First Jewish-Roman War, which culminated in AD 70 with the destruction of the Jewish temple.

ETERNITY

Second Coming of Christ & Final Judgment

The Church Age   Tribulation   Millennium

Society gradually improves

DISPENSATIONAL PREMILLENNIALISM

What is dispensational premillennialism?

This view believes that Jesus will come back to earth after a seven-year tribulation and will rule during a thousand-year millennium of peace on earth.

In addition, God will still give to the nation of Israel the land described in Genesis 15:18 (from the river of Egypt to the river Euphrates—the full extent of King Solomon's kingdom).

Most dispensational premillennialists are "pre-tribulationists"; they understand Revelation 4:1–2 to refer to the rapture. The rapture is understood as the event when Christ removes Christians from the earth before the great tribulation begins.

Some dispensational premillennialists, known as mid-tribulationists, believe the rapture will occur during the great tribulation.

What do dispensational premillennialists emphasize?

Dispensational premillennialists believe the rapture and the second coming of Jesus are *two separate events*. The rapture comes *before* the great tribulation, and the second coming occurs *after* it. During the seven years of tribulation, natural disasters and wars will occur on earth, and people who are faithful to Jesus will suffer intense persecution. Dispensational premillennialists emphasize literal interpretations of Revelation.

According to dispensational premillennialists

- During the great tribulation, many Jews will turn to Jesus Christ.
- God's promises to Abraham and his offspring were unconditional; therefore, the Jews will still receive the land described in Genesis 15:18. The establishment of the modern state of Israel in 1948 fulfilled a key end times prophecy.
- All references to Israel in Revelation refer to the nation of Israel.

What Scriptures seem to support dispensational premillennialism?

- God will remove Christians before the outpouring of his wrath during the tribulation (1 Thessalonians 5:9; Revelation 3:10).

- God's promises to Abraham and his offspring were unconditional (Genesis 15:7–21).

- The church is not specifically mentioned between Revelation 4 and 19.

When has dispensational premillennialism been popular?

This view emerged in the 1800s among the Plymouth Brethren (group of fundamentalist Bible Churches founded in the 1820s). Dispensational premillennialism increased in popularity in the late 1800s and remains widespread today.

Prominent dispensational premillennialists include:

J. Nelson Darby, C.I. Scofield, Harry A. Ironside, Gleason Archer, Donald G. Barnhouse, Hal Lindsey, Chuck Smith, John MacArthur, Charles Ryrie, Charles Stanley, Norman L. Geisler, and Tim LaHaye.

Tim LaHaye wrote that there are "two keys to understanding the prophetic Word of God. First, one must interpret the Bible literally unless the context provides good reason to do otherwise. Second, we must understand that Israel and the church are distinct! If a person fails to acknowledge these two facts of Scripture, all discussion and argument is fruitless. The issue is not so much prophecy as it is one's view of Scripture and the church."[182]

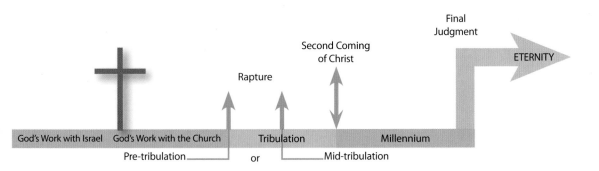

God's Work with Israel — God's Work with the Church — Rapture — Tribulation — Second Coming of Christ — Millennium — Final Judgment — ETERNITY

Pre-tribulation ___ or ___ Mid-tribulation

HISTORICAL PREMILLENNIALISM

What is historical premillennialism?

This view believes that Christians will remain on the earth during the great tribulation. The tribulation will purify the churches by rooting out false believers, and the second coming of Christ will precede the millennium. Covenantal historical premillennialists believe that the church has superseded Israel as God's people. New covenantalists see God's work with Israel as a temporary picture that pointed forward to what God had already planned to do through Jesus. Like dispensational premillennialists, historical premillennialists see the millennium—the thousand-year reign of Jesus—as a literal, future event.

The earliest church fathers envisioned an earthly millennium. During these first centuries of Christian faith, the church's theologians anticipated not only the physical reign of Jesus Christ following a time of testing but also the restoration of all creation to its original goodness in a millennial kingdom.

Historical premillennialism began to fade as later church fathers—influenced by Greek philosophy that viewed the physical world as evil and by the aftermath of some Christians' false expectations of a physical millennium—downplayed the idea of an earthly millennium.

What do historical premillennialists emphasize?

Historical premillennialists try to balance symbolic and literal interpretations of Revelation, emphasizing both what the book meant to first-century readers and how it might apply to people's lives today.

According to historical premillennialists

- God's promise to give Abraham all the land from the Nile River to the Euphrates River (Genesis 15:18) was made to the "offspring" of Abraham— one, particular offspring whose name is Jesus (Galatians 3:16). During the millennium, Jesus will reign from Jerusalem not only over the land promised to Abraham but also over the whole earth. In this way, Jesus will completely fulfill God's promise that Abraham's "offspring" would gain the land from the Nile to the Euphrates.

- The true Israelites in every age have been those who trust in Jesus as the divine Messiah-King (Romans 9:6–8; Galatians 6:16). Before Jesus arrived on earth, people trusted in Jesus by looking expectantly for a Messiah who was yet to come (Hebrews 11:13, 39–40). Most references to "Israel" in Revelation refer symbolically to the church.

What Scriptures seem to support historical premillennialism?

- The revealing of the Antichrist precedes Christ's return (2 Thessalonians 2:3–4).
- The tribulation will root out false members from the churches (Revelation 2:22–23).
- The saints are on earth during the tribulation (Revelation 13:7).
- God's promises to Abraham and his offspring were conditional (Genesis 22:18; 2 Chronicles 33:8; Isaiah 1:19–20; Jeremiah 7:6–7).
- The New Testament frequently uses "Israel" and "the twelve tribes" to refer to Christians (Matthew 19:28–29; Romans 9:6–8).

When has historical premillennialism been popular?

Historical premillennialism seems to have been the earliest view of the end times among Christians who lived just after the apostles.

Prominent historical premillennialists include:

Many early church fathers—including Lactantius (240–320), Irenaeus (130–200), Justin Martyr (100–165), and probably Papias (60–130), a disciple of the apostle John—embraced historical premillennialism.

Modern supporters include scholars such as David Dockery, John Warwick Montgomery, George R. Beasley-Murray, Robert Gundry, George E. Ladd, R. Albert Mohler, and Russell Moore.

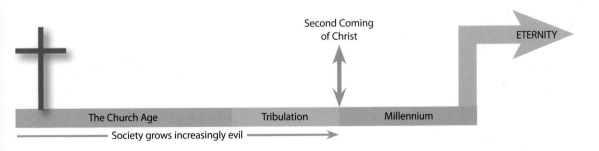

The Church Age — Tribulation — Second Coming of Christ — Millennium — ETERNITY

Society grows increasingly evil

FOUR VIEWS OF THE END TIMES

	Amillennialism	Postmillennialism	Dispensational Premillennialism	Historical Premillennialism
Will Jesus return physically?	Yes	Yes	Yes	Yes
When will Jesus return?	Anytime; a detailed time frame is not important.	After the millennium.	After a 7-year tribulation; before the millennium.	After tribulation; before the millennium.
Do the rapture and second coming of Christ occur at the same time?	Yes	Yes	No, they are events separated by either 7 years (pre-tribulation rapture) or 3$\frac{1}{2}$ years (mid-tribulation rapture).	Yes
Will there be a great tribulation?	The tribulation occurs any time Christians are persecuted or wars and disasters occur.	Tribulation is either the first-century Jewish-Roman War or the ongoing conflict between good and evil prior to millennium.	Yes	Yes
Will Christians suffer during the tribulation?	Yes, Christians will suffer and endure persecution until Jesus returns; persecution will increase in the end.	Yes, Christians are called to share the gospel, and tribulation will occur when that gospel is opposed.	Christians are either raptured before the tribulation (pre-tribulation rapture) or 3$\frac{1}{2}$ years into the tribulation (mid-tribulation rapture).	Yes, Christians will go through the tribulation and endure suffering and persecution for the cause of Christ.
Will there be a literal 1,000-year millennium?	No, the millennium refers to the reign of Christ in the hearts of his believers.	No, the millennium refers to a period of peace when the gospel reaches all people.	Yes, after the 7-year tribulation, Christ will return and reign for 1,000 years.	Yes, after the tribulation, Christ will return and reign for 1,000 years.
Who is saved?	Christians only	Christians only	Christians only	Christians only
Is the modern state of Israel relevant to the prophecies in Revelation?	No	No	Yes	No
When was this view most held?	Well-known by the AD 300s. It became widespread throughout the AD 400s. Continues to be accepted today.	May have been popular in the AD 300s and 400s, perhaps earlier. Less popular today.	Became popular in the 1800s. Has increased in popularity.	The earliest view of the end times, emerging at the end of the first century.

IMPORTANT WORDS TO KNOW

666—Number of the beast, spelled out in Revelation 13:18 as six hundred sixty-six. Greek and Hebrew did not have written numbers. Instead, either they spelled out the number, or they wrote out the number using the letters in the alphabet. For example, the first letter of the alphabet might represent the number one, and so on. Many scholars point out that, in Hebrew, the number of Nero's name can be 666 if written using Neron, the Latin spelling of the name. (Nero reigned AD 54–68. He was the first emperor to engage in specific persecution of Christians.) One good approach to this issue is to remember that six is a symbol of incompletion; 666 indicated total imperfection.

144,000—Group of believers who endure the great tribulation (Revelation 7:14). Some believe that these persons are literally 144,000 Jews—12,000 from each tribe—who embrace Jesus Christ as their Lord (see Revelation 7:4–9). Others suggest that the terms "Israel" and "twelve tribes" often refer to Christians (Romans 9:6–8; Galatians 6:16; James 1:1). Therefore, the number would point to God's people (symbolized by twelve tribes, twelve apostles, or both) multiplied by 1,000 (a number that symbolizes an extreme multitude or length of time)—in other words, the full number of those who belong to God.

Abomination of desolation—An event that desecrates the temple in Jerusalem and is a signal to Jesus' followers that soon Jerusalem will be ruined. Mentioned in Matthew 24:15, it may refer to the destruction of the temple in AD 70 by the Romans, or Roman plans to set up a statue of the Emperor in the temple in AD 40, or some future event.

Antichrist—(from Greek, *antichristos*, in place of Christ) Anyone who denies what the apostles taught about Jesus Christ (1 John 2:18–22; 4:3; 2 John 1:7). Specifically, the Antichrist is a Satanic counterfeit of Jesus Christ, described as "lawless" and as a "beast" (2 Thessalonians 2:3–8; Revelation 13:1–18; 17:3–17). The Antichrist could be a specific person who rises to power during a time of tribulation or a symbol of false teachers and leaders who will arise when the end of the age draws near.

Apocalyptic literature—(from Greek, *apokalypsis*, revealing) Jewish genre or writing, structured around visions that figuratively pointed to hidden truths for the purpose of assuring God's people of the goodness of God's plans during periods of persecution.

Armageddon—(from Hebrew, *Har-Megiddon*, Mount Megiddo) The city of Megiddo was located between the Plain of Jezreel and Israel's western coast. Deborah, Gideon, Saul, Ahaziah, and Josiah fought decisive battles near Megiddo—largely because the area around Megiddo is broad and flat. So the valley of Megiddo became the symbol of a point of decisive conflict. Some believe that a literal battle will occur near Megiddo near the end of time. Others view the reference to Armageddon as a symbol of an ultimate conflict between spiritual forces of good and evil.

Babylon—Revelation 17 presents the figure of a prostitute called Babylon riding upon a scarlet beast. The name is symbolic, yet interpretations vary:

1. **Jerusalem**: The fall of Babylon could be a symbolic reference to the fall of Jerusalem in AD 70.

2. **Rome**: After AD 70, Jewish writers often referred to Rome as "Babylon."[183] The name may symbolize the political and religious powers in every age that attempt to defy God and to persecute his people.

3. **One-world government and religion**: Babylon may be a reference to a one-world government and one-world religion, perhaps centered in the revived city of Babylon, that will emerge near the end of time.

Beasts, two—Symbolic creatures described in Revelation 11:7 and 13:1–18.

1. **The first beast**: This creature rises from the sea and has ten horns and seven heads. The seven heads seem to point to Rome, the city known for its seven hills. Some interpreters understand this reference to Rome as a literal reference to a power that will arise from Rome near the end of time; others view it as a symbolic reference to the powers in every age that defy God's dominion and persecute God's people. The beast claims blasphemous names for itself—much like Domitian, emperor from AD 81 until 96, who demanded that he be addressed as "Lord and God." One of the horns seemed to have died but then returned to life—much like the false rumor that emerged after the death of Nero that he had come back to life.[184]

2. **The second beast**: This creature rises from the earth with horns like a lamb and a voice like a dragon—in other words, a satanic parody of Jesus Christ, the Lamb of God. Some interpreters understand this creature as a literal leader who will encourage people to worship the first beast. Others view the second beast as a symbol of any religion in any time period that focuses worshipers on anything other than Jesus Christ.

Church age—The time period from the beginning of the church (about AD 30) until Jesus Christ returns for everyone who has trusted in him.

Eschatology—Study of the Bible's teachings about the events leading up to the second coming of Jesus (from Greek, *eschatos* [final] + *logos* [word or idea] = "a word about the final things").

Final judgment—The event described in Rev. 20:11-15, when God resurrects all people, judges them from the great white throne, and delivers them to their eternal destinies.

First coming of Christ—The earthly life and ministry of Jesus Christ, about 4 BC–AD 30.

Letters to the Seven Churches—After the opening vision (Chapter 1), John begins to write to the messengers (angels) of seven churches, Ephesus, Smyrna, Pergamum, Thyatira, Sardis, Philadelphia, and Laodicea. The messages review the churches' histories, give warnings and commands, and tells them to prepare for what is about to unfold. These were actual messages to real churches in existence in John's day, though some see in the seven churches patterns that apply to the church in specific past, present, or future eras.

Mark of the beast—Indication of a person's allegiance to the teachings of the Antichrist (Revelation 13:16–17). The people of God receive a similar mark, indicating their loyalty to Jesus (Revelation 7:3; 9:4; 14:1; 22:4). Some biblical students believe that the mark of the beast will be an actual mark, required by the Antichrist. (Between the Old and New Testaments, some Jews were forced to be branded with the symbol of the god Dionysius.[185]) Other interpreters of Revelation understand the mark as a reference to someone's actions ("hand") and beliefs ("forehead"). "Hand" and "forehead" seem to carry this symbolic meaning in Exodus 13:9, 16.

Millennium—The thousand-year reign of Jesus on earth, described in Revelation 20:4–6 (from Latin, *mille*, thousand).

- **Premillennial:** The belief that the millennium is a *future* event and Jesus will return *before* (pre-) the millennium.
- **Amillennial:** The millennium is a symbol of Christ's present reign among his people.
- **Postmillennial:** Jesus will return *after* (post-) the millennium. The millennium is a time in which most of the world submits to Jesus, and peace and justice reign.

Preterism—Preterism is the eschatological viewpoint that suggests some, if not all, biblical prophecies about the end times refer to specific events that happened in the first century. Some preterist interpretations include: the Antichrist refers to Emperor Nero; the tribulation refers to the Jewish War; and the Destruction of the temple occurred in AD 70 (from Latin, *praeter*, past or bygone).

Rapture—Event described in 1 Thessalonians 4:15–17, when Jesus Christ returns for his people. Dispensational premillennialists believe that the rapture and the second coming of Jesus are *two separate events*. They place the rapture *before* the great tribulation and the second coming *after* the tribulation. Historical premillennialists, amillennialists, and postmillennialists understand the second coming of Jesus and the event described in 1 Thessalonians 4:15–17 as the same event (from Latin, *raptus*, carry away).

Second coming of Christ—The bodily return of Jesus to earth to reign as king.

Tribulation—Time when disasters happen on the earth and people who are faithful to Jesus suffer intense persecution, possibly lasting seven years (Revelation 7:14).

- Premillennialists place the great tribulation near the end.
- Dispensational premillennialists typically believe that the tribulation will last exactly seven years.
- Many historical premillennialists view the reference to "seven years" as a symbol of the completeness of God's dealings with the world as the end of time approaches.

- Most amillennialists and postmillennialists treat the tribulation as a symbol of calamities and persecutions that have occurred throughout church history.

- Some amillennialists and postmillennialists are *preterists*—they believe that the great tribulation occurred between AD 63 and 70, during the Jewish-Roman conflict that ended with the destruction of the Jewish temple.

Witnesses, two—Two beings described in Revelation 11:1–14 who speak the truth about God before being killed and then resurrected. Many suggestions have been made regarding who the two witnesses might be. Here are three of the many possibilities:

1. Some believe that these two witnesses are two people who will appear during the tribulation, near the end of time.

2. Others view them as two biblical prophets—perhaps Moses and Elijah—that have been resurrected to proclaim God's truth during the tribulation.

3. Others see the two witnesses as symbols of the Law and the Prophets—both of these testified about Jesus and yet, this testimony was rejected, even to the point of killing those that appealed to this testimony (for example, Stephen in Acts 7). If so, the "resurrection" of the two witnesses would point to a time of final vindication, a point at which God demonstrates that the Law and Prophets did indeed testify about Jesus Christ.

NOTES

SECTION 1

CHAPTER 1

1. J.R.R. Tolkien, *The Lord of the Rings: One Volume Edition* (New York: Houghton Mifflin, 1994), 72.

2. Didymus, *De Trinitate*, 3:41; Epiphanius, *Haereses*, 48: 11.

3. R. Abanes, *End Times Visions* (London: Turnaround, 1998), 119, 337.

4. A. Arthur, *The Tailor King: The Rise and Fall of the Anabaptist Kingdom of Munster* (New York: St. Martin's, 1999) 67, 103–164.

5. G. Underwood, *The Millennarian World of Early Mormonism* (Urbana: University of Illinois, 1993).

6. R. Abanes, *End Times Visions* (London: Turnaround, 1998), 93–94.

7. J. Curl, "Davidians, Friends Gather in Waco to Praise Koresh," in *The Washington Times* (April 20, 2003).

8. K.G.C. Newport, *The Branch Davidians of Waco* (Oxford, UK: Oxford University, 2006) 155–339.

9. J. Berton, "Biblical Scholar's Date for Rapture": *http://articles. sfgate.com*; L. Schele and D. Freidel, *A Forest of Kings* (New York: Harper, 1990, 1992) 80–82, 430–431; see also M. Van Stone, "2012 FAQ": *http://www.famsi.org*.

CHAPTER 2

10. John Warwick Montgomery, *In Defense of Martin Luther* (Milwaukee: Northwestern, 1970), 82. For a survey of the term "*sensus literalis*" and its function in biblical interpretation, see Charles Scalise, "The 'Sensus Literalis,'" in *Scottish Journal of Theology* 42 (1989): 45–65.

11. For "historical-grammatical-rhetorical," see Roy Zuck, *Basic Bible Interpretation* (Colorado Springs: Cook, 1991) 77.

12. Origen, *De Principiis*, 4:2:4–17.

13. Thomas Aquinas, *Summa Theologica*, 1, Q. 1, A. 10.

14. Martin Luther, *Lectures on Genesis*, Chapters 1-5, 1:91, 98, 232–233. Aquinas, *Summa Theologica*, 1, Q.1.A.10; Augustine, *Confessiones*, 12. See also J. Pennington, *Reading the Gospels Wisely* (Grand Rapids: Baker, 2012).

15. Some scholars have suggested that Daniel is a fictional text written in the second century BC rather than a combination of historical narrative and apocalyptic elements written in the sixth century BC. For a simple but compelling presentation of rationale for the historicity of Daniel and for a setting in the seventh and sixth centuries, see Joyce Baldwin, *Daniel* (Leicester: InterVarsity, 2009).

16. Adapted from Robert Plummer, *40 Questions about Interpreting the Bible* (Grand Rapids: Kregel, 2010), 213–214.

17. Translated from "Muratorian Canon in Latin": retrieved October 28, 2010, from *http://www.earlychristianwritings. com/text/Muratorian-Latin.HTM*.

18. For *Iesou Christou* in Revelation 1:1 as subjective genitive, see, e.g., George Eldon Ladd, *A Commentary on the Revelation of John* (Grand Rapids, MI: Eerdmans, 1972).

19. Josephus, *Contra Apionem*, 1:19.

20. Islands mentioned by Tacitus include Gyarus and Donusa, two islands in the Cyclades chain, west of Patmos ("silano interdicendum censuit ipsumque in insulam Gyarum relegandum," "Gallus Asinius cum Gyaro aut Donusa claudendum censeret," *Annales* 3:68; 4:30); both of these islands had deficiencies of drinkable water ("id quoque aspernatus est, egenam aquae utramque insulam referens dandosque vitae usus cui vita concederetur," *Annales* 4:30). Tacitus also referenced exile to unnamed Aegean islands ("velut in agmen et numerum, Aegaei maris insulae permittuntur," *Annales* 15:71), clearly suggesting a historically-accurate basis for John's claim to have been exiled to Patmos.

CHAPTER 3

21. Adapted from Justin Martyr, *Dialogus cum Tryphone*, 80–81

22. See Theodor Herzl, *Der Judenstaat* (Leipzig: Breitenstein, 1896) and Heiko Haumann, et al., eds., *The First Zionist Conference in 1897* (Basel: Karger, 1997).

23. See Menasseh Ben Israel (Manoel Dias Soeiro), *Humble Addresses to the Lord Protector* and *Apology for the Jews*. It should be noted that Menasseh believed that a settlement of Jews throughout the world was a necessary precursor to the dawn of a messianic age. Because of this belief, he encouraged Oliver Cromwell to allow Jewish settlements in England, expecting Jewish people someday to return to Zion from their settlements throughout the world.

24. Albert Mohler, "A Call for Theological Triage and Christian Maturity": *http://www.albertmohler.com*.

25. Hippolytus, *Apostolike Paradosis*, 21.

26. Justin Martyr, *Dialogos cum Tryphone*, 70, AD 135.

27. Irenaeus of Lyons, *Adversus Haereses*, 1:10:1, AD 177.

28. Tertullian of Carthage, *Praescriptionibus Adversus Haereticos*, 13, AD 200.

29. Justin Martyr, *Dialogos cum Tryphone*, 81.

30. Justin Martyr, *Dialogos cum Tryphone*, 80.

31. Adapted from Graeme Goldsworthy, *Gospel and Kingdom* (Exeter: Paternoster, 1994), chapter 5.

CHAPTER 4

32. Three views have emerged more recently, at least in their contemporary form, though both would claim to represent the perspective found in the New Testament: (1) The modified Lutheran perspective, (2) Olive Tree Theology, and (3) progressive dispensationalism. The modified Lutheran view seems to constitute a form of new covenant theology. For more on the modified Lutheran view, see Douglas Moo, "The Law of Christ as a Fulfillment of the Law of Moses: A Modified Lutheran View," in *Five Views on Law and Gospel*, ed. Stanley Gundry (Grand Rapids: Zondervan, 1996). Olive Tree Theology contends that Gentile believers are grafted into God's covenant with Israel, thus sharing in God's blessing on Israel gaining participation in the reign over the land promised to Abraham. For more on Olive Tree Theology, see David Stern, *Jewish New Testament Commentary* (Clarksville: Messianic Jewish, 1992), 412–422, and, Daniel Cohn-Sherbok, *Messianic Judaism* (London: Cassell, 2000), 35. Progressive dispensationalism will be considered in the chapter on dispensational premillennialism.

33. Lewis Sperry Chafer, *Dispensationalism* (Dallas: Dallas Theological Seminary, 1951), 107.

34. John F. Walvoord, *The Millennial Kingdom* (Grand Rapids: Zondervan, 1983), 145. Walvoord's first two functions of "children of Abraham" have been conflated here into "natural lineage." The distinction that Walvoord notes—between natural lineage only and spiritual lineage within natural lineage—is still maintained within this grouping.

35. John F. Walvoord, *The Rapture Question* (Google eBook edition; Grand Rapids: Zondervan, 2010); "The Church Age as a Parenthesis"; for Israel's rejection of the kingdom, see Tim LaHaye and Ed Hindson, *The Popular Encyclopedia of Bible Prophecy* (Eugene: Harvest House, 2004), 57–60.

36. In this context, what is intended by "covenantal" is the covenantal continuity from the Old to the New Testament with reference to faith in the Messiah as the basis of justification which results in a fundamental unity between God's workings with believing Israel and with the church. There are some affinities between this sense of the word "covenantal" and the traditional Reformed covenantal schema that includes a covenant of redemption within the Trinity before the foundation of the world, a covenant of works with Adam and Eve, and a covenant of grace centered in Jesus Christ that extends from the protoevangelium in Eden to the return of the Messiah the end of time; however, as used here, these two functions of the word "covenantal" are not necessarily synonymous. As used here, the emphasis is on the unity and continuity of the covenant of grace.

37. R. Kendall Soulen identifies three forms of supersessionism: (1) *Punitive or retributive supersession* in which the supersession is a divine punishment for Israel's rejection of Jesus as Messiah; (2) *Economic supersession* in which Israel's destiny and history find their fulfillment in Jesus Christ and in the church; and, (3) *Structural supersession* in which the structural outline of one's theology diminishes the role of Israel. Structural supersession is more an implicit effect than an explicit theological assertion; as such, the structural view is not treated here. While agreeing with Soulen's general typology, it seems more accurate and helpful to distinguish between (a) economic supersession with fulfillment in Jesus, the consummate Israelite, and, (b) economic supersession with fulfillment in a largely Gentile church, even as it is recognized that these two categories are not completely exclusive of one another. As such, the category presented here as "supersessionism" includes *punitive supersession* as well as *economic supersession with fulfillment primarily centered in the church*. The category presented here as fulfillment in Jesus Christ represents *economic supersession with fulfillment primarily centered in Jesus Christ*. See R. Kendall Soulen, *The God of Israel and Christian Theology* (Minneapolis: Fortress, 1996), 30–33, 181.

38. Lactantius, *Divinarum Institutionum*, 4:11; see also Origen of Alexandria, *Contra Celsum*, 4:22; Melito of Sardis, *Peri Pascha*, 93–99.

39. Jeffrey Niehaus has shown that all the biblical covenants cannot be subsumed under a single covenant in "An Argument against Theologically Constructed Covenants," in *Journal of the Evangelical Society* 50 (2007): 259–273. But see also William Dumbrell's distinction between "cutting a covenant" and "confirming a covenant" in *Covenant and Creation* (Nashville: Nelson, 1984).

40. Although this position does not rest solely or even primarily on Genesis 49:10, Justin Martyr and other early Christian theologians understood Genesis 49:10 as an indication of the fulfillment of God's covenant with Israel in Jesus Christ and translated the text along these lines: "The scepter shall not depart from Judah, nor the ruler's staff from between his feet, until the One comes to whom the scepter rightfully belongs; to him shall be the obedience of the nations." For Justin, see *Apologia Prima*, 32. For other early theologians, see Jaroslav Pelikan, *The Emergence of the Catholic Tradition (100–600)* (Chicago: University of Chicago, 1971), 56.

41. Melito of Sardis, *Peri Pascha*, 39–45.

CHAPTER 5

42. The universalism of Origen of Alexandria and Gregory of Nyssa, in which all sentient beings are eventually welcomed into the new heaven and new earth (C. Bigg, *The Christian Platonists of Alexandria* 2nd. ed. [Oxford: Clarendon,1913], 273–280, 343–351), represents an exception to the overwhelming expectation of condemnation of non-believers that pervades the councils, creeds, and confessions of faith. It seems that Origen was, however, expressing his own hope rather than any exegetically-rooted expectation (Henry Chadwick, *Early Christian Thought and the Classical Tradition* [Oxford: Clarendon, 1966], 119). Clement of Alexandria may have been a universalist, though this is not at all clear in his writings (Bigg, 147–148; W.E.G. Ford, *Clement of Alexandria's Treatment of the Problem of Evil* [Oxford: Oxford University, 1971], 40, 72–73). Gregory of Nazianzus did not accept universalism but regarded it as a possibility (Bigg, 343–344; E. Plumptre, *The Spirits in Prison* 2nd ed. [London: Isbister, 1893], 138–140).

43. See, e.g., Justin Martyr, *Dialogos cum Tryphone*, 81.

44. Irenaeus of Lyons, *Adversus Haereses*, 1:10:1; see also Tertullian of Carthage, *Praescriptionibus Adversus Haereticos*, 13.

45. For a presentation and defense of this perspective, see John Cooper, *Body, Soul, and Life Everlasting* (Grand Rapids: Eerdmans, 2000). For alternative proposals from a Christian perspective, see Joel Green, *Body, Soul, and Human Life* (Grand Rapids: Baker, 2008) and Kevin Corcoran, *Rethinking Human Nature* (Grand Rapids: Baker, 2006).

46. G.K. Chesterton, *Orthodoxy* (London: Lane, 1908) 194.

SECTION 2

CHAPTER 6

47. G. K. Beale, *The Temple and the Church's Mission* (Downers Grove: InterVarsity, 2004), 67.

48. For Adam's priestly role, see James Merrill Hamilton, *God's Glory in Salvation through Judgment* (Kindle edition; Wheaton: Crossway, 2010), 1523–1542. For Adam's kingly role, see Peter Gentry, "Kingdom through Covenant," *Southern Baptist Journal of Theology* 12 (2008): 16–43.

49. *Abraham* does not clearly mean "father of a multitude." However, the author of Genesis connected the name to this meaning in Genesis 17:5. As such, either the name is to be connected to this meaning through assonance with *ab-hamon* ("father of a multitude"), or, a now-unknown Semitic term—*raham* or something similar—was known to the author which implied "multitude." See, e.g., Gordon Wenham, *Genesis 1-15* (Nashville: Nelson, 1987), 252–253, and, Thomas

Brodie, *Genesis as Dialogue* (New York: Oxford University, 2001), 240.

50. Lewis Sperry Chafer, *Dispensationalism* (Dallas: Dallas Theological Seminary, 1951), 107.

51. *Westminster Confession of Faith*, chapter 7.

52. Michael Horton, *God of Promise* (Grand Rapids: Baker, 2006), 78.

53. Dispensationalists as well as some new covenantalists might respond to the suggestion that land promises were fulfilled in the days of Joshua or Solomon by pointing out that God explicitly stated he would bring Israel back to the land after they were sent into exile for their sins (Leviticus 26:27–45; Deuteronomy 30:1–10). This full restoration to the land would have to occur after the Babylonian exile, long after Joshua's day or Solomon's day.

54. Tom Wells and Fred Zaspel, *New Covenant Theology* (Frederick: New Covenant, 2002), 1–8.

55. Abner Chou of The Master's College provided this insight.

CHAPTER 7

56. For the Garden of Eden as a kingdom in ancient Near Eastern context, see P. Gentry, "Kingdom through Covenant," *Southern Baptist Journal of Theology* (Spring 2008).

57. This is not to suggest that Satan usurped this authority without God allowing his actions. God is utterly sovereign and Satan's power is limited (Job 1:12; 2:6). The point is simply that there have been competing kingdoms from the beginning of time.

58. Adapted from J. Currid and D. Barrett, *Crossway ESV Bible Atlas* (Wheaton: Crossway, 2010), 308. Some portions also drawn from Leslie McFall, "The Chronology of Saul and David," *Journal of the Evangelical Theological Society* (September 2010).

59. "In light of Israel's rejection of Christ, he ... announced the introduction of a new form of the kingdom, one that would span the period from Israel's rejection of Christ until Israel's future acceptance of Christ at his second advent. ... The postponement interrupted Israel's national restoration. ... The parable of the wicked vinedressers (Matthew 21:33–44) signifies the withdrawal of the offer of the covenanted kingdom to Israel and its postponement to the future. ... Prophetic postponement is a tenet of classical dispensationalism." T. LaHaye and E. Hindson, eds., *Popular Encyclopedia of Bible Prophecy* (Eugene: Harvest House, 2004), 189, 299–300, 304.

60. Ladd, *The Presence of the Future* (Grand Rapids: Eerdmans, 1974), 45.

61. A. McClain, *The Greatness of the Kingdom* (1959; reprint, Winona Lake: BMH Books, 2001), 17.

62. Ladd, *The Presence of the Future*, 46–52.

63. Eugene H. Merrill, *Everlasting Dominion: A Theology of the Old Testament* (Nashville, TN: Broadman & Holman, 2006), 279–81.

64. Scholars debate whether Isaiah's "servant" is Israel, the Messiah, or both at different times, but it is impossible to deny that at least several of the "servant" references must be announcing an individual messianic person who we know as Jesus of Nazareth.

65. Ladd, *The Presence of the Future*, 60.

CHAPTER 8

66. Josephus, *Bellum Judaicum*, 6:5:3.

67. For discussion of these terms, see Grant Osborne, *The Hermeneutical Spiral* (Downers Grove: InterVarsity, 2006), 265–267; Willem Van Gemeren, *Interpreting the Prophetic Word* (Google eBook; Grand Rapids: Zondervan, 2010), chapter 3; Kim Riddlebarger, *A Case for Amillennialism* (Grand Rapids: Baker, 2003), 56.

68. Josephus, *Bellum Judaicum*, 5:5:6.

69. The arched entrance is known as "Robinson's Arch" and led into the Royal Colonnade. It is disputed whether the Romans destroyed the retaining walls or if perhaps the revolutionaries did so to fortify their own defensive position. Roman soldiers were, however, clearly the persons responsible for destroying the temple.

70. Riddlebarger, *Amillennialism*, 235.

71. Adapted from G. K. Beale, *The Temple and the Church's Mission* (Downers Grove: InterVarsity, 2004), 352–353.

72. "Architect Claims He Has Pieced Together Old Biblical Puzzle," *Los Angeles Times*, 1/6/1996.

73. Josephus, *Bellum Judaicum*, 5:5:5; 7:5:5–6.

74. These four views of Ezekiel's temple are adapted from Beale's study on the temple (*The Temple and the Church's Mission*, 335).

75. These ten occurrences of the Hebrew *chadash* ("new") in Isaiah 40–66 are found in 41:15; 42:9, 10; 43:19; 48:6; 62:2; 65:17 (2x); and 66:22 (2x).

76. Riddlebarger, *Amillennialism*, 37.

CHAPTER 9

77. Gleason Archer, Jr., *A Survey of Old Testament Introduction* rev. ed. (Chicago: Moody, 1996), 421–436; Franz Rosenthal, *Die Aramaistisch Forschung* (Leiden: Brill, 1939), 66–70; Bruce Waltke, "The Date of the Book of Daniel," *Bibliotheca Sacra* (1976): 321–323; Kenneth Kitchen, et. al., "The Aramaic of Daniel," *Notes on Some Problems in the Book of Daniel* (London: Tyndale, 1965), 31–79.

CHAPTER 10

78. Daniel used the redundant phrase "weeks of days" twice in 10:2–3 "because the author [wanted] to return to the literal and normal use of the word 'week'" (Peter J. Gentry, "Daniel's Seventy Weeks and the New Exodus," *Southern Baptist Journal of Theology* 14.1 [2010]: 33).

79. Gentry, "Seventy Weeks," 34.

80. One other view is so unlikely that it is not included here: This view identifies the decree with Jeremiah's prophecy of destruction in 605 BC (Jeremiah 25:11; cf. 25:1) or in 586 BC when the Babylonians destroyed the temple in Jerusalem. Starting the prophetic clock in this way leads to 115 BC or 96 BC. But proponents of this view do not believe the prophecy was fulfilled at either of these times. Rather, they take the numbers as approximate, rounded, or symbolic and place the fulfillment of Daniel 9:25–27 in the 160's BC with the blasphemous life of Antiochus IV Epiphanes (see 1 Maccabees 1:10–61; 6:1–16 in the Roman Catholic or Eastern Orthodox Scriptures) or with the heroic temple-cleansing of Judas Maccabeus (1 Maccabees 4:41–58). However, in Jeremiah 25, the prophet was not making a decree of *construction* but a decree of *destruction*. The prophetic word in 605 BC was that Jerusalem would fall, not that Jerusalem would rise. Further, how could the events around Antiochus IV possibly fulfill the stated purpose for the seventy sevens ("to finish the transgression," to make "an end to sin," "to bring in everlasting righteousness")?

81. Keith A. Mathison, *From Age to Age* (Phillipsburg: P&R, 2009), 275.

82. See Joyce G. Baldwin, *Daniel* (Downers Grove: InterVarsity Press, 1978; reprint, 2009), 187. Mathison highlights the 400-year prophecy of Genesis 15:13 and its apparent 430-year fulfillment in Exodus 12:40–41 as an example of a rounded number with an inexact fulfillment (Mathison, *From Age to Age*, 276). However, a rounded-number interpretation is not the same as a symbolic interpretation.

83. Gentry, "Seventy Weeks," 37.

84. Gentry, "Seventy Weeks," 36, citing Benedict Zuckerman, *Über Sabbathjahrcyclus und Jubelperiode* (Breslau: Korn, 1886).

85. Robert Anderson, *The Coming Prince* (1895; reprint, Grand Rapids: Kregel, 1975) 67–75.

86. Anderson, *The Coming Prince*, 127–128.

87. From a dispensationalist perspective, the first, second, and fourth purposes require fulfillment in the millennial age because Israel's "transgression" and "sin" will not be complete and "everlasting righteousness" will not fill the earth until the Jews embrace their Messiah at his second coming (Walvoord, *Daniel*, 221–23).

88. Miller, *Daniel*, 264.

89. If the decree of Cyrus in 538 BC is seen as the starting-point, these first seven "weeks" would have to a flexible, open-ended, or symbolic period of time, because the city of Jerusalem was not rebuilt by 489 v (49 years after 538 BC).

90. Gentry, "Daniel's Seventy Weeks and the New Exodus," 37.

91. If one accepts the ESV translation, the first "anointed one" would have to arrive within the first seven "weeks." Those who take this view see the numbers as rounded or approximate and interpret the "anointed one" of v. 25 as the revered high priest Onias III in the second century BC.

92. Kenneth T. Aitken, "*nagid,*" *New International Dictionary of Old Testament Theology and Exegesis*, 5 vols., ed. W. A. Van Gemeren (Grand Rapids: Zondervan, 1997), 3:20–21.

93. Some scholars have taken the following perspective, which the authors of this book view as highly unlikely: The Anointed One was Onias III (murdered in 171 BC by Jews in league with the pagan king Antiochus IV), and Antiochus IV was the ruler yet to come. Antiochus IV persecuted faithful Jews but made a peace agreement with less faithful Jews, according to 1 Maccabees 1:11. Antiochus IV committed a desolating abomination by claiming the title "Epiphanes"—"divine manifestation"—and erecting a pagan altar above the altar in front of the Jewish temple.

94. Young, *Daniel*, 191; Jerome, *Commentarii in Danielem*, ed. F. Glorie, in *Corpus Christianorum* 75 (1964), 9:24–27.

95. For example, compare Psalm 16:9–10 with Acts 2:25–28 and 13:35.

SECTION 3

CHAPTER 11

96. For a non-religious recognition of the universality and antiquity of messianism, see the anthropological work in W.D. Wallis, *Messiahs* (Washington, D.C.: ACPA, 1943).

97. Josephus, *Bellum Judaicum*, 1:21:3

98. In later years, carved niches would pockmark this cliff, with an idol in each niche. See J. Wilson, *Caesarea Philippi: Banias, the Lost City of Pan* (London: Tauris, 2004), 44–47, 61–66. Contrary to the claims of some commentators, the primary niches and inscriptions seem to have been carved in the second and third centuries; as such, neither Jesus nor his first disciples would have seen them.

99. "The act of anointing confers *kabod* [glory]; it is thus to be regarded as an act of enablement" (W. Grundmann, *chrio,* in *Theological Dictionary of the New Testament*, vol. 9, ed. G. Kittel, et al., trans. G. Bromiley [Grand Rapids, Michigan: Wm. B. Eerdmans, 1964], 498).

100. Psalms of Solomon may be found in several sources, including an English translation by J. Harris (*The Odes and Psalms of Solomon* [Cambridge: Cambridge University Press, 1909]) and the online Greek text at *http://sacred-texts.com/bib/sep/pss. htm* from which these quotations were translated.

101. *Damascus Document* 12:23–13:1. *Damascus Document* is derived from 4Q265, 4Q266, 4Q267, 4Q268, 4Q269, 4Q270, 4Q271, 4Q262, 4Q273, 5Q12, and 6Q15. See also 1Q28a 2:11–21.

102. *Community Rule* (4Q258) 9:9–11.

103. *Damascus Document* 19:9–11.

104. Josephus, *De Antiquitate Judaica*, 17:10; 18:1–10, 23.

105. See T. Ice, "Church Age," and J. Borland, "Church in Prophecy," in *The Popular Encyclopedia of Bible Prophecy*, ed. T. LaHaye and E. Hindson (Eugene: Harvest House, 2004).

106. A. Fruchtenbaum, "Conversion of Israel," in *The Popular Encyclopedia of Bible Prophecy*, ed. T. LaHaye and E. Hindson (Eugene: Harvest House, 2004).

107. J. Walvoord, *The Millennial Kingdom* (Grand Rapids: Zondervan, 1959), 136. See also H. Hoyt, "Dispensational Premillennialism," in *The Meaning of the Millennium*, ed. R. Clouse (Downers Grove: InterVarsity, 1977), 81.

CHAPTER 12

108. Josephus, *Bellum Judaicum*, 7:5:5–7.

109. Tim LaHaye and Ed Hindson, *The Popular Bible Prophecy Commentary*, 358.

110. Josephus, *Bellum Judaicum*, 7:5:5–7.

111. Wayne House and Randall Price, *Charts of Bible Prophecy*, 130.

112. Josephus, *Bellum Judaicum*, 3:10:9.

113. Josephus, *Antiquitates Judaicae*, 20:2:1–5; Josephus, *Bellum Judaicum*, 6:3:3–4.

114. Seneca, *Naturales Quaestiones*, 6:1–11.

115. Josephus, *Bellum Judaicum*, 6:5:3.

116. Josephus, *Antiquitates Judaicae*, 20:8:5–6; Josephus, *Bellum Judaicum*, 6:5:2.

117. Josephus, *Bellum Judaicum*, 5:9:4; 5:13:6.

118. Athanasius, *Apologia de Fuga*, 11; John Chrysostom, *Homilia*, 75:2; 76:1; Clement, *Homilia*, 3:15; Josephus, *Bellum Judaicum*, 2:20:1; 4:6:1; 4:7:3; 5:10:1; 5:13:4; 6:2:2; 6:6:1; Eusebius, *Historia Ecclesiastica*, 3:5; Epiphanius, *De Mensuris et Ponderibus*, 15; *Abot de Rabbi Nathan* (Leiden: Brill, 1975), 67–69.

119. Josephus, *Bellum Judaicum*, 6:6:1.

120. Josephus, *Bellum Judaicum*, 6:5:3; Tacitus, *Annales*, 5:13.

121. John Walvoord, *Prophecy Knowledge Handbook*, 391; Hal Lindsey, *The Late Great Planet Earth*, 53.

122. John Walvoord, *Prophecy Knowledge Handbook*, 391.

123. Chrysostom, *Homilia*, 49.

CHAPTER 13

124. The most common names, in order, were: Simon, Joseph, Lazarus, Judas, John, and Jesus. I have classified all forms of the second most frequent name "Joseph"—including "Joses," "Josah," and "Joseh"—as variants of the same name. For more information of praenominal frequencies, see T. Ilan, *Lexicon of Jewish Names in Late Antiquity Part 1* (Tübingen: Mohr, 2002), and, R. Bauckham, *Jesus and the Eyewitnesses* (Grand Rapids: Eerdmans, 2006).

125. For proof of this pattern, see T. Jones, *Misquoting Truth* (Downers Grove: InterVarsity, 2007), 79–137.

126. Justin, *Dialogus cum Tryphone*, 81:4; Irenaeus, *Adversus Haereses*, 4:20:11; Tertullian, *Adversus Marcionem*, 3:14:3.

   In the third century, a pastor named Dionysius suggested that there might have been two church leaders in Ephesus named "John." In the early fourth century, church historian Eusebius of Caesarea made a similar claim. Based partly on a misreading of some earlier references to "John," Eusebius speculated that John the apostle wrote the Gospel and 1 John while a different John—known as "the elder"—wrote 2 John, 3 John, and Revelation. See Eusebius, *Historia Ecclesiastica*, 3:39; 7:25. See also S. Smalley, *Thunder and Love* (Milton Keynes: Word, 1994), 38, and, R. Gundry, *Matthew* (Grand Rapids: Eerdmans, 1982), 611–612.

127. Tacitus, *Annales*, 15:44.

128. Suetonius, *Vita Domitianus*, 13:2.

129. Tacitus, *Annales*, 3:68; 4:30; 15:71.

130. Eusebius, *Historia Ecclesiastica*, 3:18:1; 3:20:8–9.

131. *Magnesieusin Ignatios*, 5.

132. *Odes of Solomon*, 8:13–19.

133. T. LaHaye and E. Hindson, eds., *The Popular Bible Prophecy Commentary* (Eugene: Harvest House, 2007), 517; T. LaHaye, "One Hundred Forty-Four Thousand," *The Popular Encyclopedia of Biblical Prophecy* (Eugene: Harvest House, 2004), 256–257.

134. T. LaHaye, "One Hundred Forty-Four Thousand," *The Popular Encyclopedia of Biblical Prophecy* (Eugene: Harvest House, 2004), 256–257.

135. T. LaHaye, "One Hundred Forty-Four Thousand," *The Popular Encyclopedia of Biblical Prophecy* (Eugene: Harvest House, 2004), 256–257.

CHAPTER 14

136. P. Prigent, *Apocalypse 12, Beitrage zur Geschichte der Biblischen Exegese 2* (Tubingen: Mohr, 1959), 1.

137. 2 Maccabees 7.

138. For more on the emperor cult, particularly trickery in the temples that might make an image seem to live, see S.J. Scherrer, "Signs and Wonders in the Imperial Cult," *Journal of Biblical Literature* 103 (1984): 599–610; also, Dio Cassius, *Historia*, 59:28:6; Eusebius, *Historia Ecclesiastica*, 2:13:1–4; Irenaeus, *Adversus Haereses*, 1:23; Justin, *Prima Apologia*, 26; Theophilus, *Ad Autolycum*, 1:8; S.R. Price, *Rituals and Power* (Cambridge: Cambridge University Press, 1984), 197–222; W.M. Ramsay, *The Letters to the Seven Churches of Asia and Their Place in the Plan of the Apocalypse* (London: Hodder, 1904), 98–103.

139. Athanasius, *Apologia Contra Arianos*, 3:49.

140. Augustine, *De Civitate Dei*, 20:19:2.

141. John Chrysostom, *Homilia*, 2 Thessalonians 4.

142. Cyril of Jerusalem, *Catecheseis*, 15:12.

143. 3 Maccabees 2:29.

144. G. Osborne, *Revelation* (Grand Rapids: Baker, 2002), 518.

145. For more on the mark of the beast, see B. Witherington III, *Revelation* (Cambridge, UK: Cambridge University Press, 2003), especially 184–185. For the most comprehensive study of the mark of the beast, with compelling arguments that 666 refers to Nero, see Richard Bauckham, *The Climax of Prophecy* (Edinburgh: Clark, 1993).

146. Flavius Philostratus, *Vita Apollonii*, 4:38.

147. Suetonius, *Vita Neronis*, 57; *Ascension of Isaiah*, 4:8-11.

148. For 666 to refer to Nero, the Greek *Neron Kaisar* must be spelled *NRWN QSR* in Hebrew rather than *NRWN QYSR*. It remains uncertain whether anyone familiar with Hebrew in the first century AD would have spelled *Neron Kaisar* without a *yodh* to transliterate the "*I*" in *Kaisar* (G.W. Buchanan, *The Book of Revelation* [Lewiston: Mellon, 1993], 345–346); however, the use of an atypical spelling could make sense if there were peculiar numeric qualities regarding 666, including (but not limited to) the fact that *therion* (Greek, "beast") can be calculated as "666," that characterized 666. The textual variant 616 could be an attempt to identify the beast as Emperor Caligula (R. Mounce, *The Book of Revelation* [Grand Rapids: Eerdmans, 1997], 264), but Bauckham's proposals in *The Climax of Prophecy* seem more likely than Mounce's suggestions.

SECTION 4

CHAPTER 16

149. S. Ambrose, *D-Day* (New York: Simon and Schuster, 1994). 190–195; C. D'Este, *Eisenhower* (New York: MacMillan, 2003). 527–528; E. Larrabee, *Commander-in-Chief* (New York: Simon and Schuster, 1988), 455.

150. Adapted from O. Cullmann, *Christ and Time* (Philadelphia: Westminster, 1950), 84.

151. W. Hendriksen, *More than Conquerors* (Grand Rapids: Baker, 1998), 36.

152. Augustine of Hippo, *De Civitate Dei*, 20:7

CHAPTER 17

153. From personal correspondence with Kenneth Gentry and from *He Shall Have Dominion* (Tyler: ICE, 1992).

154. L. Boettner, *The Millennium* repr. ed. (Phillipsburg: P&R, 1990), 14.

155. J. Edwards, *The Works of President Edwards in Eight Volumes*, vol. 3, ed. S. Austin (Worcester: Isaiah Thomas, 1808), 373–375.

156. Quoted in B. Withrow, "A Future of Hope," *Trinity Journal* (Spring 2001): 75–98.

157. R.J. Rushdoony, "Back to the Future," *New Wine* (November 1986): 24.

CHAPTER 18

158. L.S. Chafer, *Dispensationalism* (Dallas: Dallas Theological Seminary, 1951), 107.

159. L.S. Chafer, *Systematic Theology. Volume 1* repr. ed. (Grand Rapids: Kregel, 1976), 40.

160. C.I. Scofield, *Scofield Reference Bible* (New York: Oxford, 1909), 5.

161. C.C. Ryrie, *Dispensationalism* (Chicago: Moody, 2007), 28–34.

162. C.C. Ryrie, *Dispensationalism* (Chicago: Moody, 2007), 46.

163. For texts of pseudo-Ephraem, see E. Beck, ed., *Des heiligen Ephraem des Syrers Sermones* III (Louvain: Secrétariat du Corpus, 1972), 60–71; T. Lamy, ed., *Sancti Ephraem Syri Hymni et Sermones* volume 3 (Mechliniae: Dessain, 1897), 187–212.

164. F. Gumerlock contends that this obscure text refers to a pre-tribulational rapture ("A Rapture Citation in the Fourteenth Century," *Bibliotheca Sacra* 159 [2002]).

165. T. Weber, "Dispensational and Historic Premillennialism as Popular Millennial Movements," in *A Case for Historic Premillennialism* (Grand Rapids: Baker Academic, 2009).

166. R. Moore, "Personal and Cosmic Eschatology," in *A Theology for the Church*, ed. D. Akin (Nashville: B&H Academic, 2007), 905.

167. T. LaHaye, *No Fear of the Storm* (Sisters: Multnomah, 1992), 240.

CHAPTER 19

168. R. Moore, "Personal and Cosmic Eschatology," in *A Theology for the Church*, ed. D. Akin (Nashville: B&H Academic, 2007), 905.

169. Papias, *Fragments*.

170. Justin Martyr, *Dialogus cum Tryphoni*, 80, 110.

171. Irenaeus, *Adversus Haereses*, 5:26; 5:30.

172. Irenaeus, *Adversus Haereses*, 5:33.

173. Tertullian, *Adversus Marcionem*, 3:25; Tertullian, *De Resurrectione Carnis*, 25.

174. There have been some attempts to identify Charles H. Spurgeon as a postmillennialist; however, these assertions have been soundly refuted. See D.M. Swanson, *Charles H. Spurgeon and Eschatology*: *http://www.spurgeon.org/eschat.htm*.

175. R. Moore, "Is There a Future for Israel?": *http://www.russellmoore.com/2009/01/09/is-there-a-future-for-israel*.

176. Irenaeus, *Adversus Haereses*, 5:33–34.

177. Justin Martyr, *Dialogus cum Tryphoni*, 123, 125. Cf. R. Wilken, "In Novissimis Die Bus," in *Journal of Early Christian Studies 1* (1993): 15.

178. W. Percy, *The Message in the Bottle* repr. ed. (New York: Picador, 2000) 6, cited in R. Moore, "Personal and Cosmic Eschatology," in *A Theology for the Church*, ed. D. Akin (Nashville: B&H Academic, 2007), 923.

179. R. Moore, "Personal and Cosmic Eschatology," in *A Theology for the Church*, ed. D. Akin (Nashville: B&H Academic, 2007), 923.

CHAPTER 20

180. Augustine of Hippo, *The City of God*, 20:9.

181. L. Boettner, *The Millennium* (Nutley, NJ: Presbyterian and Reformed, 1957), 14.

182. Tim LaHaye, *No Fear of the Storm*, (Sisters, OR, Multnomah Books, 1992), 234.

183. G.K. Beale, *The Book of Revelation* (Grand Rapids, MI: Eerdmans, 1999), 19.

184. G.E. Ladd, *A Commentary on the Revelation of John* (Grand Rapids, MI: Eerdmans, 1972), 178–179.

185. 3 Maccabees 2:29.

INDEX

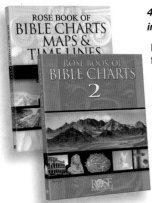

400 pages of reproducible charts in two volumes.

Dozens of popular Bible charts, maps, and time lines in two spiral-bound books.

Rose Book of Bible Charts, Maps & Time Lines
192 pages. Hardcover.
ISBN-13: 9781596360228

Rose Book of Bible Charts 2
233 pages. Hardcover.
ISBN-13: 9781596362758

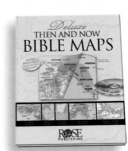

Deluxe "Then and Now" Bible Maps
Book with CD-ROM!
See where Bible places are today with "Then and Now" Bible maps with clear plastic overlays of modern cities and countries.

Hardcover.
ISBN-13: 9781596361638

New! Full-Color Rose Bible Basics Books
For personal use, Bible studies, small groups, and new member classes. 128 pages, 6 x 9-inch paperback.

Christianity, Cults & Religions
ISBN-13: 9781596362024

Names of God and Other Bible Studies
ISBN-13: 9781596362031

Why Trust the Bible?
ISBN-13: 9781596362017

The Bible at a Glance
ISBN-13: 9781596362000

Rose Book of Bible & Christian History Time Lines
Six thousand years and 20 feet of time lines in one hard-bound book. The Time Line compares Scriptural events with world history and Middle East history. Shows hundreds of facts; includes dates of kings, prophets, battles, and key events. Can be removed from cover and extended 20 feet.

Hardcover. ISBN-13: 9781596360846

Feasts & Holidays of the Bible
chart, pamphlet, and PowerPoint®

The Tabernacle
chart, pamphlet, and PowerPoint®

The Temple
chart and pamphlet

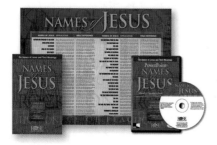

Names of Jesus
chart, pamphlet, and PowerPoint®

Names of God
chart, pamphlet, and PowerPoint®

Christ in the Passover
chart and pamphlet